Praise for

THE HUMOR CODE

"Peter and Joel's globe-spanning search for what makes things funny is a wonderful page-turner that entertains as much as it informs."

—Dan Ariely, author of *The (Honest) Truth about Dishonesty*
and *Predictably Irrational*

"This book tickled my hippocampus. Joel Warner and Peter McGraw gave me paradigm-altering insights into humor, but also creativity, business, happiness, and, of course, flatulence."

—A.J. Jacobs, author of *Drop Dead Healthy*
and *The Year of Living Biblically*

"If you've ever wondered why we laugh at what we do, you have to read this book about the DNA of humor. The odd-couple authors take us on a journey from the halls of science to the backstage of Los Angeles comedy clubs, and they show us why people can laugh amidst tensions in Palestine or a clown brigade in the Amazon. It's part Indiana Jones, part Tina Fey, and part *Crime Scene Investigation*, and it will make you smarter and happier."

—Chip Heath, author of *Decisive*, *Switch*,
and *Made to Stick*

"Engaging, wise, and of course funny, *The Humor Code* is a wonderful quest to discover who and what makes us laugh. Pete McGraw and Joel Warner are the best of company, and you'll be glad you took this trip with them."

—Susan Cain, bestselling author of *Quiet: The Power of Introverts
in a World That Can't Stop Talking*

"I've always been fascinated by how humor works. I'm not willing to say that *The Humor Code* solves the puzzle once and for all, but it comes pretty close—and along the way it's a hell of a ride."

—Jimmy Carr, stand-up comedian, television host, actor, and coauthor of
Only Joking: What's So Funny About Making People Laugh?

"*The Humor Code* is a fun narrative of how a serious scientific theory is born, tested, and lived."

—Ben Huh, CEO, The Cheezburger Network

"Spanning five continents, McGraw and Warner's quest for a unified field theory of funny may be quixotic, but like Don Q and Sancho, their misadventures are irresistible and their enthusiasm is as infectious as the laughter they chronicle. Together they manage to find the science in comedy and the comedy in science, and share it all with the reader in this playful Baedeker of humor."

—Barnet Kellman; Emmy Award–winning director of *Murphy Brown* and *Mad About You*, professor at the University of California School of Cinematic Arts, and codirector of Comedy@SCA

"*The Humor Code* is so good that I wish I wrote it. In fact, I've already started telling people I did. Luckily, Pete McGraw and Joel Warner are givers, so they won't mind. They've given us a remarkable look at what makes us laugh, with the perfect blend of science, stories, satire, and sweater vests. This book has 'bestseller' written all over it."

—Adam Grant, professor at the Wharton School of the University of Pennsylvania and bestselling author of *Give and Take*

"McGraw and Warner have done something quite remarkable and commendable. They've taken an intriguing question regarding the nature of humor and artfully mined answers from both the outcomes of scientific research and their own 'worldwide comedy tour' experiences. I've never seen anything like it."

—Robert Cialdini, bestselling author of *Influence*

"*The Humor Code* is a rollicking tour de farce that blends academic insights and amusing anecdotes to answer some of the most serious (and frivolous) questions about humor, from what makes us laugh and why we laugh at all, to how the world's cultures came to have completely different senses of humor."

—Adam Alter, *New York Times* bestselling author of *Drunk Tank Pink* and assistant professor of marketing and psychology at New York University

"If you've ever been interested in trying comedy, this book will either scare you away from it or force you to do it. I consider both options a success."

—Mike Drucker, standup comedian and
writer for *Late Night with Jimmy Fallon*

"If you're doing business in the global marketplace, *The Humor Code* is a must-read. Not only did I learn what makes things humorous around the world, now I understand why nobody in Japan ever laughed at my jokes!"

—Marty St. George,
senior vice president of marketing, JetBlue Airways

"Blending cutting-edge science and clever stories, *The Humor Code* will help you find a funnier world—whether you are on Twitter or not."

—Claire Diaz-Ortiz, author of *Twitter for Good*
and innovator at Twitter, Inc.

"Funny, poignant, and inspiring, Peter and Joel manage the tricky task of vivisecting comedy without losing the patient."

—Andy Wood, cofounder and producer of the
Bridgetown Comedy Festival

"Humor is like happiness—universal but subjective. What's great about *The Humor Code* is that it takes a scientific look at how humor differs across cultures [while] vitally connecting us at the same time."

—Jenn Lim, CEO and chief happiness
officer of Delivering Happiness

"A harrowing tale of men obsessed with understanding a gargantuan and enigmatic beast called Funny. This book might as well be titled 'Moby Dick Jokes.'"

—Baron Vaughn, comedian; as seen on Comedy Central, *Conan*,
The Late Late Show with Craig Ferguson, and his podcast *Deep S##!*

"Leave it to a reporter and a scientist to try to ruin something beautiful by dissecting it, and instead create something wonderful. *The Humor Code* is a tremendous book."

—Shane Snow, technology journalist and cofounder of Contently

"The search for what makes things funny was one we found we could not stop reading. Two thumbs up (Andrew hated it)."

—The Grawlix (comedians Adam Cayton-Holland, Andrew Orvedahl, and Ben Roy)

THE HUMOR CODE

A Global Search for What Makes Things Funny

Peter McGraw, PhD, and Joel Warner

SIMON & SCHUSTER PAPERBACKS

New York London Toronto Sydney New Delhi

Simon & Schuster Paperbacks
An Imprint of Simon & Schuster, Inc.
1230 Avenue of the Americas
New York, NY 10020

First Simon & Schuster trade paperback edition April 2015

SIMON & SCHUSTER PAPERBACKS and colophon
are registered trademarks of Simon & Schuster, Inc.

For information about special discounts for bulk purchases,
please contact Simon & Schuster Special Sales at 1-866-506-1949
or business@simonandschuster.com.

The Simon & Schuster Speakers Bureau can bring authors
to your live event. For more information or to book an event
contact the Simon & Schuster Speakers Bureau at 1-866-248-3049
or visit our website at www.simonspeakers.com.

Designed by Esther Paradelo

Manufactured in the United States of America

10   9   8   7   6   5   4   3   2   1

The Library of Congress has catalogued the hardcover edition as follows:

McGraw, Peter.
  The humor code : a global search for what makes things funny / Peter McGraw, PhD
and Joel Warner.
     pages cm
  1. Wit and humor—Psychological aspects. I. Title.
  BF575.L3M384 2014
  152.4'3—dc23

                                                                        2013031454

ISBN 978-1-4516-6541-3
ISBN 978-1-4516-6542-0 (pbk)
ISBN 978-1-4516-6543-7 (ebook)

AUTHORS' NOTE

Portions of this book—a line here, a paragraph there—previously appeared under one or both of our bylines in various publications, including *Wired*, Wired.com, *Westword* newspaper, *Salon*, *The Huffington Post*, *Psychology Today*, and our personal websites (PeterMcGraw.org and JoelWarner.com). Please don't hold it against us. We were eager to spread the word about what we were up to.

Humor can be dissected, as a frog can, but
the thing dies in the process
and the innards are discouraging
to any but the pure scientific mind.

—E. B. White, 1941

Let's kill some frogs.

CONTENTS

Introduction   xiii

1. COLORADO: Set-up   1
2. LOS ANGELES: Who is funny?   17
3. NEW YORK: How do you make funny?   41
4. TANZANIA: Why do we laugh?   67
5. JAPAN: When is comedy lost in translation?   93
6. SCANDINAVIA: Does humor have a dark side?   119
7. PALESTINE: Can you find humor where you least expect it?   149
8. THE AMAZON: Is laughter the best medicine?   175
9. MONTREAL: Punch line   197

Acknowledgments   213
Notes   218
Index   227

INTRODUCTION

People a lot smarter and more important than the two of us have pondered what makes things funny. Plato and Aristotle contemplated the meaning of comedy while laying the foundations of Western philosophy. Thomas Hobbes probed the issue within the pages of his momentous tome *Leviathan*. Charles Darwin looked for the seeds of laughter in the joyful cries of tickled chimpanzees. Sigmund Freud sought the underlying motivations behind jokes in the nooks and crannies of our unconscious.

None of them got it right. Yet for some reason, we think we can succeed where they all failed.

Who are we? A dream team of Nobel Prize–winning scientists and Emmy-laden comedy writers? Not exactly.

Let's start with my co-author: Peter McGraw, the so-called "brains" of the operation. An academic with an adventurous side, he's the guy who set this outlandish quest in motion. As a professor of marketing and psychology at the University of Colorado, Boulder, he's obsessed with making sense out of insanity, order out of chaos. His university office is impeccably organized, with piles of journal articles and academic surveys—on topics ranging from the economics of gun shows to mega-church marketing strategies—arranged by subject, stacked in perfect columns, and labeled with orderly Post-it notes. To try to understand the odd ways the world works, he's circumnavigated the globe on a ship. Twice. He's just as exacting regarding his teaching techniques. Lately, before classes, he's been telling himself he's going to a big, exciting party, to ensure his lectures are as energetic and engaging as possible. For a professor who goes by "Pete" instead of "Dr. McGraw," stuffy and long-winded doesn't cut it.

So when he started contemplating what makes things funny and found that little about it made sense, that wouldn't stand. He had to find a nice, tidy explanation.

Then there's me, Joel Warner, the more cautious half of our duo. As a journalist, I've always suspected that there's something about me that's not quite right. While my colleagues thirst for tips on dirty cops and City Hall corruption, I prefer stories on real-life superheroes and beer-delivering robots. As an upbeat newshound, I've never been fully comfortable in an industry that relishes tragedy over comedy. Maybe, I figure, if I can help Pete solve the riddle behind the lighter side of life, I won't be so confused.[1]

Considering our pedestrian backgrounds, it might seem unlikely that we can outperform some of history's greatest minds in our quest to crack the humor code. But we have a couple advantages. For one thing, we suspect we have the timing right. Although comedy has been around since the dawn of civilization, it has never been so pervasive and accessible. Comedians such as Will Ferrell and Tina Fey are among America's biggest celebrities. Satirical news shows such as *The Daily Show* and *The Colbert Report* have become news sources for an entire generation. Roughly a quarter of all television commercials attempt to be humorous, and the internet has become a 24-hour one-stop shop for laughs. Everywhere you look, somebody is making a joke—which means those jokes have never been so easy to study.

Plus, we have science and technology on our side. (And we don't just mean we have Google.) Aided by increasingly advanced technologies, scientists are piecing together the intricacies of the human

---

1. We thought long and hard on how best to write this book. A third-person account: "We ask Louis C.K. way too much about his physical anatomy"? A God's-eye-view of our hijinks: "Pete's busy getting an exfoliation scrub when Joel gets chased naked out of the Japanese spa"? We decided to go with my personal point of view: "Pete naps and I worry about dengue fever as we fly into the Amazon in a Peruvian Air Force cargo plane packed with 100 clowns."

condition. Psychologists are probing our unconscious motivations, biologists are tracking down our evolutionary origins, and computer scientists are building new forms of artificial intelligence. While these efforts are helping to solve some of the universe's greatest mysteries, they could also help us figure out why we laugh at farts.

Our plan, simply put, merges the best of both worlds, a mash-up of science and comedy—two topics that don't always get along. We'll apply cutting-edge research techniques to the wide world of humor while subjecting the zingers, wisecracks, and punch lines we've all taken for granted to hard-and-fast analysis back in the lab.

Along the way, we aim to answer tough questions that are bound to turn heads of scientists and comedians alike: Do comics need to come from screwed-up childhoods? What's the secret to winning the *New Yorker* cartoon caption contest? Why does being funny make you more attractive? Who's got a bigger funny bone—men or women, Democrats or Republicans? What is, quantifiably, the funniest joke in the world? Is laughter *really* the best medicine? Can a joke ruin your life—or lead to revolution? And, most important of all, do the French love Jerry Lewis?

As with all the best experiments, not everything will go as planned. There will be bickering, bruised egos, and, yes, more than a few bad jokes. Still, we're confident that the two of us make a good team. Pete's got a way with data, while I have a way with words. Pete's willing to pursue his research in the most outrageous circumstances imaginable, while I have the wherewithal to keep us out of trouble. At least, that's what we've told ourselves.

To cap off our expedition, we'll tackle one final challenge, one that's either the ultimate high-stakes experiment or a scheme as hare-brained as they come. We'll use our newfound knowledge to try to kill it on the largest comedy stage in the world.

But we're getting ahead of ourselves. Our journey begins, appropriately enough, with a set-up straight out of a joke:

Did you hear the one about the professor and the journalist who walk into a bar?

We walk into the Squire Lounge just as the Denver watering hole is gearing up for its weekly open-mike comedy night. Looking around, Pete grins. "This is fantastic!" he yells over the ruckus, sounding like a field biologist who's just discovered a strange new animal species. The mirrored walls display awards for "Best Dive Bar in Denver," the stench of industrial cleaner hangs in the air, and the sound of clanging beer bottles blends into the police sirens wailing through the night outside. The clientele sports tattoos and ironic mustaches, lumberjack shirts, and plastic-rimmed glasses.

Pete is wearing a sweater vest.

The professor sticks out here like a six-foot-five, 40-year-old sore thumb. He's also calm for someone who's about to do stand-up for the first time. Or for someone who's been warned that this open mike is the toughest one around. As a local comic put it to me, "If you fail at the Squire, you will not only fail hard, but then you will be cruelly, cruelly mocked."

Rolling up the sleeves of his button-down shirt, Pete orders us a couple whiskeys on the rocks. "This is a welcoming crowd," he cracks sarcastically.

I'm soon ordering another round. I don't know why I'm the more nervous of the two of us. I have little at stake in Pete's stand-up routine. We've only known each other for a few weeks, but I'd like him to succeed. I fear that's not likely to happen.

Pete's already working the room. He zeroes in on a woman by the pool table. She turns out to be another open-mike first-timer. "Did you think about your outfit tonight?" he asks. "I put this on so I look like a professor."

He glances around the room. The neon Budweiser signs on the walls cast a bluish, sickly hue on the grizzled faces lined up at the bar.

Turning back to the woman, Pete offers an unsolicited piece of advice: "No joking about Marxism or the military-industrial complex."

I'd stumbled upon Pete after having written an article about gangland shootings and fire bombings for *Westword*, the alternative weekly newspaper in Denver. I was eager for a palate cleanser. I hoped that it wouldn't involve cultivating anonymous sources or filing federal open-records requests. Yes, such efforts have brought down presidents, but I'm no 31-year-old Woodward or Bernstein. I'd rather find another story like the profile I wrote of a McDonald's franchise owner who used his arsenal of fast-food inventions to break the world record for drive-thru Quarter Pounders served in an hour. Or the coffee connoisseur I'd followed to Ethiopia in search of the shadowy origins of the world's most expensive coffee bean. (The expedition broke down several dozen miles short of its goal thanks to caffeine-fueled bickering, impassable muddy roads, and reports of man-eating lions.)

When I heard about a Boulder professor who was dissecting comedy's DNA, I'd found my story.

It's true, Pete told me when I first got him on the phone. He'd started something he called the Humor Research Lab—also known as HuRL. His research assistants (the Humor Research Team, aka HuRT) were just about to run a new round of experiments. Maybe I'd like to come by and watch.

A week later, sitting in a large, white conference room at the University of Colorado's Leeds School of Business, I witnessed Pete's peculiar approach to humor research. Four student volunteers filed into the room, signed off on the appropriate consent forms, and then sat and watched as a somber-faced research assistant dimmed the lights and played a clip from the hit comedy *Hot Tub Time Machine*. After ten minutes of scatological gags and off-color sex jokes, the students filled out a questionnaire about the film. Did they find the scene in which the BMW keys were removed from a dog's butt funny? What about the line "A taxidermist is stuffing my mom"? Or the part where a character breaks his catheter and sprays urine on everybody?

The experiment, Pete explained to me, was the latest chapter in HuRL's attempts to understand what makes things funny. Other tests included forcing subjects to watch on repeat a YouTube video of a guy driving a motorcycle into a fence, to determine when, exactly, it ceases to be amusing. Another exposed participants to a real-life ad of an anthropomorphized lime peeing into a glass of soda, then had them drink lime cola to see if they thought it tasted like pee.

For someone like Pete, there was nothing unusual about this research. Over the course of his relatively short career, he's haggled with casket manufacturers at a funeral directors' convention, talked shop with soldiers of fortune at a gun show, and sung hymns at a Fundamentalist Baptist church in West Texas, all for the sake of science.

His experiments aren't limited to his day job. The professor has a tendency to live his research, no matter the disastrous results. While he was working toward his PhD in quantitative psychology at Ohio State University, a mentor invited him to Thanksgiving dinner. Pete offered to pay for his meal just to see the reaction to the obvious faux pas.

Pete puts himself and others in uncomfortable situations to make sense of human behavior—or figure out why so much of it doesn't make sense. There have to be logical rules behind humanity's illogical decisions, he figures. He just has to find them. "It's a way to keep control in an uncertain world," Pete told me the first time we met. Growing up in a working-class town in southern New Jersey, he sometimes faced the harsh realities of that uncertain world. Yes, there was always food on the table for him and his younger sister, Shannon, but his single mother had to work two or three jobs and sometimes rely on food stamps to do it. Yes, his mom took care of them, but her headstrong and forceful manner didn't always make her household a fun place to be. And, yes, he sported high-tops and Ocean Pacific T-shirts like the other boys in high school, but by age fourteen, he was working as a stock boy at the local Woolworth's to pay for it all himself. Maybe that's why ever since, he's always been determined to keep everything tidy and under control.

I could identify with Pete's compulsive tendencies, maybe more than I liked to admit. In an industry populated by ink-stained shlubs and paper-cluttered offices, I come off as a tad neurotic. To streamline my reporting process, I've assembled a small, über-geeky arsenal of digital cameras, foldaway keyboards, and electronic audio-recording pens. In the Denver home I share with my wife, Emily McNeil, and young son, Gabriel, every bookshelf is arranged alphabetically by author and segregated into fiction and nonfiction. (I'd say this drives Emily up the walls, but she's my perfect match: as orderly and organized as they come.) In my world, unhappiness is a sink full of dirty dishes.

Pete offered me an all-access tour of his scholarly world. He explained to me that a chunk of his research could be classified as behavioral economics, the growing field of psychologists and economists who are hard at work proving that people don't make rational financial decisions, as classical economists have long suggested. Instead, they've discovered, we do all sorts of odd stuff with our money. While completing his post-doctoral training at Princeton, Pete shared an office with Daniel Kahneman, the Nobel Prize–winning psychology professor who helped establish the field. Kahneman's office would never again be so organized.

But Pete's interests extend well beyond behavioral economics. He's not just interested in why people act strangely with their money. He wants to know why they act strangely all the time. A few years ago, he became fascinated by what could be the most peculiar human phenomenon of all.

While giving a talk at Tulane University about how people are disgusted when churches and pharmaceutical companies use marketing in morally dubious ways, Pete mentioned a story about a church that was giving away a Hummer H2 to a lucky member of its congregation. The crowd cracked up. And then one of the audience members raised her hand with a question. "You say that moral violations cause disgust, yet we are all laughing. Why is that?"

Pete was stumped. "I'd never thought about it," he told me.

He decided to figure it out.

It doesn't take long for the Squire to fill up with patrons ready to cheer—or jeer—the comics tonight. Folks are soon packed in so tightly that the communal body heat overwhelms the slowly rotating fans overhead.

"Welcome to the Squire," cracks the night's MC, grinning into the microphone from the bar's cramped corner stage. "It's the only place with an indoor outhouse." He follows the bit up with a joke about accidentally smoking crack. The room roars, and he turns his attention to three innocent-looking audience members who've unwisely chosen to sit at the table closest to the stage. Soon he's detailing the horrendous sexual maneuvers the wide-eyed threesome must perform on one another. The three, it turns out, are friends of Pete's who thought it would be nice to cheer him on.

As the MC introduces the first of the night's amateurs, Pete slips to the back of the room to look over his note cards. "I'm worried my routine may be a little benign," he admits to me, as the comic on stage fires off a bit about slavery and watermelons.

I pat him reassuringly on the back, but secretly I'm glad that I'm not the one getting on stage. I'm far from spineless, but anything I've done that would be considered gutsy has been under the guise of reporting. I've always been content being the guy in the corner taking notes, the one asking the tough questions, and not the one who answers them. When one of the comedians hears there's a *Westword* reporter in the house, he can't help but make a joke about the paper's numerous medical marijuana dispensary ads. "It should just be a bunch of rolling papers," he ad-libs as the crowd laughs at my expense. I try, and fail, to turn myself invisible.

Other aspiring comics take their turn at the mike, trotting out one offensive subject after another: masturbation, misogyny, Jim Crow laws, drug overdoses.

It's Pete's turn. "This next guy isn't a comedian," says the MC, "but a moderately funny professor from the University of Colorado. Give it up for Dr. Peter McGraw!"

Pete bounds onto the stage and grabs the microphone from the stand—promptly disconnecting it from its cord. The audience goes silent as the professor fumbles with the device.

Comedy 1, science 0.

Pete is far from the first scholar to dive into the wild world of humor. There's an entire academic association dedicated to the subject: the International Society for Humor Studies. Launched in 1989 as an outgrowth of an earlier organization, the World Humor and Irony Membership, or WHIM, the ISHS now includes academics from disciplines ranging from philosophy to medicine to linguistics, a group that has little in common other than a shared fascination with humor and a tendency to be snubbed by colleagues in their own fields for their offbeat scholarly interests.[1]

Altogether they're a productive lot, organizing an annual international conference covering topics like "The Messianic Tendency in Contemporary Stand-Up Comedy" and "Did Hitler Have a Sense of Humor?"; founding *HUMOR: The International Journal of Humor Research*, a quarterly publication chock-full of fascinating reads like "The Great American Lawyer Joke Explosion" and "Fartspottings: Reflections on 'High Seriousness' and Poetic Passings of Wind"; and compiling the soon-to-be-released *Encyclopedia of Humor Studies*, a 1,000-page behemoth covering the whole of humor research from absurdist humor to xiehouyu (a humorous Chinese figure of speech).

What's fascinating about the ISHS, though, is that its members can't seem to agree on a single theory of what makes things funny.[2]

It's not as if the experts don't have enough humor theories to choose from. Over the centuries, efforts have been made to explain why we laugh at some things and not at others. The problem, however, is that the world has yet to agree on the right answer. Plato and Aristotle introduced the superiority theory, the idea that people laugh at the misfortune of others. But while their premise seems to explain teasing and slapstick, it doesn't work for a simple knock-knock joke.

Sigmund Freud, the father of psychoanalysis, had a different view. In his 1905 work, *Jokes and Their Relation to the Unconscious*, he argued that humor was a way for people to release psychic energy pent up from repressed sexual and violent thoughts. His so-called relief theory works for dirty jokes—it's one of the few cases in polite society in which folks are at liberty to talk about their naughty bits. The theory also apparently works for Freud's own witticisms. In 1984, enterprising humor scholar Elliot Oring set about psychoanalyzing the 200 or so jests, riddles, and pithy anecdotes in *Jokes and Their Relation to the Unconscious*. He concluded that the famously private psychotherapist had hang-ups around money lending, sex, marriage, personal hygiene, and, last but not least, Freud's self-described "instructress in sexual matters," his randy old Czech nanny.[3]

Score one for relief theory. Still, it's hard to fit a lot of things people find funny, like puns and tickling, into Freud's model. It doesn't help that the rest of Freud's theory of the unconscious has been abandoned by research psychologists.

Most experts today subscribe to some variation of the incongruity theory, the idea that humor arises when people discover there's an inconsistency between what they expect to happen and what actually happens. Or, as seventeenth-century French philosopher Blaise Pascal put it when he first came up with the concept, "Nothing produces laughter more than a surprising disproportion between that which one expects and that which one sees."[4] Incongruity has a lot going for it—jokes with punch lines, for example, fit this model well. But even the incongruity theory falls short when it comes to tickling or play fighting. And scientists have found that in comedy, unexpectedness is overrated. In 1974, two University of Tennessee professors had 44 undergraduates listen to a variety of Bill Cosby and Phyllis Diller routines. Before each punch line, the researchers stopped the tape and asked the students to predict what came next. Then another group of students was asked to rate the funniness of each of the comedians' jokes. Comparing the results, the professors found that the predictable punch lines were rated considerably funnier than those that were unexpected. The level of incongruity of each punch line was *inversely* related to the funniness of the joke.[5]

There's another dilemma with all these theories. While they all have their strengths, they also share a major malfunction: they short-circuit when it comes to explaining why some things are not funny. Accidentally killing your mother-in-law would be incongruous, assert superiority, and release pent-up aggressive tensions, but it's hardly a gut-buster.[6]

It might seem that there's no way to cover the wide world of comedy with a single, tidy explanation. But for someone like Pete, a guy who yearns for order, that wouldn't do. "People say humor is such a complex phenomenon, you can't possibly have one theory that explains it," he told me. "But no one talks that way about other emotional experiences. Most scientists agree on a simple set of principles that explain when most emotions arise." It's generally accepted that anger occurs when something bad happens to you and you blame someone else for it, while guilt occurs when something bad happens to someone else and you blame yourself.

It has to be the same for humor, Pete figured. There has to be a simple explanation that the authorities have long overlooked. He thinks he found it by doing a Google search for "humor theory."

One of the first results led to "A Theory of Humor," an article published in a 1998 issue of *HUMOR: The International Journal of Humor Research*, written by a man named Thomas Veatch.[7] Veatch posited what he called the "N+V Theory," the idea that humor occurs when someone perceives a situation is a violation of a "subjective moral principle" (V) while simultaneously realizing that the situation is normal (N). To prove that his idea worked, Veatch, who had a PhD in linguistics from the University of Pennsylvania, laid out point after compelling point, meandering from computational linguistics to developmental psychology to predicate calculus. It's heady, compelling stuff, and to Pete, Veatch's theory was closer to the truth than anything he'd come across. But it hadn't rocked the field of humor scholarship. Why had Veatch and his N+V Theory sunk into obscurity?

While Veatch had once taught linguistics at Stanford University, he'd since dropped off the academic radar. It took several weeks of online sleuthing and unreturned voice mails to get Veatch on the phone from his home in Seattle.

The N+V Theory started with a simple joke, Veatch told me:
Why did the monkey fall out of the tree?
Because it was dead.

"I first heard it in '85 or '86, and I laughed for like an hour," said Veatch. That didn't make sense to him, so he thought long and hard about it—as he did about most things. Growing up, Veatch says, he was a loner who read every book in his grade-school library. It was the first inkling of a prodigious mind that, according to Veatch, would later dream up the MP3 player long before anyone had heard of MP3s and devise a phonetics chart that he believes can teach literacy to downtrodden people around the world.

Before those endeavors, he decided to explain the dead-monkey joke. So he sat down in his Stanford office one day in 1992 and came up with the N+V theory. The concept seemed to explain the joke. The lifeless monkey was a violation, but the situation was normal because dead monkeys will fall out of their trees. The premise seemed to work for every other kind of humor Veatch could think of, too. So in 1998, he published his theory in *HUMOR* and waited for a response. And waited. And waited. And waited.

It wouldn't be the last time Veatch's plans wouldn't go as expected. After his stint at Stanford, he tried to make a go of it in the business world, but his attempt to build a speech-synthesizing e-mail reader fell through, as did Teachionary, a language-learning program he developed. He's since tried other jobs: construction manager, carpenter, pizza delivery guy, plumber's helper.

Veatch's tale seems like a testament to just how daunting a task it is to define humor once and for all. But his predecessor's fate hardly gave Pete pause. Veatch's theory engrossed him. As far as he could tell, Veatch had nearly hit the theoretical bull's-eye. But something about it still seemed not quite right.

Pete's department chair, Donnie Lichtenstein, summed up the problem when doctoral student Caleb Warren tried to illustrate Veatch's theory by referring to a fictional story used in psychological surveys that often got people chuckling. As the tale goes, a man decides to use his kitten as a sex toy, with the feline purring in enjoyment. That situation may be funny, said Lichtenstein, but nothing about it is normal.

So Pete and Caleb set upon improving Veatch's work and ended up with a new comedic axiom: the benign violation theory. According to this amended theory, humor only occurs when something seems wrong, unsettling or threatening (i.e., a violation), but simultaneously seems okay, acceptable, or safe (i.e., benign). When something is just a violation, such as somebody falling down the stairs, people feel bad about it. But according to Pete and Caleb, when the violation turns out to be benign, such as someone falling down the stairs and ending up unhurt, people often do an about-face and react in at least one of three ways: they feel amused, they laugh, or they make a judgment—"That was funny."

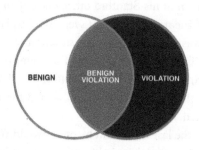

To them, the term "benign," rather than "normal," better encapsulated the many ways a violation could be okay, acceptable, or safe—and gave them a clear-cut tool to determine when and why a violation such as the feline-turned-sex-toy story can be funny. While heavy petting with a kitten may not be normal, according to the story, the kitten purred and seemed to enjoy the contact. The violation was benign—no kittens were harmed in the making of the joke. Later, when Pete and Caleb used this story in an experiment, participants who read a version in which the kitten whined in displeasure at the heavy petting found the tale far less funny than the "happy kitty" scenario.[8]

Then there's the story of the church-raffle Hummer that got Pete pondering what makes things funny in the first place. The idea of mixing the sanctity of Christianity with a four-wheeled symbol of secular excess strikes people as a violation. But when Pete presented the raffle story to regular churchgoers as well as people who rarely go to church, those less committed to Christianity were more likely to find a holy Hummer benign and therefore found it funnier.[9]

Immoral behaviors are not the only kind of humorous situation that could be explained by the benign violation theory. A dirty joke trades on moral or social violations, but it's only going to get a laugh if the person listening is liberated enough to consider risqué subjects such as sex okay to talk about. Puns can be seen as linguistic violations that still make grammatical sense, though they're typically only funny to cerebral types and grammarians who care about the nuances of the English language. Sarcasm violates conversational rules by meaning the opposite of what's said. No one is going to be amused by a crack like "You're good at basketball? Yeah, right!" if they don't notice the exaggerated tone and grasp the intended meaning. Nor is the guy who thinks he's good at basketball.

And tickling, long a sticking point for other humor theories, fits perfectly. After all, tickling involves violating someone's physical space in a benign way. People can't tickle themselves—a phenomenon that baffled Aristotle—because it isn't a violation. Nor will people laugh if a creepy stranger tries to tickle them, since nothing about that is benign.

Pete's ideas about tickling were recently boosted by, of all things, a tickle robot. Cognitive neuroscientists at University College London devised an apparatus in which subjects could control, via a joystick, a mechanical arm brushing a piece of foam over their other hand. When the arm corresponded to the joystick movements, participants didn't find the feeling all that ticklish, but the more the experimenters delayed or shifted the direction of the arm's movements from that of the joystick, the more ticklish folks rated the sensation.[10] These findings meshed with the idea that laughter occurs when tickling is a benign violation: adding a small delay or change in direction of the robotic arm added just enough of a violation to make it ticklish.

Almost as soon as Pete unveiled the benign violation theory, people began to challenge it, trying to come up with some zinger, gag, or "yo momma" joke that doesn't fit the theory. Although Pete is willing to engage in such rhetorical debates, he's weary of doing so. For one thing, humor theorists had been relying far too long on such "thought experiments," trying to shoehorn as many jokes as possible into their theory of choice. But outside of philosophy, thought experiments only get you so far. For another, says Pete, it's fine to criticize the theory, but you'd best offer up a better alternative. And Pete's confident that the benign violation theory outperforms incongruity, relief, superiority, and all other humor-theory contenders. To prove it, he and Caleb turned to science—hence the founding of HuRL. "Your intuition often leads you astray," Pete said to me. "But within the lab, you can set theories against one another."

In one HuRL experiment, a researcher approached subjects on campus and asked them to read a scenario inspired by a story about legendarily depraved Rolling Stones guitarist Keith Richards. In the story, Keith's father tells his son to do whatever he wishes with his cremated remains—so when his father passed away, Keith decided to snort the ashes. Meanwhile, the researcher, who didn't know what the participants were reading, gauged their facial expressions as they perused the story. Then the subjects were asked about their reactions to the story: Did they find the story wrong, not wrong at all, a bit of both, or neither? As it turned out, those who found the tale of Keith and his obscene schnozz simultaneously "wrong" (a violation) and "not wrong" (benign) were three times more likely to smile or laugh than either those who deemed the story either completely okay or utterly unacceptable.[11]

Pete and Caleb became more confident. Pete came to believe the benign violation theory could even help people improve their schtick. As he puts it, folks could use his theory to make upsetting concepts more amusing by making them seem more benign. He calls this tactic the Sarah Silverman Strategy, after the comedian who gets away with jokes on abortion and AIDS because the way she tells them is so darn cute. On the flip side, he believes that pointing out what is wrong with our everyday interactions with soup chefs and "close talkers" can help make those experiences hilarious. Pete calls this technique the Seinfeld Strategy.

HuRL's research has started to gain traction. Pete and Caleb's first paper on the benign violation theory appeared in one of the top mainstream psychology journals. Meanwhile, some of Pete's fellow humor researchers are starting to take notice. "I absolutely consider it significant; it furthers the field," Don Nilsen, co-founder of the

International Society for Humor Studies and co-author of the *Ency-clopedia of 20th-Century American Humor*, told me. "I don't think there are any examples of humor that don't fit this."

The benign violation theory has also been endorsed by a very different sort of humor expert: Ben Huh, CEO of the Cheezburger Network, the multimillion-dollar silly-picture web empire that includes sites such as "I Can Has Cheezburger?" and "FAIL Blog," with whom Pete has shared his research. "I'm a guy who makes his living off of internet humor, and McGraw's model fits really well," Huh told me over the phone. Lately he's been using the model to determine which content could be the next big meme. Take a post about a church funeral getting interrupted by a parishioner's "Stayin' Alive" ringtone. "The benign violation theory applies to that," said Huh: it's clearly a violation for "Stayin' Alive" to come on during a memorial for someone who'd just died, but it's more benign—and therefore funnier—than if somebody purposely turned on the theme to *The Walking Dead*. All in all, says Huh, "He's just a lot more right than anyone else."

But the theory doesn't impress everyone. The skeptics include Victor Raskin. In the world of humor scholarship, Raskin is a titan. Among other achievements, the Purdue University linguistics professor founded the journal *HUMOR*, edited the influential tome *The Primer of Humor Research*, and helped develop the general theory of verbal humor, one of the preeminent theories of how jokes and other funny texts work. He's also, I discovered, not one to mince words. "What McGraw has come up with is flawed and bullshit—what kind of a theory is that?" he told me in a thick Russian accent. To Raskin, the benign violation theory is at best a "very loose and vague metaphor," not a functional formula like $E=mc^2$. It doesn't help that among the tight-knit community of humor scholars, Pete's few years dabbling in the subject is akin to no time at all. "He is not a humor researcher," grumbled Raskin. "He has no status."

Status or not, I decided to reserve judgment on Pete's theory until I saw it in action. I wanted Pete to put his theory to the test. I asked him to accompany me to a Denver stand-up show so he could use his theory to critique the comedians.

He offered one better. "How about I get up on stage myself?"

"That," I replied mischievously, "would be a very good idea."

"**Thank you very** much," Pete says into the Squire's microphone, once he gets it reconnected and begins his act. "Being a professor is a good job. I get to think about interesting things. Sometimes I get my mind on something non-academic. Lately, I have been thinking a lot about nicknames."

"First, a good nickname is mildly inappropriate," he says. "An ex-girlfriend referred to me to her friends as 'Pete the Professor.' Not inappropriate, and not good. Now, if she referred to me as 'Pete the Penetrating PhD-Packing Professor'—mildly inappropriate, and thus a good nickname."

But Pete trips over the words "Pete the Penetrating PhD-Packing Professor" and doesn't get a laugh. Nor do folks chuckle at the other funny names he tries out: Terry the Dingleberry. Thomas the Vomit Comet.

He throws out a line about "a well-endowed African American gentleman," hoping to get some snickers, but it's too pedestrian for a crowd used to hearing about late-term abortions and the joys of meth. He does get a few laughs when he says that most good nicknames involve alliteration and then pauses to explain the meaning of "alliteration"—although it's possible folks were just laughing at the professor's presumption.

People turn away and get lost in small talk. By the time Pete gets to the end of his four-minute routine—with a zinger about a 35-year-old virgin nicknamed Clumpy Chicken—he's lost much of the audience.

"Thanks. Have a good night," Pete says, then leaves the stage amid polite applause. He's replaced by the open mike's MC, who's eager to punch the crowd back up. He has the perfect target.

"I thought you were going to talk about your humor theory!" the comic calls after the professor. "He has this theory, see . . . well, who cares. Obviously, it's WRONG!"

The crowd's back, laughing uproariously. But the MC's not finished.

"All you black people, that's a sweater vest he's wearing, not a bulletproof vest."

He waits a beat. "So go ahead and shoot him."

Standing at the bar after his act, Pete considers his performance. "You can't just get up there and expect to kill."

But why didn't he kill? He spends the night mulling it over. "I clearly underestimated the audience and the challenges in creating sufficient violations," he tells me later. "This means the Seinfeld Strategy would have needed to be multiplied severalfold." Of course, trying to outdo the other comedians in Squire-appropriate violations wouldn't have been a good move, either. Once word got out about the professor who spouts one-liners about slavery and crack cocaine, Pete might have had to start looking for another job.

Pete's stand-up attempt gives the usually confident professor pause. It's clear, he tells me once the article comes out, that he has a ways to go before he understands the vagaries of comedy—and HuRL alone won't take him the rest of the way. There's a big, comical world out there, he says, and if he wants to figure out what really makes things funny, he's got to venture beyond the confines of his lab.

But he can't do it alone. Just as his scholarship needs to be vetted by his academic colleagues, he needs an objective observer, someone willing to call him out if his conclusions don't pass muster.

Someone, in other words, like me.

I'm in. The adventure sounds like a blast, plus it may help me figure out why I am such a screwed-up, hopelessly lighthearted reporter. It will be like *Eat, Pray, Love*, but with awkward guy hugs and dick jokes.

Still, I offer a condition. At the end of the journey, Pete has to again try his hand at stand-up. But this time, at a slightly bigger stage than the Squire: The Just for Laughs comedy festival in Montreal, the biggest comedy event in the world. Comics work for years to earn a shot there, and a single routine can make or break a comedy career. If Pete thinks that he's going to crack the humor code, he has to get up at the festival—and win one for science.

It's a half hour to show time, and Louis C.K. looks miserable. The comic is slumped alone in a chair in the dingy greenroom of Denver's Paramount Theatre, the toll of weeks on the road apparent on his face. Clearly, all he wants to do is eat his ham sandwich and get ready for his show. But instead he has to contend with the likes of us—an overexcited professor and a nervous journalist who've just barged in to ask him to deconstruct what he does on stage.

It's a wonder we got back here at all. C.K., with his stand-up specials and hit FX series *Louie*, is one of the biggest names in the stand-up business. Every one of the 1,800 or so seats for the show tonight at the Paramount Theatre—one of the largest and swankiest venues for comedy in the region—has long been sold out.

It makes sense to start our search for the secrets of humor by talking to comedians like C.K. In many ways, stand-up is the perfect petri dish for figuring out why we find things funny. It's comedy boiled down to basics—just a comedian and an audience, no backstory, no sets, no editors or producers or censors, a place where you either score a laugh or you don't. Stand-up is one of the country's most prominent cultural inventions. Thanks to *The Tonight Show* and *Seinfeld*, the work of American comedians now influences comedy all over the world. Plus, judging from his performance at the Squire, Pete could use a few tips.

So, what turned Louis C.K. into *Louis C.K.*? How does someone *be* funny? Is it an innate talent, something you're born with or that arises from the right conglomeration of instincts and personality traits? Or is it something that develops over time, either through absorbing the right rules or personal trial and error? And what about other variables to consider, such as childhood baggage and the quirks of various comedy clubs? How do they all influence someone's ability to be hilarious?

We're here hoping that C.K. can provide us with some answers. Heck, maybe the king of stand-up will be so taken with our endeavor that he'll show us the secrets to being funny. Our quest will be over as soon as it's begun.

Knowing that he has only a few minutes, Pete launches into the benign violation theory, but he only gets halfway through before C.K. cuts him off. "I don't think it's that simple," he grumbles. "There are thousands of kinds of jokes. I just don't believe that there's one explanation."

His research dismissed, his theory shot down, Pete casts about for something to talk about. "So I was actually chatting with some of your fans in the lobby, and I asked them what questions I should ask you . . ." he begins.

My stomach drops. When an older woman who had made one too many trips to the Paramount's bar heard we were interviewing C.K., she shrieked out a question. But surely there is no way Pete would ask it.

I'm wrong.

"So one woman wanted to know how big your penis is."

C.K. cracks the faintest of smiles but shakes his head. "I am not going to answer that."

"I wouldn't, either," Pete responds. "But I've heard that if you don't answer that, it means it's small."

Now there's no smile.

Sensing we've overstayed, we head for the door. Clearly, we're going to have to look elsewhere to figure out what makes people funny. So, we figure, why not go where many comedians go to try to break into the big time, to hone their acts and get noticed by agents and talent scouts and TV execs? Why not go where up-and-comers go to become the next Louis C.K.?

And with that, we're off to Los Angeles to see how many more people Pete will alienate with penis questions. For science.

"Welcome to the La Scala of comedy," says Alf LaMont. 'This is where it all happened."

We're standing in front of the Comedy Store, a black bunker of a building surrounded by palm trees. Beside us, Maseratis and BMWs glide through the night along the Sunset Strip, the billboard-lined mile-and-a-half stretch of pavement curving through West Hollywood that's always been steeped in a heady cocktail of fame and vice.

This part of town has long been a place of wise guys and movie stars, beatniks and go-go dancers, groupies and glam rockers—and, here at the Comedy Store, some of the pivotal moments in stand-up history. Los Angeles is bursting at the seams with comedy. There are stand-up shows big and small every night of the week at comedy clubs and improv theaters and cabaret clubs, even in the Masonic lodge of a local cemetery. There are podcast tapings and comedic web-video shoots and several major comedy festivals. There's even a new academic concentration in comedy at the University of Southern California. The seeds of this bustling comedy scene can be traced here, to this spot, in 1972, with the opening of the city's first dedicated comedy club.

"All the other comedy clubs got rid of their history, or never had it to begin with," says LaMont, head of marketing for the Comedy Store. "Here, it seeps through the very building." It might not be the only thing seeping through the cracks. LaMont, who resembles a carnival barker with his handlebar mustache, escorts us through a maze of scuffed floors and dingy hallways, describing the club like an out-of-control circus: Here, by the front entrance, are black-and-white photos from when the building housed Ciro's, a celebrity nightclub with Mob ties, years before comics Sammy Shore and Rudy DeLuca rented the space and turned it into a stand-up joint.

And here, scrawled on the walls, are the signatures of up-and-coming comics who flocked to the Comedy Store when Shore's wife, Mitzi, took control of the operation and it became known as the proving grounds to get on *The Tonight Show Starring Johnny Carson*. This who's who of comedy includes David Letterman, Jay Leno, Andy Kaufman, Steve Martin, Elayne Boosler, Richard Lewis, Robin Williams, Arsenio Hall, and Richard Pryor. Here's the bullet hole resulting from the time Sam Kinison got into an argument with Andrew Dice Clay and pulled a gun. ("Sam wasn't trying to kill Andrew," says LaMont. "I don't think.")

"And here," says LaMont, guiding us to a forlorn spot in the Comedy Store's parking lot, "is where things stopped being funny." In 1979, comics formed a labor union and demanded to be paid for their performances, something the club had never done. The Comedy Store eventually began compensating comedians, but some union members were blacklisted. That included Steve Lubetkin, who, on June 1, 1979, jumped from the roof of the thirteen-story Continental Hyatt House next door, landing on the pavement where we're standing. He left behind a note: "I used to work at the Comedy Store. Maybe this will help to bring about fairness."

We stop in the Original Room, a space up front that's known as the toughest room in the country. To show us why, LaMont has us walk on stage and he lowers the lights. Looking out, all we see is pure darkness, with a single, blinding spotlight shining straight at us like an oncoming train. "It's important to hear the audience, not see it," LaMont tells us.

LaMont's tour ends in the Comedy Store's Belly Room, a murky shoe box of a performance space up a rickety flight of stairs at the back of the club. We're here to meet Josh Friedman, a clean-cut 22-year-old financial consultant who's a friend of a friend. The year before, Friedman had tried out on a whim for a stand-up competition and ended up winning the contest at a big downtown club. Now he wants to see if he has the potential to go further—which is why he's here in the Belly Room about to perform for the first time.

We take our seats, and the show begins. Soon the young comic is up. Friedman begins with a tale of a drunken night in Shanghai that ends with him taking a spin on what he thinks is a stripper pole, ripping out a support beam, and knocking out an old Chinese lady. Then he goes on to point out that people who complain that Doritos are like crack don't know what they're talking about: "You eat too many Doritos and it's like, 'My stomach hurts.' You smoke too much crack and it's like, 'My teeth are gone.'" He ends with a bit about his doctor asking to look at his penis: "I was like, 'Oh, my God, this guy is trying to molest me!' And then I realized how ridiculous I was being. He's not some random guy off the street. He's my optometrist!"

The six-minute set isn't bad, but we're biased. We like Friedman. For the real verdict, we'll leave it up to a couple of pros we've invited to the show. One is Sarah Klegman, a young dynamo of a manager for Levity, one of the biggest comedy agencies in LA. The other is Jeff Singer, a hip-looking guy with black plastic glasses who's the executive talent scout for the Just For Laughs comedy festival. These two spend their days watching stand-up reels and grilling club owners, their nights haunting open mikes and talent showcases, looking for the next big thing. And we want to know if Friedman has a shot at the title.

Klegman and Singer, who both watched the performance impassively, divide their comments into good and bad news: the good news is that Friedman has impressive confidence for someone so green. Now for the bad news. He's too long-winded with little payoff, says Singer. "In a six-minute set, you have to get funny quick." And that line about Doritos and crack? "He telegraphed that like a bad boxer."

Klegman has her own critiques. He has no personality on stage, no particular voice, she says. Plus, his beats were off. If he's going to tell stories, "he's gotta dance into it." Finally, he missed an opportunity with his appearance: "He looks like a gay fourteen-year-old," says Klegman. "He should talk about that."

If Friedman is serious about comedy, say Klegman and Singer, he has to get to work. He needs to get on stage four times a week, minimum. If he keeps at it, who knows, maybe he'll be worth their time—five to eight years down the road.

That seems like a lot of time and effort to see if someone has what it takes to be funny. Could there be an easier method, a way to measure somebody's sense of humor, like modern-day baseball scouts use on-base percentages or unintentional walk and strikeout rates to predict a player's future performance?

One stumbling block is that no one seems to agree on what having a sense of humor means. Does it suggest you're good at telling jokes—or good at getting them? Does it mean you find everything funny? Or that you laugh a lot? Most of the time, if you say somebody has a good sense of humor, you're giving them an all-around compliment. (Or, if you're selling your friend on a blind date, it means the date is not very good-looking.)

It doesn't help that the term "humor" has had all sorts of different connotations. It wasn't until the early nineteenth century that humor became widely used in its modern sense, as a virtue. Before that, "humour," from the Latin word for "fluid," referred to bile, phlegm, and other bodily fluids believed to wreak havoc on people's moods. A "humourist" was someone whose body fluids were so imbalanced they acted mentally ill. A "man of humour" was someone skilled at impersonating an insane person.[1]

Despite the confusion, researchers have made valiant efforts to measure people's sense of humor. In the 1980s, Yale researcher Alan Feingold tried to rate humor as an ability to remember funny things: "What comedian said, 'I get no respect!'?" "Complete this joke: 'Take a long walk on a short ____.'" But mostly what he found was that those who scored high watched a lot of funny movies and TV shows.[2]

Tests that require people to produce humor, such as coming up with cartoon captions or crafting jokes, might make more sense, but so far, no one's figured out a standardized way to do so. More effort has been put toward questionnaires that ask people to gauge their own sense of humor. But one of the problems with this method is that according to self-report measures, everyone in the world is hilarious. Researchers found that when asked to rate their own sense of humor, 94 percent of people claim it's average or above average.[3] Apparently, if everybody applied themselves, we'd be a nation full of Carrot Tops.

Klegman and Singer say they don't need to use quantitative measures. Friedman doesn't have what it takes. They can feel it in their guts. Later, at a greasy late-night diner, Singer elaborates on the subjective part of his job, the stuff he can't quantify. "There are a lot of intangibles," he says over bacon and eggs. "In comedy, you are looking for something that pops, something that will play to the masses, something that will make someone a star." Sometimes, he says, "you can look at someone and there is something unique in their soul. It's in their DNA."

He doesn't see that looking at Friedman.

"Okay, class, what's the most important thing in stand-up comedy?" Greg Dean asks his students.

"Your relationship with the audience," they respond in unison.

"What's your reason for being on stage?" Dean continues.

"To tell the audience what's wrong," they answer.

Dean, sitting in a director's chair on stage at the Santa Monica Playhouse, looks satisfied. The dozen or so people sitting around us in the small theater's stadium-style seats are halfway through his five-week intro stand-up class, and they seem to be getting it. The students here are retired lawyers, dock workers, and the unemployed. But they all want to get into comedy. That's why they've come here, to take what's reportedly the longest-running stand-up class in the country. And today, Dean, named best comedy teacher at the Los Angeles Comedy Awards, is going to teach them about riffing, the art of interacting with your audience.

"Stand-up comedy is the most terrifying thing on the planet, and riffing is the most terrifying element of stand-up," announces Dean. He's a big, imposing guy, but he comes off as gentle and a little geeky. That doesn't make what comes next any less intimidating: Each student has to get up on stage and start riffing like they're working the room. "And remember," says Dean, as he pulls out a stopwatch, "Be playfully mean."

Earlier today, we'd visited Dean at his house, a small bungalow in Hollywood filled with small yipping dogs, whiffs of incense, and the flotsam of a life lived oddly. There are circus hats and juggling pins and Buddha statues and two suits of armor standing guard by the fireplace, remnants of a career that includes a stint as a Ringling Bros. circus clown, a one-man comedy act called the "Obscene Juggler," a warm-up act for Chippendale dancers, and personal assistant for self-help guru Tony Robbins. For Dean, it all culminated in what he calls his life's work, "a taxonomy of comedy that other people can build on."

To explain what he meant, Dean started diagramming jokes on a whiteboard he'd set up in his living room. He explained that his joke-writing method arose from number-one benign violation critic Victor Raskin and his linguistic theory of humor—the idea that a joke involves two different and opposite scripts, or frames of reference, with one script usually suggested by the set-up and the opposite script often revealed by the punch line. Take an example Raskin uses in his hefty book on the subject, *Semantic Mechanisms of Humor*:

"Is the doctor at home?" the patient asked in his bronchial whisper.

"No," the doctor's young and pretty wife whispered in reply. "Come right in."

The script suggested by the set-up is that the patient wants the doctor at home so he can be treated by him. The second script revealed by the punch line is that the patient doesn't want the doctor home, so he can be treated in a different manner by the doctor's wife.[4] All Dean did was turn Raskin's theory into a step-by-step joke-writing process. The first step, Dean told us, is coming up with the first scripts, or set-up. "Any statement will do," he said, writing one on the board:

My wife is an excellent housekeeper.

The obvious meaning of this phrase, what Dean calls the "Target Assumption," is that the wife is great at housework. But what else could "housekeeper" mean, he asked us; how could this key word, what he calls the "Connector," be construed? What about if "housekeeper" means someone who literally keeps the house? He calls this step, coming up with a second script, the "Reinterpretation," and it's key to finishing the joke, which he wrote on the board.

My wife is an excellent housekeeper.
When we got a divorce, the bitch got the house.

The system is an elegant way to take obtuse scholarly theory and put it to good use. Even Raskin has nice things to say about it. "Greg is a very nice man, and I have always been flattered by his attention," he responded when I e-mailed him on his thoughts about Dean's work. Still, Raskin being Raskin, he added, "He is no scholar, and the way he understands the theory is very simplistic."

Dean admits that his joke-writing trick doesn't a comedian make. That's why in his classes and his book, *Step-by-Step to Stand-Up Comedy*, he also tackles all sorts of other stuff, like how to hold a microphone and use words with hard consonants because "k" sounds are funnier than "r" sounds, and how to "tag" your punch lines with follow-up punch lines to turn jokes into ongoing bits. And how to riff.

The first on stage for Dean's riffing exercise at the Santa Monica Playhouse is a student named Jack. He looks around the room and focuses on a guy near the front.

"What's your name?" asks Jack, grasping an imaginary microphone.

"Er, Herb," the guy ad-libs.

"And what do you do, Herb?"

"Work in a salon."

"Oh, *really*," purrs Jack, flashing bedroom eyes at Herb. "I never would've guessed—you look so strong and tough!"

The bit's a hit, as are many of his classmates' ad-libbed riffs. Pete and I are impressed. But does that mean that Dean and his comedy-class colleagues are on to something? Is rote instruction the best way to become funny? Questions like this leave many established comics fuming. There's no shortcut to stand-up, they declare; the only way to do it is to put in your years at the clubs, working your way from show opener to feature to headliner, developing your voice through endless nights of blood, sweat, and other sorts of liquids. Does it make sense to pay somebody to teach you what to do, they argue, when some of the most famous comedians of all, like Lenny Bruce, Richard Pryor, and Steve Martin, are the ones who broke all the rules?

These critics might have a point—or they might not. Sooner or later, aspiring comics need to put in stage time. But could taking classes or working with an expert speed up the process? It's hard to know, says Pete. Nobody's ever tested it. "None of these processes are scientific," he says. And without the science, it's tough to make promises about anything.

Take a basic concept that many comedy teachers agree on: you need to stick a big, pregnant pause between your set-ups and punch lines—sometimes as long as several seconds. As Dean notes in his book, quoting from his comedy-expert predecessors, "Timing is knowing when to stop speaking in the midst of a routine in order to allow thinking time for the audience to prepare itself for the laugh that is coming up."[5] On the surface, this advice seems obvious: when someone tells a joke, he or she pauses between the set-up and punch line—right?

Recently, Salvatore Attardo, linguistics professor at the University of Texas A&M and former editor-in-chief of *HUMOR: International Journal of Humor Research*, along with his wife, Texas A&M colleague Lucy Pickering, decided to find out. The two analyzed recordings of ten speakers reciting a pre-written joke as well as a gag they came up with on the spot. What they found was unexpected: the participants didn't pause before punch lines, and the mean length of time between set-ups and punch lines was in fact slightly shorter than the pauses between sentences in the set-up.[6]

"It was absolutely counterintuitive for us," Attardo told me on the phone. For more than a year, they couldn't get anyone to publish their results, because no one believed them. When they presented their work at academic conferences, they were told, "You must have gotten the worst joke-tellers in the universe." But their findings withstood scrutiny, and with additional analysis, Attardo and Pickering also found that punch lines aren't marked by any sort of unusual pitch, speed, or volume.[7] There's nothing differentiating a punch line from the rest of a joke other than it's supposed to be funny.

So why do we assume otherwise? The best theory Attardo's heard is that it could be thanks to one of the most famous one-liners of all: comedian Henny Youngman's iconic 1930s quip, "Take my wife—please."

"This joke only works if there is a long pause," said Attardo. "Because Youngman was so famous and it was such a prominent joke, people essentially said, 'Because there is a huge pause in that joke, there is a pause in all jokes.'"

So maybe it's time for people everywhere to retire the idea of pausing before punch lines. Or as Youngman might put it, take Attardo's research—please.

I'm a dog. I'm not just any dog, I'm Boy George's dog.

Pete and I are on stage at the Upright Citizens Brigade Theatre at the foot of Hollywood Hills, in an unobtrusive storefront space across the street from the ornate headquarters of the Church of Scientology. The location is fitting. These days, people flock to the classes at UCB Theatre and its counterpart in New York like religious converts. The country's only accredited improv and sketch-comedy school, UCB teaches roughly 9,000 students a year, with many more on the wait-list. Improvisation appears to have eclipsed stand-up as the way to get hilariously huge; Mike Myers, Tina Fey, Stephen Colbert, Steve Carell, Dan Aykroyd, John Belushi, Will Ferrell, Kristen Wiig, Jimmy Fallon, and Conan O'Brien are just some of the celebrities who came out of improv groups. And right now, UCB Theatre, founded by comedy star Amy Poehler and her colleagues in 1999, is on the top of the improv hierarchy, boasting alumni that have gone on to write and perform for *Saturday Night Live*, *The Office*, *The Daily Show with Jon Stewart*, *The Late Show with David Letterman*, *The Ellen DeGeneres Show* . . . the list goes on.

We're participating in an improv class taught by Joe Wengert, a wonkish, bespectacled guy who's one of UCB LA's top instructors. We're among some of the program's most advanced pupils, the ones most likely to be tomorrow's comedy elite. Since improv is all about creating performances on the spot, for my first assignment of the day, Wengert teams me with student Darwyn Metzger and tells the two of us to act out a made-up movie called *Wilmer Grace and His Dog*. "Set in the late 1980s," somebody suggests. "Starring Boy George," adds another. "And his dog."

Instinctively, I drop to my hands and knees, ready to be Boy George's dog: "Woof!" Darwyn looks at me like I'm an idiot. I've just broken one of improv's most important rules: "Yes, and . . ." The seemingly obvious thing to do if you're trying to be funny with somebody else is to disagree with them, for the same reason disagree-ments are useful to me as a writer: Arguments are funny! Conflict is interesting! But in improv, it's all about letting the interaction of the performers progress to see what sort of things unfold. An argument stops that process cold. Instead, improvisers are trained to agree with whatever their colleagues say, then use it to further the action: "Yes, and . . ." "No" is a no-no. But I didn't even get that far. By pretending to be a dog that can't do anything but bark, I'd killed all potential interaction between Darwyn and me before we'd even begun.

It's not about being funny, it's about being honest. That's what Charna Halpern told me weeks earlier on the phone: "There is nothing funnier than the truth." Alongside the late improv master Del Close, Halpern co-founded the influential Improv Olympic Theater in Chicago, now known as iO; helped develop the "Harold," the three-act long-form technique that's the triathlon of improv; and wrote the definitive book on the subject, *Truth in Comedy: The Manual of Improvisation.* The improv system laid out in *Truth in Comedy* reads like a self-help book: Be honest. Agree with one another. Stay in the moment. Welcome silence. Listen to your inner voice. There is no such thing as a mistake.

There's a reason the rules sound so life-affirming, said Halpern: improv is all about building bonds with one another, forming order out of the chaos. "We are saving our corner of the world," she said. Halpern has run improv workshops for warring factions in Cyprus, and once flew to Switzerland to teach the physicists working on the $9 billion Large Hadron Collider particle accelerator to loosen up. "I should get a Nobel Prize," she declared. It's unclear whether she was joking.

Our UCB class lasts for hours, but the time flies. Improv is play, and it's a lot of fun. Afterward, at a nearby coffee shop, the students seem ready to do it all again. "I love using another person to succeed or fail on stage," one of them tells us. "It's freeing," says another. "It's like therapy light," raves a third.

We haven't heard anything like this from the stand-up comics we've been talking to in LA, folks who seem like a whole different comedic species than these improvisers. "It's a different beast," a UCB student says about stand-up. "It is flexing two completely different muscles."

Are different people really funny in different ways? Scientists believe so, and they've gotten good at parsing those differences. Take the Humorous Behavior Q-sort Deck, a 100-item test developed at the University of California, Berkeley, that measures how people use humor in their everyday lives. Pete and I subjected ourselves to the Q-sort Deck, discovering its procedure is every bit as ungainly as its name. Going through the assignment's 100 cards, each labeled with a different humor statement, and organizing them in piles from least to most representative of how I use humor, I was soon asking questions I'd never asked before: Do I laugh heartily from head to heel? (Probably more than I care to admit.) Am I bored by slapstick comedy? (Who isn't?) Do I find humor in the everyday behavior of animals? (Is it possible to say no to this once you've been exposed to the miracle website "Animals Being Dicks"?) To ensure I was as honest as possible, I recruited my wife, Emily, to help out. Soon she was grumbling, "Why in the world are we doing this?"

Once I had my answers, added up the totals, and plugged in some mathematical formulas that brought back nightmares of high school algebra, I had my five humor-style scores for the five different ways people tend to create and appreciate humor. Incredibly, my results were almost identical to Pete's. We both scored positively for "socially warm versus cool" and "competent versus inept" humor styles, meaning we both use humor to encourage positive morale, and we're both witty (although Pete is more confident in his schtick than I am in mine). Unfortunately for those we chat up at cocktail parties, we both scored negatively for the "reflective versus boorish" style, suggesting our humor can be unappealingly competitive and clownish, and we're both a bit negative in "benign versus mean-spirited" humor, so we're equally likely to tell cruel jokes. The only difference was in "earthy versus repressed" humor, which means Pete likes dirty jokes while I'm a bit of a prude.

So maybe the UCB students are right. There are different comedic muscles. And it does seem that different muscles come into play in stand-up and improv. But Wengert the UCB teacher, who has a thriving stand-up career on the side, thinks the two share more similarities than most people realize. "All good comedy talks about what is wrong and what is funny about a situation," he tells us later. "A lot of times, the approach for both is, what bothers you about this situation, what's truthful about it."

Again and again, we've heard that the best comedians are at some level outsiders, the people who can stand apart from everyone and everything and ask themselves, "What's funny about this?" As scholar Stephanie Koziski noted, comics have more in common with anthropologists than either group is likely to admit: "The comedian and the anthropologist share a way of seeing. This involves the capacity to stand outside themselves and to empathize with people who are different in order to more fully understand their actions and beliefs."[8]

Maybe that's why ethnic and cultural outsiders in America, those with one foot in the mainstream and one foot outside, have long thrived in comedy. A 1979 *Time* magazine article estimated that while Jews constituted just 3 percent of the U.S. population, they were responsible for an astounding 80 percent of all comedians.[9] While Jewish comic supremacy has surely since declined, their ranks have been replaced in part by African Americans, Asian Americans, Hispanic Americans and, more recently, Muslim Americans. Among this influx was Chris Rock, who grew up in a working-class section of Brooklyn but was bused to predominantly white schools. That made him an outsider in both places, a painful situation for a young kid, but a great state of affairs for a future stand-up icon.

Of course, you don't have to be a minority to be a great comic. But either way, it seems helpful to cultivate what W.E.B. Du Bois called your "double-consciousness," your "two-ness."[10] Yes, in the United States this phenomenon has been a bad thing, something that's kept people fractured and suspicious and struggling with self-identity. But on the bright side, it also makes for good comedy.

For something that's conceptually so basic—joke-telling in its primal form—all we hear from stand-up comics in LA is how complicated it is to do their job right. In comedy, they explain, context is everything. There are too many outside variables, they tell us, too many ways those simple jokes can get mucked up by quirks of the comedy club or audience or a million other factors. "Comedy is seldom performed in ideal circumstances," wrote Steve Martin in his memoir, *Born Standing Up: A Comic's Life*. "Comedy's enemy is distraction, and rarely do comedians get a pristine performing environment. I worried about the sound system, ambient noise, hecklers, drunks, lighting, sudden clangs, latecomers, and loud talkers, not to mention the nagging concern, 'Is this funny?'"

And more than anything else, comedians seem to worry about the space they're trying to be funny in. Is it a "good" room or a "bad" room? But what does that even mean? What constitutes a comedy club, after all, is all over the map. In Los Angeles alone, we've visited venues ranging from brightly lit halls to shadowy bars to back-alley alcoves to black-box theaters to the back room of a comic book store. But if the comedians we've talked to had it their way, clubs would all look more or less the same: a densely packed, dimly lit space with low ceilings, red curtains, and nothing at all that's blue. As Jordan Brady, a comedian turned director whose 2010 documentary *I Am Comic* explored comedy-club designs, put it to us, "A great club experience is best served dark and intimate."

What's funny about these suggestions is that they go against best practices in retail-space design. Research shows that consumers are happiest—and therefore most likely to spend money—in environments with open layouts, high ceilings, and blue-hued color schemes.[11] But as Pete points out, an ideal comedy club isn't designed to get people to buy stuff, even if some drink-shilling club owners wish otherwise. It's to help them have an emotionally arousing experience: to laugh.

And from that perspective, the comics might be on to something. Experiments have shown that people exposed to warm color schemes, especially those with red, are more likely to become aroused and excited, while cool colors like blue are calming and sedative. And the last thing you want of a comedy audience is everybody feeling calm and sleepy.[12] Furthermore, darkened clubs might help people feel more concealed and therefore less inhibited in what they're willing to laugh at. In experiments, people in poorly lit rooms and wearing sunglasses were more likely to do devious things because they felt anonymous.[13] Being packed into a comedy club might have the same disinhibiting effect. When people are in large groups, they are more likely to do embarrassing things such as act like monkeys, make rude noises, and suck on baby bottles.[14] Apparently, if you get enough folks together, everything turns into a frat party.

To see if the comedians knew what they were talking about, Pete figured there was only one thing to do: build his own comedy club. Incredibly, the Denver Art Museum let him do so. During one of the museum's monthly after-hours social events, in which the building remains open late and a cash bar serves up drinks, Pete, working with his collaborator Caleb and graduate student Julie Schiro, took over a small 15-by-50-foot gathering space, filling it with rows of chairs and setting up a movie projector stocked with comedy footage: an *Ellen DeGeneres Show* sketch in which the actor Dennis Quaid terrorized a café barista ("Dennis Quaid wants a coffee!"); a compilation of "epic fail" videos, most of which involved people hit in the groin; and clips of babies making ridiculous faces as they gummed on lemons. Throughout the night, they had groups of museum visitors "attend" their comedy showcase, varying aspects of the room for different performances—changing lighting levels and switching the color of the background behind the movie clips. (Pete had hoped to modify room temperature, but the museum wouldn't go for it. Something about damaging millions of dollars' worth of art.)

Sure enough, combining low lighting with a red backdrop seemed to make some of the clips funnier—but not all of them. And none of the differences reached levels of statistical significance. Plus, an outside variable threw off the results, one Pete never anticipated in an upright place like an art museum: As the night progressed, people became increasingly drunk and rowdy. "That's great for a comedy club," says Pete, "but bad for science."

What about the people who fill the comedy clubs, we wonder—those who come to hear the jokes? Is there a difference between a good comedy audience and a bad one? Hollywood believes there is—and has lately been throwing time and money at the issue. Which is why, just after dawn one morning, Pete and I drive to a warehouse in a bland Burbank industrial zone to have our chuckles evaluated by the laughter queen of Los Angeles.

"Have you practiced laughing?" I ask Pete.

"I practiced yesterday, while I was stuck in traffic," he says. "It was kind of embarrassing."

I haven't practiced. And it's 7 a.m., and I haven't had coffee. There is nothing at all to laugh about.

Lisette St. Claire greets us at the warehouse's entrance, showing us around its cubicle-filled interior—the headquarters of Central Casting, the giant staffing company that's Hollywood's go-to place for extras and stand-ins. "This is the heart of Hollywood," she says. "Eighty-five to 90 percent of everything that's shot in LA, we have a finger in it." That's why she's seeing us so early. In a few hours, things will get busy around here. Folks will begin to line up outside for a shot at being cast as "Homeless Man Number Two." Sometimes, for certain jobs, St. Claire casts herself. "It's fun," she says. "You get to be a hooker one day, a doctor the next."

Her most unusual assignment of all fell into her lap thanks to *The Nanny*, the 1990s sitcom starring Fran Drescher. Years earlier, Drescher had been assaulted in her home by armed robbers. She wasn't keen on having random people in her studio audience. The show asked Central Casting to provide prescreened audiences for the show.

For St. Claire, the casting director assigned to the task, not any old audience would do. "I was not about to send just anybody. I wanted people who were really good," she tells us. St. Claire's overzealousness on the matter makes sense: from her outsized personality to her riot of curly hair to her storied history as a onetime mud wrestler, she's not the sort to do the bare minimum.

She started auditioning people, looking for dominating, infectious laughs. If chosen, folks got $75 for a day's worth of chuckles, slightly better than your typical extra. If folks made the cut, she put them into one of three tiers: top-level Group A, second-string Group B, or "when hell freezes over" Group C.

Her formula was a hit. Her phone started ringing, with three to four shows a week turning to Central Casting's cacklers instead of, say, a laugh track. "We couldn't get enough people with good laughs out," she says.

St. Claire's live laughers have a better scientific track record than the canned version. In one study, researchers found that the sound of strong laughter caused people to rate a Steven Wright comedy routine funnier—but only if they believed the laughter wasn't pre-recorded.[15]

So, do our laughs make the cut? St. Claire turns to me. "Laugh like you're about to pee your pants."

I try my best, feeling goofy and awkward as I cackle as loud and long as I can. It's hard not to feel like a fool when you're laughing at nothing whatsoever.

When I'm laughed out, it's Pete's turn. He slaps his knee and rears his head back, mouth agape. No wonder his college friends nicknamed him "T-Rex."

"Not bad," St. Claire says with a polite smile. "I'd put you both in Group B."

The laughter queen is being kind.

No trip to Los Angeles is complete, we figure, without a road trip to Las Vegas. So on a bright California morning, we lock our apartment, pack up our rental car, and, trading hackneyed shouts of "Vegas, baby!" head out onto the road . . . only to find ourselves stuck in five-lane, bumper-to-bumper, no-end-in-sight traffic. At 11:37 a.m. on a Saturday. "This is not the exciting *Swingers*-style trip we envisioned," grumbles Pete as we idle in a sea of cars. He points to a homeless man pushing two shopping carts piled high with odds and ends down the sidewalk. "That guy is beating us."

Eventually we make it through the congestion and, after hours of cruising through desert vistas of gnarled Joshua trees and craggy mountain peaks, we make it to Sin City. It's like a fever dream in the middle of nowhere: gargantuan casinos soaring overhead, kitschy music blaring from all directions; lurid neon flashing—and, in the middle of it all, featuring a smile as bright as any of the signs on the Las Vegas Strip, a huge billboard for the man we've come to see: "Funny Man George Wallace for President!"

As entertainment journalist Richard Zoglin wrote in *Comedy at the Edge*, "Stand-up comedy may be the only major art form whose greatest practitioners, at any given time, want to be doing something else"—whether that be a sitcom star, a film icon, or a late-night talk-show host. But it's difficult to break out in such a way, to become mega-stars with multimedia empires. For one thing, once you've reached the top, it's hard to stay there. Unlike rock stars, comics can't just do greatest-hits tours, since old jokes are, well, old.[16]

Still, some comedians have managed to become fabulously rich. But maybe they had an unfair advantage. Is a white comic, for example, more likely to strike it rich than a black comic? To find out, Pete decided to mine the data from an online list of nearly 200 comedians' net worth, ranging from the $800 million fortunes of Jerry Seinfeld and Larry David to the $5,000 income claimed by Andy Dick.[17] Working with undergraduate research assistant McKenzie Binder and cognitive scientist Phil Fernbach, he sliced the info every which way. Not surprisingly, they found the biggest predictor of success was age. The longer folks had been in the business, the more money they'd earned. Being involved in endeavors other than stand-up, such as starring in or producing films, also correlated with higher net worth. Gender didn't have much effect, but then again, only 10 percent of the comedians listed were female. A few other traits, though, did seem to offer marginal help. Comedians who were atheistic or agnostic, were married, or, yes, happened to be white, tended to be richer. But these effects mostly went away when Pete and his collaborators controlled for the other relevant characteristics. Put another way, Chris Rock wouldn't make more money if he were white, but he would make more money if he wrote, produced, and directed more movies.

George Wallace, a former ad-agency salesman who started in comedy in late-1970s New York alongside his roommate and friend Jerry Seinfeld, seems to have handled his ascension to the comedy firmament with ease. While he's never starred in a sitcom or big movie, he sells out the biggest theaters, has appeared on the biggest talk shows, and was named among the 100 greatest comics of all time by Comedy Central. And here in Las Vegas, at the Flamingo Resort and Casino, where he has a running show we have tickets for tonight, he holds court like a king over his flashy fiefdom.

Some say Vegas, with all its distractions, is one of the toughest places for a comic to perform. But not so for Wallace. As soon as the comedian, in a gray suit and signature beret, steps on stage in the

Flamingo Showroom with its 60-foot ceilings and red plush seating, he's in his element. The near-capacity crowd eats up his cracks about NBA stars, televangelist Joel Osteen, and what he'd do if he were president. Every "yo mamma" joke lands a laugh, every time he trots out his catchphrase, "I be thinkin' . . ." folks go wild. It's a bit hokey. But Wallace is fun, he's boisterous—and most of all, he seems happy.

Such a persona goes against one of the most endearing stereotypes in all of comedy: the road-weary, liquored-up, drug-addled, and all-around screwed-up comic. As British humorist Jimmy Carr and his journalist co-author Lucy Greeves put it in their far-reaching book *Only Joking: What's So Funny About Making People Laugh?* "In a room filled with people, the comedian is the only one facing the wrong way. He's also the only one who isn't laughing. For normal people, that's a nightmare, not a career aspiration."[18] In many famous cases, that nightmare hasn't ended well. Lenny Bruce overdosed on drugs. Mort Sahl lost himself in obsession over the John F. Kennedy assassination. Richard Pryor set himself on fire while freebasing cocaine and nearly killed himself. The comedy industry accepts these potential outcomes as a given. The Laugh Factory, one of the biggest comedy clubs in LA, has an in-house therapy program. Two nights a week, comics meet with psychologists in a private office upstairs while lying on a therapy couch once owned by Groucho Marx. "Eighty percent of comedians come from a place of tragedy," Laugh Factory owner Jamie Masada, a colorful guy in hip sneakers and jeans, told Pete. "They didn't get enough love. They have to overcome their problems by making people laugh."

But could Wallace, with whom we've been granted a sit-down, be the exception? The proof comedians don't have to be miserable? After his Flamingo show, casino personnel pull us backstage and whisk us through a maze of corridors, past stretching cabaret dancers and a mariachi band set, into a well-appointed dressing room with Wallace's name on the door. The towering, grinning man inside greets us, happy to chat. "I had the perfect childhood," Wallace says. "My ultimate goal was to work Las Vegas, and now I'm here." He rambles on with a confident swagger, like a rambunctious grandpa overflowing with stories. Plus, he says with a wink, "I'm the most successful comedian you've ever met, and I can go pee without anyone bugging me." He points to a photo on the wall of his friend Seinfeld. "He can't go pee."

In the early hours of the morning, we thank Wallace for his time, figuring it's time for us to go. "Don't leave!" he cries. "I'm going to be lonely!" He says this jokingly, but there's something in his voice. Maybe the most successful comedian we've ever met has no one else to talk to, nowhere else to go.

Even Wallace could have a trace of unhappiness buried beneath his layers of contentment and success. Does this mean funny people are inherently unhappy? Gil Greengross, an anthropologist from the University of New Mexico, looked into the matter by subjecting comics recruited from a local stand-up club to established personality surveys. He found that comedians on the whole don't report having more childhood problems than typical university students, nor do they appear to be more neurotic. He did find that they tended to be slightly more introverted and disagreeable than others, an odd finding considering that they're always making jokes in front of crowds. But, as Greengross put it when I talked to him, "The personalities they project on stage might not be their personalities in daily life."[19]

Our time with the Upright Citizens Brigade Theatre students left Pete wondering if improvisers would score differently on such tests. So he partnered with Greengross, as well as HuRL graduate student Abby Schneider and decision-research scientist (not to mention improv alum) Dan Goldstein to undertake what they believe is the largest-ever data collection on amateur and professional funny people. They had more than 650 UCB students—from absolute beginners to members of the theater's house teams—complete online surveys measuring personality traits like agreeableness, neuroticism, self-awareness, and tenacity. When the data came in, Pete and his colleagues found just one area of difference between the two types of humorists: the students specializing in improv tended to be more conscientious than the stand-up comics. The improvisers, the data showed, were more likely thorough, efficient, and deliberate (i.e., they were good at coming up with what comes after "Yes, and . . ."). But there's a downside: Conscientious people tend to be perfectionists. Take it from the two of us: that's not always a good thing.

But other than that, UCB instructor Joe Wengert turned out to be right: the personalities of stand-up comedians and improvisers are far more alike than different. Despite their cheerful and engaging on-stage demeanor, the improv students ended up being just as disagreeable and introverted as stage comics.

So are all comedians jackasses? Not necessarily. In his solo research, Greengross found one other bit of data: Those comedians who seemed to have the most success, in that they reported having the most shows booked, were those who tended to use friendly, more affiliative humor in their daily lives and were more open-minded, agreeable, and extroverted than their counterparts.[20] As Greengross put it to me, "There might be something in the combination of being nice to others, and not being an asshole, that pushes you over the top."

We heard the same thing from Chris Mazzilli, the cool-as-ice co-owner of Gotham Comedy Club, the poshest stand-up joint in New York City. "It's a business," Mazzilli told us about comedy. "A lot of people don't treat it as such." If you want to be successful, he concludes, "don't be an asshole." Yes, comics make their living by creating conflict and turmoil in front of an audience, but if they hope to succeed with managers, agents, club owners, producers, and directors, that conflict and turmoil had better stay on stage.

So why is it that people assume successful comics are the opposite, that they're screwed up both on stage and off? It could be because by nature of their career, all they do is talk about what's wrong with themselves, says Pete: If you're going to mine your life for comedy material, for benign violations, you're going to start with the violations—relationship struggles and health problems and other topics—that people don't talk about in polite company, but are great for a laugh.

To test his hypothesis, Pete recruited grad student Erin Percival Carter and Colorado State University professor Jennifer Harman to run an experiment in which they had 40 people come up with a short story they might tell to others at a get-together. Half had to recount a funny story, while the others just had to be interesting. Among the humorous stories were tales of a dog swallowing a box of tampons, a guy getting caught singing in the men's room to Cyndi Lauper's "Time After Time," and someone deciding one drunken night to let a buddy burn a lightning bolt into his forehead so he'd look like Harry Potter. When others read the stories and chose which authors seemed the most "messed up," the funny storytellers were rated significantly more screwy than the others.[21]

But maybe these storytellers were viewed as screw-ups simply because they weren't very good at telling funny stories. So the team re-ran the experiment, this time employing the talents of our new friends at the Upright Citizens Brigade Theatre. Alex Berg, UCB LA's artistic director, was so excited about the partnership, he launched a whole UCB "science department" to handle it (cute, we know). Once again, when the findings came in, the UCB performer who penned a funny story about teaching grade-school kids to swim when he didn't know how to swim himself was judged to be significantly more messed up than the UCB member who described in a serious manner saving a guy who'd fallen onto the subway tracks—even though both stories were actually written by the same person.

In conclusion, maybe we're all equally screwed up. The rest of us just aren't as motivated as comedians to share those screw-ups with others in the guise of jokes.

That is, except for the Harry Potter lightning-bolt guy. He needs professional help.

On our last night in Los Angeles, we head back to the UCB Theatre to catch the hottest stand-up show in town: "Comedy Bang Bang." The small black-box theater is crammed with twentysomethings in hipster T-shirts and baseball hats, swigging booze from brown paper bags beneath the venue's prominent "No drinking" signs. As usual for the show, nobody knows who's going to perform. But that doesn't matter to folks in the know. Tickets for the event sold out days ago, as they do most weeks.

When the show starts, Pete and I sit in back, taking it all in. We've seen so much stand-up lately we act like snooty connoisseurs, nodding and whispering to each other, "Oh, that's funny," rather than laughing like normal people.

Then, at the end of the night, the big special guest: Aziz Ansari, co-star of the sitcom *Parks and Recreation* and, alongside Louis C.K., one of the biggest comedy names around. He's here to work on material.

Ansari works the audience, asking what dating sites people frequent, and segues into an extended bit on internet matchmaking. He complains that as a child he was ignored by pedophiles, something he doesn't understand: "For child molesters, I must've been like the hot chick at the bar." The crowd eats it up, but with one graphic molestation joke, he takes it too far. The laughter dies.

"Oh, come on!" he cracks in mock annoyance, gesturing at a digital recorder he has running nearby. "Other people have laughed at that. I've taped it. Want me to play it for you?"

Later, Pete realizes something: "Comedians are using science." While comics like Louis C.K. might deny there's a formula behind what's funny, they've all developed their own formulas—by experimenting bit by bit, recording their shows night after night and gauging the results. As we've learned here in LA, it's not about whether or not you're funny, it's *how* you're funny: how you learn the ins and outs of the business, how you develop your comic perspective, how you mix honesty and humor, how you deal with bad venues, and how you handle your shot at fame. And the only way to learn is through hard, repetitive, empirical work. "Comedians are experimenting every time they go up on stage and try a new bit and they gauge how the audience responds," says Pete. "They tweak it, see how it changes, tweak it, see how it changes."

Yes, non-scientific stuff plays a role, too. Several months after our trip to Los Angeles, comic hopeful Josh Friedman sends us an e-mail. He's turned his attention to improv, he tells us: "As an art form and personal activity, I find I enjoy it a whole lot more," he writes.

The talent scouts' gut feeling was right. He didn't have stand-up in his soul.

Call it whatever you want, but experimentation is integral to being funny. "To say that science can't help comedy is to ignore what comedians have learned throughout the years," Pete says.

Yes, comedy's a bit messy, a bit dangerous. But then again, so is science.

Pete and I are staring at a cartoon from the *New Yorker* magazine, willing our brains to come up with the perfect caption for a drawing of a wolfman sitting in a barbershop.

The caption has to fit—but it also has to be funny. And how do you do that? In Los Angeles, we poked around in the strange and off-kilter minds of the gatekeepers of comedy and came away with a rough idea of what makes them tick. But how do they create those jokes and routines in the first place? Not to mention, how do people come up with all the other forms of comedy—narrative poems and plays and animated cartoons and novels and sketches and sitcoms and short stories and movies and satire and caricatures and puns?

That's what Pete and I aim to find out—starting by creating a funny caption for a wolfman getting a haircut. How about, "Be sure to cover up my bald spot"? Or, "Somewhere in here, I lost my keys"? Or maybe something a little more risqué—a request for a Brazilian wax?

What we're doing isn't all that unusual. Thousands undertake this task every week. Since 2005, when the *New Yorker* began devoting the last page of its weekly issue to a cartoon caption contest, the magazine has received more than 1.7 million total caption submissions from people all over the world. And at this point, 1.7 million minus 300 or so have lost. Comic actor Zach Galifianakis might be funny enough to earn $15 million for *Hangover 3*, but his submission for a 2007 cartoon of a dog throwing a stick ("He's his own best friend") didn't get a finalist nod. Michael Bloomberg turned himself into one of the richest people in the world and a three-term mayor of New York, but he swears he can't come up with an idea good enough to submit.[1]

Sure, it's possible to win the *New Yorker* Cartoon Caption Contest, but keep in mind that your chances are 5,666 to one. It's about the same chance as getting a hole in one—if you are very good at golf.

Disregarding the odds, Pete and I are taking a shot at it, but this particular contest is special: we're doing it on the twentieth floor of a gleaming skyscraper in New York City's Times Square—more specifically, in the offices of *The New Yorker*. We're sitting in a swanky conference room with floor-to-ceiling undulating glass walls. All around us are well-dressed doctors, engineers, and other professionals sipping mimosas from champagne flutes and trying to outwit each other captioning drawings of man-sized babies and guys wearing horse costumes. We're taking part in a live caption contest, part of the annual *New Yorker* Festival—Lollapalooza for the New York literati.

Attendees have been broken into a dozen or so teams of eight people, and our table is stymied. Floundering, we've been experimenting with different strategies. For the first round, we tried brainstorming a single list of captions. But that soon devolved into wild tangents and rambling, and our final list was pitifully short. So for round two, each team member submitted a caption and we consolidated the best options. Output was much improved, but it felt like a homework assignment. And it didn't get us on the leaderboard. So far, not one of our options has cracked the three finalists.

Maybe we shouldn't be too hard on ourselves, since creating things that are funny is really hard. For starters, how people create *anything* unique and brilliant is downright mysterious. For centuries, the talents of artists and inventors were thought to be either a gift from the gods, a satanic trick, or some sort of comic book–type genetic mutation. Creating stuff that is supposed to be hilarious is especially strange. Humorists will slave endlessly to find just the right combination of words or images that will get people to laugh, a body spasm that seems to occur subconsciously. It's as if the point of the Sistine Chapel ceiling were to get the Pope to sneeze.

Add to that, as Pete's discovered in his research, most things just aren't funny. In a marketing study with his collaborator Caleb Warren, he had research assistants ask undergraduates to create funny advertising headlines for the made-up company "ThriftOnline." Of all the headlines generated, only 10 percent were deemed by a second group to be gut-busters. (Best of the best? "Because looking this bad never had to be expensive.") The vast majority instead skewed toward stinkers such as "Come get your nerd."

So, then, what's the secret to making people laugh—especially when your audience numbers in the hundreds of thousands? How does someone come up with material that's novel enough, inoffensive enough, and hilarious enough to tickle funny bones the world over? Is it better to use a team-based approach, bouncing humorous ideas back and forth? Or is one single funny person all you need? And what about the giant industry that's sprung up around comedy, from Hollywood films to sitcoms to meme-filled websites? Has the rise of big-budget comedy made things funnier—or dampened the joke?

We hope to find the answers here in New York, a mass production and distribution center of American comedy, a place teeming with the film studios, television sets, publishing operations, ad firms, and theater stages that help generate, shape, and dispense one of the nation's biggest cultural exports. It's why we're at the *New Yorker* offices, racking our brains about werewolves getting haircuts. Sure, we don't really fit in with the swanky crowd, but we happen to be pals with *New Yorker* cartoon editor Bob Mankoff.

In a famous episode of *Seinfeld*, the character Elaine comes up with a *New Yorker* cartoon and in the process tangles with the magazine's cartoon editor. Although Bruce Eric Kaplan, a longtime *New Yorker* cartoonist, wrote the episode, the editor is nothing like Mankoff. The *Seinfeld* Bob Mankoff is an uppity *New Yorker* stereotype in a sweater vest and sports coat. The real Bob Mankoff is cool and engaging, if a bit intense, sporting a tailored jacket and wavy locks of shoulder-length salt-and-pepper hair. (Regarding his portrayal in this book, Mankoff quipped, "The main thing I will be concerned with is how my hair is represented.")

The *Seinfeld* version of Bob Mankoff resists all attempts to explain the *New Yorker* cartoons, insisting, "Cartoons are like gossamer. And one doesn't dissect gossamer." But the real version of Bob Mankoff has never met a thread of gossamer he hasn't sliced, diced, and stuck under a microscope. A onetime PhD student in experimental psychology—he taught pigeons how to sort addresses by ZIP code—he's a member of the International Society of Humor Studies. We'd first met Mankoff when he was making the rounds of humor conferences, presenting on the science of why LOLCat images would never be set among the publication's rarefied Adobe Caslon typeface.

No wonder we get along. And when he offered us a behind-the-scenes look at the *New Yorker*'s cartoon operation, we didn't hesitate. After all, the magazine looms large in the world of American humor creation. Before the *New Yorker* was filled with names like Truman Capote, E. B. White, and Malcolm Gladwell, it started as the 1920s version of *The Onion*. As Ohio University communications professor Judith Yaros Lee wrote in *Defining* New Yorker *Humor*, the humor publication was one of the first to target a specific socioeconomic demographic (college-educated, upwardly mobile urban professionals), and to match this population's sense of humor, the magazine's jokes were groundbreakingly intelligent, topical, and a bit dangerous. In the world of published comedy, the *New Yorker* was a turning point. According to literature professor and author Sanford Pinsker, when the first issue rolled off the press on February 21, 1925, "The 'character' of American humor changed."[2]

Part of that transformation was due to the magazine's cartoons. Harold Ross, the *New Yorker*'s founder, once joked that because of all the visual gags, his magazine had been described to him as "the best magazine in the world for a person who cannot read."[3] But they weren't just silly drawings. The entire cartoon medium changed thanks to the *New Yorker*'s one-two punch of a concise, clever image combined with a witty, short caption. As Lee put it to me over the phone, "The central discovery of the *New Yorker* cartoon was not the one-line caption, but rather the idea that the caption and the drawing worked together to convey a comic idea." That combination stuck around, revolutionizing the funny-drawing industry, and has come to define what most people now recognize as cartoons. No wonder former *New Yorker* editor Tina Brown once noted that *New Yorker* cartoons are "a sort of national treasure."[4]

And Mankoff offered us the keys to the vault.

To start, Mankoff suggests we try our hand at this live caption contest. Pete jumps right in, filling his yellow legal pad with captions and bouncing ideas around our table. Meanwhile, I'm staring wide-eyed at the blank page in front of me, feeling like a Pop Warner benchwarmer who's been dropped in the middle of the Super Bowl. As a writer, the *New Yorker* is my Valhalla. Being here leaves me feeling awed and unworthy. And that I'm being asked to come up with concise writerly brilliance after two flutes of mimosa? Forget about it.

Thanks to Pete, however, we've come armed with a few tricks. Not long ago, Mankoff handed over to HuRL all the submissions for a recent caption contest, one featuring a man and a woman struggling through a desertlike parking lot and coming to section "F," with no car in sight. With the help of cognitive scientist Phil Fernbach, Pete compared the several thousand losing entries to the 43 captions short-listed by the *New Yorker* as potential finalists. They found that the short-listed entries tended to have four things in common: They were novel, in that they didn't rely on words common in other entries such as "park" and "desert." They were concise—on average, 8.7 words long, a full word shorter than the rest. They didn't go overboard with punctuation; losing entries were nearly twice as likely to use question marks, and nearly seven times more likely to use exclamation points. And they featured imaginative imagery, playing with abstract concepts that weren't represented in the drawing.

"I am shocked—shocked—by the results," responded Mankoff sarcastically. "When I went to cartoon college, I was taught that long, heavily punctuated, commonplace captions were the key to success." (The final results of the contest that HuRL analyzed suggests a final secret: have lots of experience writing. The winning caption—"I'm not going to say the word I'm thinking of"—was submitted by none other than the late celebrated film critic Roger Ebert, his first win in 108 attempts.)

Considering the four criteria Pete discovered, maybe our caption ideas for the wolfman in the barbershop aren't so bad after all. Take this caption: "Be sure to cover up my bald spot." It's a concise eight words, doesn't bother with exclamation points or question marks, is pretty abstract, and seems novel. Who knows, maybe we have a winner.

Our colleagues at the table agree, and submit it to the judges. And sure enough, when the results are in, there's our caption, standing strong at second place!

I'm thrilled, until I realize that at the *New Yorker*, second place will never cut it.

So where do the mass-market jokes begin that get churned out from New York's sprawling comedic sausage factory? Where do the raw doodles originate that become polished *New Yorker* cartoons? According to Bob Mankoff, many of them come from a second-story walk-up in Park Slope, Brooklyn. When we stop by one morning, a 28-year-old named Zachary Kanin meets us at the door. Kanin's small and compact, built like a high-school wrestler. There's a somberness to him, a quiet seriousness, which we weren't expecting. Mankoff, after all, calls Kanin a comic genius.

In Kanin's apartment, which he shares with his wife, an enormous blackboard scrawled with a lengthy to-do list takes up much of the living-room wall:

Banjo (done)
Start band (done)
Order dresser
Go on *Wheel of Fortune*
Get sexy (done)

The last item sounds ominous, if not a bit racy: "July 24th: Banan-ageddon!" Kanin explains it refers to the time when he and his wife bought too many bananas. They figured if they didn't eat them all by July 24, they'd have a bananageddon on their hands.

Kanin has already accomplished a lot of things that aren't on the board. Like attending Harvard and serving as president of its illustrious humor magazine, the *Harvard Lampoon* (at five three, Kanin is proud to point out he's the shortest-ever president). And scoring the job when Mankoff called the *Lampoon*'s offices his senior year in college, looking for a new assistant. And once at the magazine, becoming one of its youngest-ever staff cartoonists.

According to Mankoff, cartooning is "idea creativity on overdrive." Scientists, inventors, and artists don't have to come up with that many good ideas to get by. A good year for a research professor like Pete entails publishing one peer-reviewed journal article. As a journalist, I am in good shape if I come up with a dozen solid magazine articles a year. Cartoonists? We're talking about a different order of magnitude. If someone like Kanin hopes to cut it at the *New Yorker*, he or she has to come up with dozens upon dozens of funny ideas each week.

Kanin shows us where he tries to do so: a room at the back of his apartment not much larger than a storage closet. On a small white desk, a MacBook is surrounded by piles of drawings in various stages of germination. There's a doodle of an overweight man grasping his rumbling stomach. A Chewbacca look-alike is wearing a hobo outfit. An amoeba-like tree sprouts branches with mouths. In the margins of the pages, Kanin has scribbled down random words and phrases, hints of other odd ideas: "tap dance," "hard work," "trunk of car."

Each week, Kanin will spend hours here, doodling away until he has 100 ideas in various stages of completion, the best eight to ten of which he'll submit to Mankoff. Sometimes he lets his hand draw freely to see what it comes up with. Other times he plays with a vague concept over and over, maybe endless variations of birds, in the hope they turn into something.

If his work is good enough, the resulting cartoon won't require a caption at all, since the entire joke is contained in the drawing. This week, for example, he plans on submitting a captionless cartoon that features two people walking toward the same street corner from opposite directions. One is walking ten bowling pins on leashes. The other is walking a bowling ball.

"As a cartoonist, these are the most pleasing," Kanin tells us. "It's a puzzle you solve with just the drawing.

How, exactly, did Kanin come up with the image of people walking bowling balls and pins? How do we take all the un-funny elements of the world and distill from them humor? Any sizable bookstore has several shelves devoted to answering the question. There are how-to guides and step-by-step workbooks and so-called comedy bibles, designed mostly for wannabe comedy writers for TV and film. A few compile interviews with as many funny creative people as possible. The most interesting of these is one of the oldest: William Fry and Melanie Allen's 1975 work *Life Studies of Comedy Writers*, and mostly it's because in it, Norman Lear, the television titan behind *All in the Family*, *Sanford and Son*, *The Jeffersons*, and *Good Times*, compares comedy writing to an orgasm: "Everything is gushing, everything is just gushing." As Archie Bunker might have said, those were the days.

One of the longest-lasting theories of how we make things funny doesn't come from a comedian or humor researcher or comedy aficionado at all. It comes from a man named Arthur Koestler. And it's not all that surprising that Koestler tried to deconstruct humor creation. During his 78 years, there was little he didn't do. As an Austrian-born journalist and international man-about-town, he hobnobbed with Langston Hughes and W. H. Auden and rode a Zeppelin to the North Pole, all before being imprisoned by Franco's forces during the Spanish Civil War. Later, while fleeing the Gestapo in France, he swallowed some suicide pills he'd received from famed philosopher Walter Benjamin. The pills killed Benjamin, but not Koestler, allowing him to continue on with his eventful life—taking LSD with Timothy Leary, getting drunk with Dylan Thomas, buddying up with George Orwell, giving political advice to Margaret Thatcher, teaching a young Salman Rushdie, and sleeping with Simone de Beauvoir.

In between all that activity, Koestler managed to tackle the philosophy of making jokes in his 1964 book *The Act of Creation*. Koestler described humor as "the clash of two mutually incompatible codes"—the fusion of two frames of reference that for the most part have nothing to do with each other.[5] For Koestler, the point where the two frames of reference bisect each other equals the punch line. Puns are the simplest case, since they play with two different meanings of the same word. Greg Dean's joke-creation process that we learned about in Los Angeles fits, too, since it involves combining two opposing scripts with a single connecting concept. But the theory also works with visual humor. Take the captionless cartoon Kanin is submitting this week: it plays with two incompatible frames of reference—the tendency of people to take their dogs for walks, and the sport of bowling. There's nothing inherently comical about either, but intersect the two concepts—have pet walkers and bowling paraphernalia run into each other all at once—and you've found something funny.

Pete's fond of Koestler's work as one way to approach humor creation, but he's not ready to concede it's the be-all, end-all of humor-creation theories. Not surprisingly, he prefers his own benign violation approach: come up with something that seems wrong to you, then find a way to make it okay (or vice versa). He's also quick to point out that the process of combining two otherwise disconnected concepts sometimes just results in gobbledygook. Other times it results in smartphones ("cell phone" plus "internet browser").[6]

Koestler believed the "clash of two mutually incompatible codes" wasn't just about making jokes. He saw it as the recipe behind many other forms of human creation, from scientific innovation to artistic genesis. As he wrote, when two planes of reasoning intersect, "the result is either a *collision* resulting in laughter, or their *fusion* in a new intellectual synthesis, or their *confrontation* in an aesthetic experience."[7]

However you build jokes, creativity helps. What's fascinating is that the reverse is true, too: humor helps with creativity. In a 1987 experiment, psychologist Alice Isen and her colleagues had subjects try to solve a classic puzzle: attach a candle to a blank wall using only the candle, a box of tacks, and some matches. Folks who first watched a funny blooper reel were more successful at solving the task—tack the box to the wall and then use a match to melt the candle onto the box—than those who exercised or watched a math video.[8] And in a more recent MIT study on idea generation, improvisational comedians asked to brainstorm new products generated, on average 20 percent more ideas than professional product designers, and the improv comic's ideas were rated 25 percent more creative than those of the pros.[9]

But beyond watching *America's Funniest Home Videos* or doing improv all day, how else can budding humorists put their minds in the best possible position to combine all these disparate concepts? Koestler believed cleverness played a factor, as well as being worldly or well-read enough to have many frames of reference.

This recipe for humor production seems so simple (acquire a lot of information, then combine it in unusual ways), it's a wonder that no one has programmed a computer to do it for them. In fact, folks have been hard at work designing robo-jokesters for decades. There's JAPE, the Joke Analysis and Production Engine; STANDUP, the System To Augment Non-speakers' Dialogue Using Puns; LIBJOB, the lightbulb-joke generator; and DEviaNT, the Double Entendre via Noun Transfer program. And for computer programmers looking for just the right witty acronym for the next big comedy computer, there's the HAHAcronym Generator.[10]

Unfortunately, all these attempts have proven is that, yes, computers can tell jokes, but only dumb ones. Consider the following computer-generated zingers:

What kind of animal rides a catamaran?

A cat.

What is the difference between leaves and a car?
One you brush and rake, the other you rush and brake.[11]

If robots ever conquer the world, we're in for a dystopian future of horrible puns. That's because jokes, like puns, involve simple, fixed data sets like word lists and definitions, where computers excel. But most comedy trades in concepts that aren't simple or fixed at all. The best comedy mines a wide world of attitudes, assumptions, morals, and taboos, and getting any computer to *get* the joke—much less to come up with its own and know when and to whom to tell it—would require uploading into it all of humanity.[12]

Maybe that's why Koestler figured creating jokes wasn't as simple as being intelligent and creatively combining different subjects. Successful humor creators also have to be comfortable with "thinking aside," he wrote.[13] It's not about following rules. It's about breaking them—shifting perspectives, exploring the absurd, and probing the outer limits of what's acceptable.

Kanin is well versed in thinking aside. "My best ideas seem to be combinations of items that come out of nowhere," he says as we take a walk through Park Slope, meandering past the triumphal arch and martial statuary of Grand Army Plaza. And yes, he admits, he does tend to be a bit adventurous and inquisitive. If he were dropped into an alien metropolis, he says, "I would want to go in every room in every building in the city." Of course, he admits with a smirk, then he might be going about this cartooning thing all wrong: "Here I am, sitting in a single room, drawing pictures and not getting around."

We ponder this as Kanin stops by a streetside fruit vendor, buying three bananas. We each eat one, to help prevent Bananageddon.

The mass-market humor churned out by Kanin and all the other humorists, big-time and small, who populate New York not only has to make people laugh; it also has to sell. It has to sell *New Yorker* issues and Broadway tickets; it has to turn books into bestsellers and websites into viral sensations; it has to fill movie theaters and primetime television blocks. And nowhere is the line between what's funny and what sells finer than on Madison Avenue, where the country's ad firms attempt to churn out one humorous marketing message after another to encourage everybody to buy, buy, buy.

But does it work? When it comes to creating humor for advertising, does funny sell?

A few weeks before our trip to New York, Pete received an unexpected call from the National Campaign to Prevent Teen and Unplanned Pregnancy, the country's biggest nonprofit focusing on teenage pregnancy. The Washington, DC–based organization had launched a new birth-control campaign that pushed the comedic envelope to get the attention of 18- to 29-year-old men. There were YouTube videos of talking condoms and *Saturday Night Live* Digital Short–inspired hip-hop songs and cartoons of Coca-Cola douches. But the folks in charge weren't sure the public service announcements were working. Did adding all those jokes make for more compelling marketing messages?

The advertising industry seems to think so. In 2008, U.S. advertisers spent somewhere between $20 and $60 billion on humorous marketing.[14] By that time, more than three-quarters of all Super Bowl ads were designed to be funny.[15]

There might be a method to this marketing madness. Researchers have nailed down a few ways in which funny ads succeed. Humorous marketing does tend to get people's attention, and if the source of humor is well connected to the message, folks are more likely to remember the ads and recall the products being advertised.[16] As the ad world is quick to point out to their clients, humorous ads are also more enjoyable and more likely to be discussed. But as for all the other things funny marketing is supposed to do—like getting people to actually buy the product—conclusive proof just isn't there.

The best humorous marketing is all about nuance and positioning, believes Pete. As he's found with his colleague Caleb Warren, it's not the comedy that matters; it's how the comedy is carried out. According to the benign violation theory, humor is caused by something potentially wrong, unsettling, or threatening. That means even if an ad is funny, if marketers aren't careful, they could end up hurting the brand.[17]

It's one of the reasons, although far from the only one, that a 1999 commercial for the shoe chain Just for Feet is considered among the worst of all time. In the spot, a Humvee full of white hunters chases down a Kenyan distance runner, tranquilizes him, and slaps a pair of Nikes on his feet. The fallout was so extensive that Just for Feet sued the ad agency Saatchi & Saatchi for malpractice to the tune of $10 million.[18]

Aside from high-profile flops, though, it's difficult to figure out whether most funny ads succeed or bomb. That's why the National Campaign to Prevent Teen and Unplanned Pregnancy had come to Pete. The organization wanted to know for sure if its new funny ads were working—so it was hoping HuRL would run experiments on condom jokes in PSAs.

Of course, we replied. Anything in the name of science.

Pete decided to focus on one of their latest spots, a web video featuring a spokesman losing it while reading cue cards about birth control statistics among young adults. ("One in five guys believes having sex standing up reduces the chance of pregnancy. . . . What, are you *bleeping* kidding me?! That's the stupidest thing I've heard in my *bleeping* life!") Pete thought the video might be turning off its intended audience, since it made the people who don't use birth control the butt of the joke.

We worked with the production team behind the PSA, producing three new versions of the video. Two employed a gentle, affiliative form of teasing: "One in five guys believes having sex standing up prevents pregnancy. . . . Seriously? You know better! Just take two seconds and go, 'Yeah, you know what, that's not how sperms work.'" The final video was a control version, a straight reading of the facts in a somber fashion.

With the help of cognitive scientist Phil Fernbach and graduate student Julie Schiro, Pete recruited a group of 18- to 29-year-old males and assigned each to watch one of the four videos. The results were surprising: subjects who watched the dry, boring control version of the PSA were far more likely to seek out more information about sexual health than those who saw any of the funny versions. As Pete figures, while the funny versions might have been attention-grabbing and entertaining, they also signaled that the situation wasn't serious. Teen pregnancy was something to laugh about, not ponder. Pete has taken to referring to the results as the "Jon Stewart Effect," after the allegation that while political-satire shows like *The Daily Show* might get people to pay attention to unpleasant news, the comedy involved could make them less likely to right the wrongs that they're learning about.[19]

Does that mean we'd all be better served if commercials and ads were just a solemn laundry list of facts? Probably not. Maybe a better way to create effective funny marketing is to think of it like a good wedding toast, suggests Pete. Start with attention-grabbing jokes, then put all kidding aside and make your point.

Tuesdays have always been cartoonist open-call day at the *New Yorker*. As far back as the 1930s, artists referred to it as the "Tuesday Inquisition." It made the magazine's founder, Harold Ross, so nervous he was constantly rearranging the desks to make the place as presentable as possible.[20] For the cartoonists who show up on Tuesdays, it's the first step in a multistage selection process, the first gauging of whether the cartoon is funny enough to appear in the magazine and earn its creator upward of $1,000.

On a Tuesday, we go with Zach Kanin to cartoonist open call.

I always pictured the *New Yorker* offices as a big, ornate smoking lounge, with everyone sipping cognac in leather arm chairs and pontificating on the decline of the Euro. In reality, it looks like every other newsroom I've ever worked in: a maze of nondescript, slightly messy cubicles, with oddball marketing swag tucked away in random nooks and review copies of books stacked here and there in precarious towers. It's the inevitable detritus of an unceasing production schedule, of a place where there's never downtime for deep cleaning.

A dozen or so cartoonists mill about in front of Bob Mankoff's office, catching up and waiting to be called in. Most are regulars, though it's not unusual to find a new face or two in the crowd. The weekly event is open to anybody. You don't have to hoof it all the way here to have your work considered, but getting a chance to meet with the cartoon editor of the *New Yorker* is an opportunity most aspiring cartoonists aren't likely to pass up.

Mankoff, looking sharp in a seersucker jacket and collared shirt, calls the cartoonists one by one into his small office, which has a view of Midtown and piles of drawings sprawled across every surface. First up is Sidney Harris, who's been publishing cartoons in the *New Yorker* since 1962. Mankoff greets him like an old friend, reminiscing about the weekly pilgrimages Harris and his colleagues, cartoons in hand, used to undertake around New York decades ago, from the *New Yorker* offices to *Look* magazine, from *Saturday Evening Post* to *National Lampoon*. Mankoff throws in a good-natured barb, razzing the old-timer about how he's not good at drawing deer. "Leonardo couldn't draw a cat!" harrumphs Harris before handing over his latest cartoon submissions.

Then there's Sam Ferri, a younger guy who's had success in other publications such as *Time Out* and *The New York Press*, but is still trying to break into the *New Yorker*. With him, Mankoff takes more time. He scrutinizes Ferri's submissions—dense vignettes of New York daily life that are strikingly different from the cartoons that usually make the magazine. Here and there he offers feedback: "Make your stuff less fussy." "You don't need these extra lines on this guy's arms." But he tells Ferri not to give up, to keep going in this unique direction, even though it may take a while to pay off. "You are doing something different, and you are doing something harder," Mankoff says with a sigh. "There are no medals for that."

Mankoff knows what it's like to be in Ferri's shoes. On his wall is a framed copy of one of Mankoff's own cartoons published in the magazine, one of the most popular among those purchasing online reprints. In it, a CEO says into his telephone, "No, Thursday's out. How about never—is never good for you?" It took Mankoff years to produce stuff like that. When he was still a struggling cartoonist, he submitted more than a thousand cartoons here before he ever got one accepted.

Last one in is Kanin. "Zach, of course, is my protégé," says Mankoff as he flips through his submissions. "I taught him everything I know. It took me half an hour." He pauses on Kanin's cartoon featuring the bowling ball and pins meeting at the street corner. He likes it—a lot. "But here is the problem," he says, pointing to the leash that's tied around the bowling ball. "How is it going to roll? The fact checkers might catch that." He's not joking. Like everything else in the magazine, *New Yorker* cartoons must endure the rigors of the publication's infamous fact-checkers. One time, a cartoon featuring a talking bluebird nearly got nixed—not because birds can't talk, but because the bluebird involved wasn't the correct size for the genus *Sialia*.

Mankoff likes to joke, "Basically what I do is I reject cartoons." Truthfully, he's quite good at doing it. When he first became cartoon editor, the famous playwright David Mamet sent him a letter noting, "I've taken the liberty of sending you this batch of cartoons." Mankoff responded, "Thank you very much for your submission. I've taken the liberty of sending you a play." But sitting here in his office, it's clear he's doing far more than just rejecting. He's working with each cartoonist, editing them, helping them understand what separates regular cartoons from *New Yorker* cartoons.

The criteria for Mankoff aren't as simple as what's funny and what's not. As he's the first to admit, the funniest cartoons often don't make it. As in advertising, the comedy here is all about context. "The cartoons in the rejection pile make no point aside from being funny," Mankoff tells us after the open call over lunch at a fashionable French restaurant, where he orders a veggie burger and herbal tea. The ones that make it in are funny, too, but also have a point. For Mankoff, it's all about insight—a great *New Yorker* cartoon has an "aha!" moment, alongside the "ha ha." That "aha!" it turns out, is crucial; a large body of psychological research suggests that making creative connections, whether it's understanding a witty punch line or solving a tricky math problem, is an innately pleasurable experience.[21]

It's why Mankoff is fond of Kanin's bowling-ball image: it's a smile-and-nod joke. It takes two common cartoon tropes—bowling and street-corner mishaps—and combines them in a cunning way. It's the sort of gag that fits into the witty yet respectable legacy handed down by some of the *New Yorker*'s comedy giants—the doughy simplicity of James Thurber, the shadowy macabre of Charles Addams, the eccentric doodles of Saul Steinberg. "One of the objectives of the *New Yorker* is to advance cartooning as an art," Mankoff says. He hopes to do that by working hand in hand with cartoonists, essentially creating comedy by committee.

That's the de facto way of doing things in the big business of humor creation—comedy by committee, jokes via brainstorm. Sitcoms are produced by writers' rooms, funny movies by one or more screenwriters plus a director, editors, producers, and all sorts of hangers-on. Probably only in stand-up is joke creation still mostly a solitary exercise, and even there, many comics work with other comedians and writers to fine-tune their routines.

The communal comedy strategy makes sense. If you're aiming to come up with something that's going to make millions of people laugh, a good way to go is the shotgun approach: stick ten funny people in a room and hope for the best. Do you want to risk your multi-million-dollar film, TV or magazine budget on a single schmuck with a good sense of humor?

Still, Mankoff knows that all his communal work here, culling and editing and crafting burgeoning talent like Kanin's, isn't going to produce even a single cartoon that everyone everywhere is going to find hilarious. "It turns out it's funny enough," he says, and he's not saying that to be pessimistic. *New Yorker* cartoons are different from stand-up comedy, he tells us, where each joke has to work with just about everyone in the comedy-club audience. There are just too many *New Yorker* readers, too large a comedy audience, to have any cartoon appeal to everyone. "These are like heat-seeking missiles," Mankoff says of the cartoons. "For each one of these, there will be one you don't like, but like a heat-seeking missile, it will find its home." Sure, maybe you don't love the *New Yorker* cartoon of one amoeba saying to another, "You're wasting your time. I'm asexual." But if Mankoff's done his job right, enough other people will, snipping it out and fastening it to their refrigerator or tacking it to their cubicle wall or even purchasing a copy from the *New Yorker*'s online "Cartoon Bank" database, which Mankoff helps run.

And Mankoff, for one, believes Kanin's bowling-ball cartoon is funny enough that it will find a home among the magazine's readers. So it makes the cut, landing in the pile of submissions that will move up the production chain. Let's just hope the fact-checkers don't get too picky about the bowling-ball leash.

Mass-produced comedy also comes with its fair share of risks. While attending an academic conference in Chicago, Pete visited the headquarters of Groupon, the gigantic daily-deal website known for injecting comedy into its online deal descriptions. He visited a cavernous editorial office staffed with hundreds of 20- and 30-year-olds, all of whom seemed to be wearing hoodies, tight sweaters, and ironic glasses. "Groupon is run by hipsters!" he told me when he returned.

Since every day Groupon puts out the equivalent of a 400-page novel in marketing copy, the challenge, according to Groupon editor in chief Aaron With, is getting all those hipsters to write like a single, tight-sweater-wearing Kurt Vonnegut. It's why With developed an editorial manual that lays down specific rules about how to inject hilarity into Groupon's materials. The guide reads like a Groupon coupon making fun of editorial manuals: produce 20 percent humorous content to 80 percent informative content. Include a funny moment every two to four sentences. Stay away from the natural hipster tendency to write about unicycles, mimes, mullets, Snuggies, ligers, hipsters, zombies, pirates, and ninjas. And unicorns—definitely don't write about unicorns.

Later, Pete spoke with one of the longest-running writers for Groupon. When he asked him what the hardest part of the job was, the writer responded, "Making something that is actually funny."

Still, compared to most mass-market attempts at humor, Groupon is freewheeling. There are just too many people involved, argue critics of Hollywood comedies and sitcoms, too many writers and directors and producers and network executives and studio chiefs and key advertisers. The goal of these gargantuan operations? Maximize the number of people chuckling and minimize those offended. In the television development world, there's a term for this practice: "Least Objectionable Programming." The results don't usually equal hilarity, but then, that's not the point. It's to move movie tickets and score high Nielsen ratings.

Jokes can suffer within the factory system of funny. But what about the comedians themselves? What does the production process do to the folks who come up with the jokes to begin with? We figure the best person to ask is Todd Hanson, the guy behind one of the most celebrated examples of modern American comedy. For the last 21 years, Hanson has been a writer for the satirical newspaper *The Onion*. Many people consider being among the anointed few to come up with fake *Onion* news articles such as "Drugs Win Drug War" and "Study Reveals: Babies Are Stupid" to be a dream job. If that's the case, Hanson, who's been an *Onion* writer longer than anybody, should have the perfect gig—right?

A beleaguered-looking Hanson ushers us into his Brooklyn apartment. "There's massive trauma going on," he tells us, rubbing his eyes. He looks like he just got out of bed. Either that, or he's been up for days. The catastrophe, he tells us, is that the company that now owns *The Onion* is consolidating its operation. That means the writing staff will be relocating from New York to the corporate headquarters in Chicago. There is much more at stake than just changing ZIP codes, says Hanson, slumping into a ratty couch surrounded by empty whiskey bottles and overflowing ashtrays. He rolls up the left sleeve of his T-shirt, revealing a tattoo that reads "Satire." "I didn't want to get this tattoo till I felt like I earned it," he says. When *The Onion* relocated in 2001 from its original home in Madison, Wisconsin, to New York, he says, "I felt like I earned it." But now, with the impending move . . . his head slumps, his voice trails off.

Hanson pulls it together to walk us through *The Onion*'s production schedule. On Mondays, everyone on the writing staff gets together and offers up 25 potential funny headlines. Of the hundreds submitted, the vast majority are rejected by the group, never to be suggested again. The best fifteen, however, evolve into full stories for the paper. But the person who came up with a winning headline usually isn't the one to write the story. Another person will edit it, and then nobody in particular will get a byline.

"Everything at *The Onion* is in a collaborative voice," explains Hanson. It's a dignified approach, one that does away with the cutthroat nature of most comedy writing teams. It's part of the reason that Hanson and his colleagues are responsible for sticking the landing on one of the most difficult comedic feats in recent memory: figuring out how to be funny right after the September 11, 2001, terrorist attacks.

Hanson watched the Twin Towers disappear from the Manhattan skyline from his Brooklyn window that morning, seemingly taking with them all potential for humor. *Saturday Night Live, The Daily Show*—all the late-night talk shows halted production. *Time* magazine declared, "The Age of Irony Comes to an End." *The Onion*, as the flagship of everything ironic, seemed to be included in that death knell. The staff had just arrived in New York, and hadn't yet put out a single issue in their new home. Now, before they had a chance to do so, says Hanson, "We wondered, 'Is this the end?'"

Timing in comedy has always been tricky. When is it too soon to joke about something, and when is it too late? The trauma of the 9/11 attacks brought the conundrum to a different level. Mark Twain is famously credited with saying, "Humor is tragedy plus time." But would *any* amount of time be enough to make the tragedy of 9/11 funny?

As Pete points out, however, timing is far from the only variable that can be tweaked to help land a joke in its comedic sweet spot. The secret, he says, is understanding that in comedy, emotional attachment is key. To make a joke more or less funny, you can make the violation involved more or less benign by shifting the psychological distance between the violation and the person perceiving it. Waiting for days, months, or years before tackling a taboo subject is an obvious way to make an event feel distant and thus safer. But there are other, less drastic ways to do so, too.

To prove it, Pete has been running experiments in HuRL. In one study, participants read about a young woman who texted "Haiti" to a mobile charity program more than 200 times without realizing that the nearly $2,000 donation would be added to her cell-phone bill. People found this story more amusing when the woman was described as a stranger rather than a close friend. In other words, an extreme violation like accidentally spending $2,000 was funnier when researchers increased the psychological distance between the person experiencing the tragedy and the person who's supposed to laugh.

But the reverse happened, too. In the same study, other participants read a story about a woman texting "Haiti" five times and accidentally charging $50 to her account. These participants were more likely amused when the woman was described as a friend rather than a stranger. This means less threatening situations such as a $50 mistake can be made funnier by shrinking the distance between the subject of the joke and the person who's supposed to get it.[22]

So maybe folks have it all wrong when they ask whether a joke is "too soon." Maybe a better way to put it is, "When is the subject matter too close for comfort, and when is it too distant to matter?"

Hanson and his colleagues looked at 9/11 this way. "To me, it's not about timing; it's about validity," Hanson tells us. "If what you are saying is honest and legitimate and has a valid point, it's going to be valid the day after, and it's going to be valid 500 years later." That's why less than two weeks after the towers came down, they tackled the tragedy head-on, creating a whole issue devoted to the terrorist attacks.

Around that same time, comedian Gilbert Gottfried caught flack for making a crack about taking a flight that made a stop at the Empire State Building. In their 9/11 issue, the staff at *The Onion* didn't make the same mistake. They didn't joke about the planes hitting the towers or the civilians who died that day. The subjects were too raw, too close for comfort. Instead, they turned the horrifying terrorists into fools ("Hijackers Surprised to Find Selves in Hell" read one article) and cracked wise about the strange aura of confusion and despair that had settled over the country. Hanson wept when he wrote an article titled "God Angrily Clarifies 'Don't Kill' Rule."

The day after the issue came out, *The Onion*'s fax machine went ballistic with grateful comments, and fan mail started to flow in by the thousands. To this day, it remains the most commented-on issue in *The Onion*'s history.

That was a career highlight for Hanson. Since then, things have gone downhill. *The Onion* is no longer the plucky upstart it once was. It now boasts a national readership in the hundreds of thousands, a major web presence and a daily web broadcast called *The Onion News Network*. In 2003, Hanson co-wrote an *Onion* film. But for years, the movie was stuck in development limbo, then released straight to video. Hanson has since disowned his part in it. Now market forces and consumer segmentation play a part in *The Onion*'s wit, and it's no longer so easy for Hanson to be so honest without stepping on corporate toes. "Now they measure comedy in terms of quantity, not quality," he says.

For Hanson, the move to Chicago might be too much. He admits that he's not sure how much longer he can be a part of *The Onion*. But if he leaves, what else could he do? While some *Onion* writers have gone on to jobs at *The Daily Show* and *The Colbert Report*, Hanson might not be built to handle a move like that. He's 42 years old and has never done anything in his professional life other than dream up make-believe news stories. In many ways he's stuck with *The Onion*, just as he's stuck with his "Satire" tattoo, which is starting to seem more like a battle wound than a badge of honor.

We've been talking for hours when Hanson's phone rings. "I'm okay," he says into the receiver when he picks it up. It's his therapist. Every night he's supposed to call her at a specific time. When he doesn't, she calls him—just to make sure he hasn't done anything drastic.

When Hanson hangs up, he's on the verge of tears. "The world is a sad place," he says to us. He's being honest and legitimate, but nothing about it is funny.

Our time in New York nearly over, we decide to let loose, to get a little debaucherous. Of course, to be productive, we aim to do it the scientific way.

The idea arose from our obsession with the TV show *Mad Men*. Is the show correct in its portrayal of well-dressed 1960s ad guys whiling away the noon hour with liquid lunches of Old Fashioneds, then popping back into the office and whipping off a whimsical ad campaign for Lucky Strike cigarettes? Does this sort of depravity really lead to successful humorous advertising? More specifically, can booze fuel comedy creation?

As anyone who's ever been to a comedy club can attest, alcohol and laughs go hand in hand. And scientists know booze can boost humor appreciation, since it lowers inhibition, decreases anxiety, and increases positive mood. In a 1997 study, social drinkers watched twenty minutes of the goofball comedy *The Naked Gun*. Those who were two drinks in found O.J. Simpson's bumbling Officer Nordberg significantly funnier than those who watched stone-cold sober.[23]

But little research has been done on the other side: whether Lenny Bruce–style decadence leads to Lenny Bruce–level jokes. We decide to look into the matter—by arranging an evening of drinks with a couple of creative directors at advertising powerhouse Grey New York, the firm responsible for making E-Trade synonymous with talking babies and producing a DirecTV ad featuring a baby in a dog collar that former U.S. president Bill Clinton called the most hilarious commercial he'd ever seen. As enticement, we tell the folks at Grey we'll foot the bill for our night on the town.

The ad guys are eager to participate, and before we know it, they've invited along their entire creative team, all on our dime. They also have a destination in mind: "Let's go to the Hurricane Club," they tell us. The name evokes a cozy corner bar, hopefully one that won't put too much strain on our wallet.

When the evening arrives and we step into the Hurricane Club, we realize we're in trouble. Waiters in white dinner jackets glide under crystal chandeliers, delivering exotic drinks served in carved-out coconuts, watermelons, and red peppers. Pete glances at the drink menu and laughs nervously. "This is going to cost us."

Putting our anxiety aside, we launch into the experiment. We show the ad team a Venn diagram we've been using to illustrate the benign violation theory:

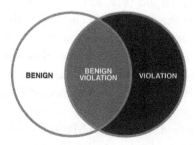

Next we tell each participant to polish off a cocktail and come up with a funny new Venn diagram that illustrates and promotes the benign violation theory. We want them to deconstruct a joke into its benign and violation parts, with the intersection labeled "funny." The ad creatives also have to fill out a survey rating how funny they consider their ad idea. After that, they down another cocktail and draw a new diagram. Repeat, and repeat, and repeat.

They're off, in a flurry of mai tais, bellinis, and mojitos. What we don't expect is how seriously everybody takes it, especially the Grey creative directors. The bosses heckle their underlings and demand that everybody give 110 percent, dammit. In the stress and depravity that ensues, everyone goes *waaay* over the line in terms of decency. Here's one of the completed Venn diagrams:

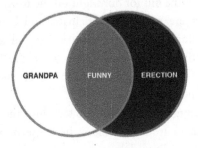

Compared to other diagrams, that's sedate. So here we are, in one of the city's ritziest juice joints with some of New York's most powerful creative minds, watching comedy—or at least attempts at it—get made. And judging from some of the preliminary results, it's one more bit of proof that most things in the world aren't funny. So if you aim to be hilarious like these ad creatives or *New Yorker* cartoonist Kanin, the best thing to do is to come up with as many jokes as possible, then come up with more. Or as Pete likes to put it, think up as many violations as possible, and then find lots of ways to make those violations okay. Most will end up as duds, but every now and then you'll come up with your own version of Kanin's bowling-ball cartoon.

As for that cartoon? It turns out Mankoff might have been right when he called Kanin a comic genius. The bowling-ball gag makes it up the production chain, past the ornery fact-checkers, and gets the green light from *New Yorker* editor David Remnick, who makes the final decision with Mankoff on the twelve to twenty cartoons in each issue. A few months later, on the bottom right corner of page 85 of the *New Yorker*, there's the bowling-ball walker and the bowling-pin walker, strolling toward their inevitable street-corner collision. But by this point, Kanin is probably too busy to notice it. He's taken a new job, one that might be even more celebrated in the annals of comedy creation: he's been hired as a writer for *Saturday Night Live*.

At the Hurricane Club, is all the booze we're buying turning the ad team into Kanin-level humorists? They believe so. The more drinks they down, the funnier they rate their comedy attempts. But later, when Pete submits the Venns to an online survey panel, he finds the inebriated ad team is off the mark. According to the panel's respondents, the shenanigans went downhill by the time the ad team reached its fifth drink. Take, for example, one creative director who went by the code name Blaze. After his third drink, Blaze rated himself about halfway up the drunkenness scale and came up with this gem:

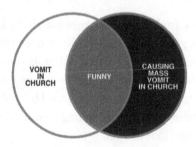

Blaze gave this a 4 out of 7 on the funniness scale, and the online-survey respondents rated it 3.5. Pretty similar. However, after his fifth and final drink, Blaze drew a diagram and rated it an utterly hilarious 7. The online panel disagreed, awarding it an average humor rating of 1.95 and an offensiveness rating of 4.2.

What was the Venn behind such wildly diverging opinions?

Don't say we didn't warn you:

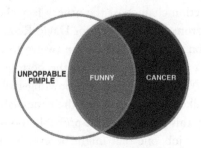

So there you have it. Proof that alcohol makes things funnier, but only for those making the funny. All it cost us was $1,272.96—the most expensive bar tab either of us has ever paid. It inspired us to create one final Venn, one we're still waiting on to see if it comes true:

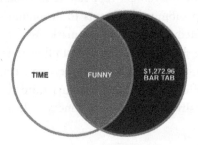

We come away from New York knowing that a killer funny bone isn't necessarily a gift from the gods. But it does take a whole lot of work—and, paradoxically, a whole lot of fun. If you're going to combine esoteric topics in clever and funny ways, you need to live large. Read up on odd topics. Explore new places. Head off on wild adventures. If nothing else, have long, rambling conversations over drinks.

Just don't offer to foot the bill.

Good news greets us in Uganda as we disembark our plane: "Uganda has defeated the outbreak of Ebola," announces a large placard standing in the airport's main hall. "Please have a nice stay."

Well, that's a relief.

We actually have a different malady in mind—one far less lethal than Ebola, but evocative nonetheless. We're here in East Africa on the trail of the so-called 1962 Tanganyika laughter epidemic. As the story goes, in 1962 in the northwest corner of Tanganyika (a country now known as Tanzania), hundreds of people began laughing uncontrollably. The affliction, if you could call it that, spread from one person to the next, and nothing seemed to stop it. Schools shut down. Entire villages were caught in its throes. When the laughing stopped months later, a thousand people had come down with the "disease."

Since then, the Tanganyika laughter epidemic has captured imaginations the world over. Newspaper articles have been written about it, radio shows have explored it, and documentaries have dramatized it. But many of these accounts detailed the incident from afar, relying on secondhand sources, scraps of information, and rumors. Few people have investigated the event themselves, tracking the laughter all the way to its source. That's why we're here.

To be honest, we're a bit skeptical of the whole account. Uncontrollable laughter, jumping from person to person like a devilish possession, doesn't make sense. But *something* happened in Tanganyika in 1962. There are enough firsthand accounts and medical reports to confirm that. But what that something is—and what, if anything, it has to do with humor—is still up for debate.

We're hoping our time here will provide us with clues about laughter in general, a phenomenon that's mysterious in itself. We've investigated a lot of funny stuff between all that stand-up in Los Angeles and all those cartoons in New York, but the laughs generated by professional comedy are just a fraction of the chuckles, giggles, and titters in our daily lives. Why is that? Why would we have developed this odd vocal mannerism? Why do we have an innate need to vocally share what we find funny with others? And why, come to think about it, do laughter and humor not always go hand in hand? Why did hundreds of people in 1962 East Africa start laughing when nothing was funny at all? And why is laughter so contagious, so compelling, that it can act like an out-of-control disease?

It began with three schoolgirls.

On January 30, 1962, at a mission-run girls' boarding school in Kashasha village not far from Lake Victoria, three schoolgirls "commenced to act in an abnormal manner." That's how it's described in a 1963 *Central African Journal of Medicine* article titled "An Epidemic of Laughing in the Bukoba District of Tanganyika," the most authoritative account of the incident. More specifically, according to its authors, local medical officers A. M. Rankin and P. J. Philip, sudden and repeated bouts of laughing and crying seized the girls. The phenomenon soon spread to their classmates. The attacks would last for a few minutes to a few hours, and one poor girl reportedly experienced symptoms for sixteen straight days. Victims couldn't focus on their schoolwork and would lash out if others tried to restrain them. They claimed things were moving about in their heads, that somebody was out to get them.

By March 18 of that year, 95 of the school's 159 middle and high school girls had been affected. At that point, to temper the ailment's spread, the school shut down. It reopened on May 21, only to close again when dozens more came down with symptoms. By that point, the epidemic had spread beyond the school.

Kashasha seems as good a place as any to start our investigation, so on our first full day in Tanzania, we head to the village, a small community on a forested ridge overlooking a sweeping, misty valley. Right off the main road we find the school, still in operation, though it hasn't housed a girls' school in decades. Now it's a vocational school. Classes aren't in session on this overcast, drizzly day, so the campus's small grassy yards are empty, and the shuttered doors to the tinsmith workshop and masonry store creak in the wind. But out of the rain, in the school's small office, we find principal Jason Kamala, a stocky man in a casual green shirt. "I have heard much about the big laughter you are after," he declares in accented English, letting loose with a hearty laugh of his own. He gives us a tour of the tidy but timeworn property, recounting what he knows. He's told this tale before.

The girls' school, run by German missionaries, was a model institution, he tells us, one of the first boarding schools in the area. Still, says Kamala, life under the school's strict religious rules wasn't easy. He shows us the former dormitory, a long, weather-beaten building that now houses carpentry and welding workshops. When this was a boarding school, he says, there were no windows on the sides of the building facing toward the village, "so they would not see boys and men on the road." Similarly, students weren't allowed to use the latrine at night because it was too close to the exterior fence.

Kamala takes us to a classroom on a far corner of the property, a basic affair with cracked walls and broken windows. He points to the wooden chairs inside. They are the same as the ones used in 1962, and they are tremendously uncomfortable. The chair backs pitch forward at an awkward angle to promote proper posture—or, as Kamala puts it, to make "good-shaped girls."

The three girls who started it all were sitting in this classroom when they burst out laughing and couldn't stop. Bewildered, the teacher rang her school bell, sending the students into the yard outside to calm everyone down. Tracing the students' path, Kamala positions himself in the yard. Here, he says, other pupils looked at the laughing trio and began cackling themselves. The lawn was soon full of out-of-control cackles. "They laughed and laughed and laughed," says Kamala.

William Rutta, the Tanzanian guide we've hired to accompany us in East Africa, is listening in his fashionable brown sports coat, scribbling away in a small notebook. When I'd first e-mailed him about being our guide, Rutta, the owner of a local safari and tourism company called Kiroyera Tours, had assured me he knew all about *omuneepo*, the local word for the laughing disease. But now that we're here, it's obvious this information is as new for him as it is for us.

But that's okay. As Rutta would say, "Hakuna matata"—Swahili for "no worries." The local phrase, made famous by its use in the Disney film *The Lion King*, is Rutta's favorite saying, at least when he's escorting *mzungus*—white people—like us. Everything so far on our trip can been summed up by "hakuna matata." In Uganda, when Rutta picked us up at the airport, the country was in the midst of a mid-level crisis that had led soldiers to fire into crowds of angry protestors? Hakuna matata. That the road between Uganda and Tanzania was being built as we drove along it, leading to hours of stopped traffic punctuated by high-speed dashes through heavy machinery and construction craters? Hakuna matata. That when we tried to cross into Tanzania, the Ugandan border-patrol office was empty, with a sign at the window saying everybody was out to lunch for an indeterminate amount of time? Hakuna matata.

Continuing his tour of the school grounds, Kamala tells us that while he wasn't at the boarding school in 1962, he witnessed *omuneepo* himself—here, at the vocational school, in 1981. "It happened with three boys," he says. "They were looking at you like this"—Kamala stares at us, wide-eyed—"then they started laughing: '*Ha ha ha ha!*' Then you found tears coming. And these boys were so stiff, their whole bodies were so tough. We had to tie them in ropes and put them on mattresses until they recovered." He's heard of other cases, too. Every few years a new report of *omuneepo* pops up at some school or village in the region. Some are just a few years old.

As for what causes these incidents? Kamala just shrugs. "Maybe those who laugh have an element of madness coming into their brains."

There is something almost akin to madness in how and when we laugh. It's not as simple as a basic reaction to something funny. Oftentimes we don't laugh when we come across something humorous, like how all those witty *New Yorker* cartoons we considered in New York left us with appreciative smiles. And laughter sometimes comes when nothing is funny at all. Type "uncontrollable laughter" into YouTube and you'll find clips of newscasters cracking up for no apparent reason in the middle of stories about war zones and political scandals. There's nothing humorous about these moments. Their jobs could be on the line, but they can't stop cracking up.

No one has illustrated laughter's strange tendencies better than Robert Provine, a neuroscientist and psychology professor at the University of Maryland, Baltimore County. A few years ago, Provine took a look at the current state of laughter research and wasn't impressed. "People had been struggling with explaining laughter for thousands of years. I thought it was time to try something else," Provine told me. "I wanted to do something that would get me into empirical science and away from essay writing." So Provine engaged in what he called "sidewalk neuroscience," tracking and observing real-world laughter. He and his collaborators used tape recorders to capture more than a thousand "laugh episodes" in bars and shopping malls and cocktail parties and class reunions. And he had dozens of student volunteers note in a "laugh log" the circumstances around every time they tittered, chuckled, or guffawed.

His findings, detailed in his book *Laughter: A Scientific Investigation*, were surprising, even to Provine. Fewer than 20 percent of the real-world laughter incidents he catalogued were in response to anything resembling something funny. Far more often, people were giggling or chuckling at innocuous statements such as "I'll see you guys later," "I see your point," and "Look, it's Andre!" Not only that, but in all these cases, the person who produced the laugh-provoking statement was 46 percent more likely to be the one chuckling than the person listening. And while laughter might seem like something that can erupt at any point in response to something funny, in only eight of the 1,200 laugh episodes did the laughter interrupt what somebody was saying. Instead, in 99.9 percent of the time, laughter occurred in tidy, natural breaks in the conversation, punctuating the speech like a period or exclamation point.[1]

Provine concluded that the laughter of our everyday lives wasn't for the most part a by-product of anything resembling jokes. Instead most of it occurs in the give-and-take we have with others that in hindsight doesn't seem funny at all. This finding puts the challenge of being a professional comedian in a whole new light. A comic is physically removed from the audience; he or she is talking *at* them, not *with* them, and for the most part isn't supposed to laugh during the routine. Comedians are essentially trying to score laughs in the exact opposite way that most people do. Now, we don't believe it's time to reinvent stand-up along the lines of everyday conversations. As we learned the hard way, chatting one-on-one with Louis C.K. is far from a hilarious experience.

Pete thinks the benign violation theory might play a role in Provine's unusual findings. The seemingly unfunny bits of dialogue that triggered most bouts of laughter might still be benign violations, says Pete—just violations that are so benign they're only laughable when you're right there, in the moment. It's the ultimate version of "you had to be there."[2] Whether or not this is the case, Provine's discoveries suggest that laughter is inherently social, that at its core it's a form of communication. Sure enough, when Provine went through the laughter logs he'd collected, he found his participants were 30 times more likely to laugh in the presence of others than when they were alone. Among the few solitary instances of laughter, nearly all occurred in response to TV shows or other media—in short, electronic proxies for other people. When people were truly alone, laughter all but disappeared.[3]

Provine found one other piece of evidence that he believed demonstrated laughter's social power, one other bit of proof that suggested laughter's communal sway was far more dramatic than most people realize. As he noted in an article in *American Scientist*, "The Tanganyikan laughter epidemic is a dramatic example of the infectious power of laughter."

Is he right? Was what started here 50-odd years ago in this boarding school an instance of laughter's social power gone haywire? We have more investigating to do.

The town of Bukoba, the administrative center of this corner of Tanzania and our base of operations, lies on the western shore of Lake Victoria, the world's second-largest freshwater lake. It's a beautiful spot: verdant tropical hills on one side, an endless expanse of blue on the other. It's like an African version of a Mediterranean seaside town, albeit one with bumpy dirt roads, corrugated metal roofs, and the smell of burning trash lingering in the breeze. Our accommodations, on a palm frond–dotted rise overlooking the town, bills itself as "the only luxurious tourist hotel" in the region, although "luxurious" is up to interpretation. There are enough mosquitoes buzzing about to inspire us to pop antimalarial pills like Tic Tacs, and there's at least one room—mine—that doesn't have hot water. (Eventually I get a new room, but then I'm confronted with the opposite problem: a shower that only scalds.)

Bukoba, when we wander about it, exudes an easygoing backcountry feel, a community-wide version of our guide Rutta's "hakuna matata" mentality. This makes sense, considering it's about as far from Tanzania's capital, Dar es Salaam, as you can get. In a place like this, we figure something as disruptive as a laughter epidemic should be easy for folks to recall.

Luckily, we're traveling with somebody who knows everybody. Rutta, who lives in Bukoba, has a copy of Dale Carnegie's *How to Win Friends and Influence People* in his van's center console, and he's been putting the self-help book to good use. He has two cell phones, one or both of which is always going off. It's difficult to make it across town with him in a timely fashion, since he's always stopping to say hello to somebody. "You're like the mayor!" exclaims Pete. Rutta just chuckles as he answers a call.

But in and around Bukoba, even with the unofficial mayor's help, people don't have much to offer regarding *omuneepo*. "All I can say is, it was sort of a miracle," a former school administrator who

witnessed some of the cases tells us with a shrug. It was a super-
natural phenomenon, counters an elderly Muslim cleric we meet
later. He believes it was spirits of people's ancestors causing trouble.
Local education and medical officials aren't much help, either. The
incident occurred in Kashasha half a century ago, they say—why
are we bothering about it now? Plus, they add, are we sure we have
the right Kashasha? There's another Kashasha, they tell us, far away
from here, in a part of the country that's not their problem. Maybe
we should go there, they suggest, insinuating it might be best if we
don't come back.

People around here clearly have far more pressing things to worry
about, like typhoid and malaria and illiteracy and AIDS, than a bad
case of the laughs. To be sure, excessive laughing can be a sign that
something is wrong with you. Pathological laughter, when nothing
is funny at all, can be a symptom of all sorts of unpleasantness: Parkinson's Disease. Multiple sclerosis. Pseudobulbar palsy. Alzheimer's.
Certain kinds of schizophrenia. Aftereffects of a pre-frontal lo-
botomy. A type of brain tumor called hypothalamic hamartoma that
triggers "gelastic epilepsy." Angelman syndrome, formerly known as
"happy puppet syndrome," since the people who have it act like the
jolly playthings of some invisible puppeteer. *Kuru*, or "the laughing
sickness," an incurable and deadly brain disorder that once swept
through the highlands of Papua New Guinea, believed to be triggered by locals consuming their dead relatives.[4]

But the laughter episodes here in Tanzania don't seem to have
anything to do with these ailments. A. M. Rankin and P. J. Philip, the
doctors who wrote about the situation in the *Central African Journal
of Medicine* in 1963, tested for infections, viruses, food poisoning, and
waterborne diseases. They found nothing.[5] Plus, in many of these
other conditions, uncontrollable laughter leads to far more serious
side effects. In Tanzania, the laughter just led to more laughter. Or
as Rankin and Philip put it, rather dryly, "No fatal cases have been
reported."

One evening, maybe to make up for all the dead ends in Bukoba,
Rutta takes us for a night on the town. He directs us into the dark,
smoky back room of a downtown Bukoba bar where, on a cleared-out

space in the center of the floor, women take turns dancing to African pop songs in skimpy outfits and heels. The place reeks of grilled meat, courtesy of a closet-like kitchen in the corner, where a sweat-drenched cook is churning out endless plastic trays heaped with charred flesh. In between musical numbers, the women hurry behind a curtain hanging from the back wall and reappear a few moments later in a full costume change. At one point, a dancer emerges in a plaid shirt and cowboy boots and performs a country line dance to Dolly Parton's "Coat of Many Colors." The operation resembles a chaste if still misogynistic version of an American strip club. And eventually, to spice it up, the women decide to make the only two *mzungus* here part of the show. So one by one, Pete and I get pulled into the spotlight.

That's how we find ourselves on stage at an African burlesque show, staring at a room of frowning men gnawing on blackened animal pieces and wondering what the hell we're doing up here, blocking their view. And so we dance. Pete waltzes with one of the dancers like he's Al Pacino in *Scent of a Woman*. I play coy with the ladies on stage and shake my butt at the audience. Pete trots out "the lasso," twirling an invisible rope and using it to capture one of the dancers. All for the sake of science.

We return to our seats amid the sounds of chuckles and claps. We weren't the sexiest dancers to grace the stage, but we were the funniest. And that has to count for something, since humor wouldn't have evolved in humans if it wasn't appealing from a sexual-selection standpoint—if it weren't, at some level, "sexy."

Sure enough, a survey of 700 men and women discovered that people considered humor among the most important of all characteristics when choosing a partner, romantic or otherwise.[6] And studies of happy marriages, especially those lasting more than a half century, find spouses often ascribe their marital bliss in part to laughing together.[7] This finding makes sense, says Pete: if you and your partner can make each other laugh, that suggests you have a similar sense of humor and therefore share compatible values, beliefs, and interests. Plus you're both adept at making the other person happy.

Unfortunately, research also suggests the opposite: humor can signal doom for a relationship. Studies have found that dating couples who exhibit strong senses of humor—and not mean-spirited humor, mind you, but positive and friendly humor—are more likely than others to break up. As paradoxical as that sounds, it's not absurd. Since humor is such a highly regarded personal trait, it's more likely that others will be enticed by these attractively funny people and will lure them away from their partners.[8]

But what, exactly, is evolutionarily attractive about a sense of humor? What use from a survival-of-the-species perspective is the ability to recognize what's funny and then bark about it? Some evolutionary theorists have posited that humor must have developed to demonstrate intelligence and creativity through wit, while others see laughter as a vocal adaptation of social grooming, a way to build bonds with one another without having to pick critters off each other's hides. The list of theories goes on: laughter could have been a "disabling mechanism," a way to signal that poking that crocodile with a stick is so laughable it might threaten our genetic survival. Or it could have been a way to determine winners and losers on the social strata—differentiating between those who deserve to laugh at others and those who deserve to get laughed at without resorting to prehistoric gladiator battles.[9] Or it could have been a signal of false alarm, a vocal demonstration that the rustling in the bushes wasn't a saber-toothed tiger as expected, just a harmless antelope.[10] One of the newest theories suggests that laughter could be the brain's version of an error message, that it evolved as a way for the mind to notice, reward the discovery of, and verbally signal mistaken leaps to conclusion.[11]

All these ideas are compelling in their own ways, but most lack hard evidence to verify their claims. If Pete were a betting man, he'd put his money on an idea put forward in 2005 by an undergrad named Matthew Gervais and his advisor, evolutionary biologist David Sloan Wilson, at Binghamton University in New York. In 29 heady pages in the *Quarterly Review of Biology*, the two wove together findings from neuroscience and positive psychology and multilevel selection theory to synthesize a novel and compelling account of how and why we developed the ability to laugh. It's the sort of virtuoso academic performance that makes a science geek like Pete gush, "That paper is amazing."

What's possibly most intriguing of all about their theory is that its key piece of evidence originated, of all places, from the work of a quirky nineteenth-century fellow named Guillaume Duchenne, a guy who went around zapping people's faces with electrodes. Duchenne, a French physician, became obsessed with figuring out what happened to human bodies when he shocked them with the hot new gizmo of the time: a portable battery and induction cable. Luckily for him, he worked at a women's hospice, so he had access to a lot of prone bodies to zap. He must have been quite the charmer. All the ladies wanted to be electrocuted by the "little old man with his mischief box."

Applying the prongs of his mischief box to people's faces, Duchenne evoked and captured one kind of smiling—the voluntary kind, the type of expression we produce when we grin or chortle to be polite. This mannerism, he discovered, involves the face's zygomatic major muscles raising the corners of the mouth. But Duchenne discovered there was a second variety of smiling and laughing, one that occurs when we find something truly entertaining or funny. This expression was more complex, utilizing both the zygomatic major muscles and the orbicularis oculi muscles that form crow's feet. It's why people say a real smile is in the eyes. Duchenne was never able to reproduce with his electrodes this second form of expression, now known as a Duchenne smile or Duchenne laughter, and he came to believe it was "only put at play by the sweet emotion of the soul." It was one of many scientific discoveries by the erstwhile electrocutioner, though Duchenne might have taken things too far in his book *The Mechanism of Human Physiognomy*. He had a beautiful model pose as Lady Macbeth while he zapped her face into different theatrical expressions.[12]

More than a century later, Gervais and Wilson saw Duchenne's discovery as evidence that laughter evolved at two different points in human development. First, they posited, at a point sometime between 2 and 4 million years ago came Duchenne laughter, the kind triggered by something funny. An outgrowth of the breathy panting emitted by primates during play fighting, it likely appeared before the emergence of language. This sort of laughter was a signal that things at the moment were okay, that danger was low and basic needs were met, and now was as good a time as any to explore, to play, to start laying the social groundwork that would lead to civilization. And this part of laughter's evolution could tie with Pete's idea that humor is elicited by benign violations, said Gervais, now a doctoral candidate in biological anthropology at UCLA. "There could be a violation or incongruity of expectation going on, but what's being signaled by the laughter is that it's not serious, or it's benign," Gervais told me. "What the humor is indexing and the laughter is signaling is, 'This is an opportunity for learning.' It signals this is a non-serious novelty, and recruits others to play with and explore cognitively, emotionally, and socially the implications of this novelty.

"I think it's an important part of the human story that humans are learners," he continued. "And something like an appreciation of humor is a process that encouraged exploration and learning for a species that has a brain built to learn."

But then, sometime between 2 million years ago and the present, theorized Gervais and Wilson, the other sort of laughter emerged—the non-Duchenne sort, the kind that isn't dependent on something being funny. As people developed cognitively and behaviorally, they learned to mimic the spontaneous behavior of laughter to take advantage of its effects. They couldn't get it right—they couldn't simulate the eye-muscle movements of real laughter and smiling—but it was close. It's similar to the way some moths evolved "owl eye" patterns on their wings to scare away predators—but in the case of non-Duchenne laughter, the point wasn't to scare away, it was to bring others closer. Mimicked laughter was a way to manipulate others, to hot wire their vulnerability to be entertained—sometimes for mutually beneficial purposes, sometimes for more devious reasons. As Gervais and Wilson put it in their paper, "non-Duchenne laughter came to occur in aggressive, nervous, or hierarchical contexts, functioning to signal, to appease, to manipulate, to deride, or to subvert."[13]

It's a compelling, if not the most cheerful, account of why we laugh. If Gervais and Wilson are right, what about the laughs we inspired at the African strip club? Were the chuckles the old kind, the involuntarily stuff of genuine amusement? Or the non-Duchenne, darker version—laughter meant to appease, or worse still, to deride? I'm hoping for the former, but I have a feeling it might be the latter.

Since we're in Africa, we figure we ought to go on a safari. Rutta is happy to oblige, one morning aiming the van toward Rubondo Island National Park, a 176-square-mile nature preserve off the coast of Lake Victoria. As we zoom up and down the rolling green hills skirting the lake, Pete fires up some Tupac Shakur on his iPod. "In the citaaay, the city of Compton!" sings Rutta, a big hip-hop fan, as we blow past longhorn cattle and vervet monkeys scampering about on the side of the road. "You know," Rutta says to Pete, "most professors don't act like you."

"Thank you," says Pete.

We eventually stop at a small, mud-bedraggled port, where we charter a small red-and-white motorboat to take us across a thin strait to Rubondo Island. Two somber-faced men in gray parkas sit behind us in the boat, armed with sizable old machine guns. We decide not to ask what threat, human or animal, necessitates that kind of firepower. When we reach the island, a four-wheel-drive safari jeep takes us through its densely forested interior. As we rumble down a two-track dirt road, foliage whipping at the windows and overhead vines sliding along the roof, I eye Rutta's stylish camouflage shirt-and-pants combo and safari vest. As usual, he's dressed for this excursion far better than we are.

We hope to spot some of the chimpanzees that inhabit the island, maybe even get a chance to tickle them. As we've noted, it's believed that human laughter evolved from the distinctive panting emitted by our great-ape relatives during rough-and-tumble play to signal it's all in good fun and nobody's about to tear anybody else's throat out. In a clever bit of scientific detective work, psychologist Marina Davila-Ross of the University of Portsmouth in the United Kingdom digitally analyzed recordings of tickle-induced panting from chimps, bonobos, gorillas, and orangutans, as well as human laughter, and found the vocal similarities between the species matched their evolutionary relationships. Chimps and bonobos, our closest relatives, boasted the most laughter-like kind of panting, while the noises of gorillas, further down our family tree, sounded less like laughing. Orangutans, our truly distant ancestors, panted in the most primitive way of all.[14]

Even if we don't find one of our hairy relations out here in the jungle, maybe we can at least find a rat or two and tickle them. There are scientific antecedents to support such a venture. In 1997, psychologist Jaak Panksepp entered his lab at Bowling Green State University in Ohio and told undergrad Jeffrey Burgdorf, "Let's go tickle some rats." The two and their colleagues had already discovered that lab rats emitted a unique ultrasonic chirp in the 50-kilohertz range when they played. Now they wondered if they could prompt these squeaks through tickling. Sure enough, when the researchers began poking at the bellies of the rats in their lab, their ultrasonic recording devices picked up the same 50-kilohertz sounds. The rats eagerly nestled their fingers for more. Soon, as the news media trumpeted the existence of rat laughter, people the world over were opening up their rat cages and engaging Pinky and Mr. Pickles in full-scale tickle wars.[15]

"I don't necessarily call it laughter; I call it a signal of positive affect," Burgdorf told us when we visited him at Northwestern University's Falk Center for Molecular Therapeutics in Chicago, where he now works as a biomedical engineering professor. Burgdorf's careful choice of words makes sense. He and Panksepp faced serious critical pushback when their rat-tickling activities first went public. But whatever you want to call it, Burgdorf, a quick-witted guy with a boyish face and a sign on his office door that reads "Know-It-All," has been obsessed with that strange rat noise he first stimulated in 1997. "How do I know that it's really a sign of positive affect?" he said to us. "That's been the question of my career."

So far, it seems he's on to something. He found the 50-kilohertz chirping changed when one of the animals involved in rough-and-tumble play was much larger than the other, when it was no longer fun and games and instead outright bullying—or as Pete would say, when the physical violations were no longer benign. And when given a choice, Burgdorf's rats would push a bar to play a recording of the

50-kilohertz chirp as opposed to other rat noises, suggesting they had a preference for the sound. Finally, when Burgdorf and his colleagues used electrodes, opiates, and other manipulations to stimulate the reward centers of rats' brains, the rats produced that same laughter-like noise.

And now, here in this lab, with its key-card-required security doors and freezers of bio samples and warning signs for radioactive materials, Burgdorf is using his rats and their special squeaks to test a new depression medication designed to increase positive mood. Clinical trials are already in phase two, and if all goes well, the drug might hit the shelves in three or four years. That's right: Big Pharma is using laughing rats to develop a happy pill.

Tickle-loving rats, joke-playing gorillas, even stories of dog laughter—these reports could just be the beginning, said Marc Bekoff when we met him at a coffee shop in Boulder, Colorado. Bekoff, a colleague of Pete's at the University of Colorado, where he's a professor emeritus of ecology and evolutionary biology, is one of the world's foremost experts on animal emotions. And he, for one, believes we're on the cusp of discovering that lots of animals have a sense of humor, maybe even all mammals. He pointed to Darwin's idea that the difference between human and animal intelligence is a matter of degree, not of kind. Or as Bekoff put it, "If we have a sense of humor, then non-human animals should have a sense of humor, too." Considering the groundbreaking discoveries that ethologists like Bekoff are making about animal behavior, from dogs understanding unfairness to baby spiders displaying different temperaments to bees being taught to be pessimistic, the idea of thousands of inherently funny species might not be all that far-fetched.

Unfortunately, cruising through the wild kingdom of Rubondo Island in our safari jeep, we don't spot any chimps, rats, dogs, or other animals to tickle. So we park the vehicle by a guesthouse near the water, and Rutta suggests the three of us go bushwhacking. We set off into the woods, climbing over tree trunks and pushing through foliage, hot on the trail of . . . well, anything at all safari-worthy. Along the way, Rutta points out a heaping pile of elephant dung, which Pete nearly steps in. Then Pete tries swinging Tarzan-style from a hanging vine, and somehow doesn't end up killing himself. After that, Rutta guides us to a shallow cave in a cliffside he's visited before, pointing out a collection of bones scattered about its floor. "Dead people," he explains, remnants of a time when foreigners like us weren't so welcome on the island. Now I'm starting to wonder about those rifles our escorts brought along.

"If I don't almost get eaten, I will be disappointed," declares Pete as we tromp through the underbrush. A few minutes later, I feel a stinging pain on my leg, then another. Looking down, I find black soldier ants swarming my feet and legs, crawling into my shoes and under my socks and biting hard any time they come across skin. Pete's covered in them, too. We slap at our legs, cursing in pain as the little buggers make a meal of our calves. Meanwhile Rutta, diligent safari guide that he is, pulls out his camera and starts taking photos of our misery.

Our walk in the jungle a bust, we return to the guesthouse and try a different tack: we pay the pilot of a small dinghy moored by the shore to take us around the island's shoreline. Motoring along the coast, we find wildlife: cormorants and egrets and ibis perched by the shore, African fish eagles swooping overhead, hippo snouts bobbing among the waves, and giant crocodiles slipping into the greenish water as we cruise by. Off in the distance, we glimpse a freakish sight: gigantic black clouds rising from the water's surface, as if the lake were on fire. These are African lake flies, explains Rutta, hatching by the millions. But then our pilot notices another kind of cloud forming overhead—storm clouds.

He turns the boat around and heads back, but he's not fast enough to outrun the storm. The wind whips up, and rain begins pelting our faces. The pilot guns the outboard motor, but that just sends more water sloshing into the boat. The rain beats down harder and harder, and soon we're plowing through an endless gray curtain of water. "These are three-foot, four-foot swells!" hollers Pete over the engine as the dinghy rocks wildly back and forth in the waves. Suddenly, in the midst of our soggy misery, I start laughing. Maybe it's the absurdity of the situation, or maybe I'm going insane with fear. Either way, Pete joins in, and Rutta does, too. Here we are, facing a possible watery grave in the middle of Lake Victoria, and we're cackling like maniacs. And we can't seem to stop.

We make it back to shore just as the squall moves on. As the sun reemerges from the clouds, we strip to our pants and lay out our waterlogged clothes out on the shore to dry. "I was thinking, 'Is this a good thing or a bad thing?' until I heard you laugh," Pete tells me as we stretch out in the sun, his iPod blasting more 1990s hip-hop. "It's an example of how laughter signals things are okay."

Rutta has another interpretation. "It's *omuneepo!*" he declares, nodding his head to Biggie Smalls.

When the Kashasha boarding school shut down during the laughter outbreak in 1962, the schoolgirls went home—and along with them went *omuneepo*. At Rwamishenye girls' middle school just outside Bukoba, a third of the 154 pupils came down with symptoms after several of the Kashasha students returned to their homes nearby. That school closed, too, and one of the pupils from that institution returned to her village twenty miles away, where she spread the ailment to her family, including a relative who'd walked ten miles to witness the symptoms. Soon two boys' schools nearby were overrun and shut down, too. "At the time of writing this paper the disease is spreading to other villages, the education of the children is being seriously interfered with, and there is considerable fear among the village communities," noted Rankin and Philip in their *Central African Journal of Medicine* article. There's no indication when, exactly, the laughing finally stopped or how many people were affected, but some reports put the total at approximately 1,000 victims.

No community suffered as much as Nshamba, a village southwest of Bukoba. There, according to Rankin and Philip, 217 villagers came down with the ailment after several of the Kashasha schoolgirls returned to their area homes. So, on a rainy African morning with gray clouds hanging low overhead, we roll into Nshamba, a busy community crisscrossed by red dirt roads.

Since many of the victims were young women, we head off in search of female villagers. We find a group in front of a coffee co-op, kneeling on a tarp and sorting by hand through large mounds of green coffee beans, looking for runts. Yes, they tell us through Rutta, they know of the laughing disease. One of them even suffered from it: the woman in the corner in the brown hairnet. We're eager to hear more, but the women turn back to their work, ignoring us. We're flummoxed, until Rutta explains that they're thirsty. They could use some sodas.

We catch on. Pete wanders over to a local shop and returns with a crate of Pepsis, Fantas, and Sprites. The women cheer. Once they've cracked open their soda-pop bribes with their teeth, they are eager to chat. We sit down with the woman in the brown hairnet, who tells us she came down with the disease in July 1996. She felt a pain in her back and head and then, three days later, lost control of her body—laughing, crying, speaking in strange languages. Only when she was taken to the hospital and given a shot of quinine did she recover.

This wasn't *omuneepo*, says Rutta. It was cerebral malaria. His second brother came down with it, causing him to run around like a maniac until he collapsed in exhaustion.

Our search through the town continues, past free-range chickens scurrying about and women eyeing us from doorsteps, chewing bits of sugarcane. We learn that the person we should talk to is a woman named Amelia. We're told she was the first person in Nshamba to come down with the ailment once it was brought here by the school-girls. When she recovered she became a healer, treating others with the disease. There's only one problem: Amelia now lives far away from here, we're told, in a distant part of the region. And she's crazy.

Meanwhile, children have been gathering about us, drawn by the spectacle of the two white guys, apparently not a common sight. As we make our way back to the van, they break out in singing: "*Mzungu*, eh, eh, eh! *Mzungu*, eh, eh, eh!" Whether the song's making fun of us or not, Pete joins in the festivities, jumping about wildly as the small children laugh with glee.

These children, as young as they are, see the humor in what's going on here: two *mzungus*, out of their element, dancing about like maniacs. Laughter develops in infants far earlier than language, usually between just ten and twenty weeks of age. (Aristotle was off when he declared babies begin laughing on their fortieth day.) To be clear, what these babies are laughing at isn't humor as we understand it; they just find certain stimuli pleasurable. (For those stuck alone with their baby nephew without any idea of what to do with him, take note: according to observational studies of what 150 infants in the first year of life laughed at, kissing the kiddo's tummy and playing "I'm gonna get you!" are winners. Bouncing the tyke on your knee? Not so much—nor is it very safe.)[16]

According to Paul McGhee, who has spent years studying how humor develops, children don't begin to recognize things as funny until about halfway through age two. That's when they understand that objects have meanings that can be rearranged in funny ways (like using a banana like a telephone). But that's not the end of it. According to McGhee, there are still three other developmental humor stages to come. Early in their third year, kids typically start using their developing language skills to mislabel objects, similar to the way I still inanely point to horses I see on long car trips and call them cows, just to piss off my wife, Emily. Then soon after, children grasp conceptual humor, based on the idea that objects have attributes that can be rearranged in an amusing fashion. And by this point, these kids are laughing all the time. Studies of five-year-olds have shown they laugh, on average, 7.7 times per hour, while the average American adult laughs just eighteen times a day.[17]

At around seven years, children develop the ability to juggle multiple concepts and meanings in their minds at once, so they finally get the whole shebang: plays on words, double meanings, puns, and complicated jokes.[18] Still, children often need several more years under their belts before they fully get the joke behind tricky concepts like irony and satire. That's not too surprising, considering that sarcasm is often so difficult to grasp, even for adults, that there are efforts afoot to create new forms of punctuation to indicate it. That includes the SarcMark, which looks like an upside-down "e" with an eyeball. This, to us, is a great idea. ℰ

As obvious outsiders in Nshamba, it's to our advantage to joke and laugh not just with these kids, but with grown-ups here, too. That's because laughter and humor are powerful social signals, indicating to the world in big, bold letters that things are okay. As sociologist Rose

Coser once put it, "Laughter and humor are indeed like an invitation, be it an invitation for dinner, or an invitation to start a conversation: it aims at decreasing social distance." Humor and laughing are so good at this, so adept at increasing positive feelings and social intimacy, that they seem to operate like a remote control, with someone else's mind as your personal boob tube. A few years ago, researchers in London had people listen to laughter while an fMRI scanner monitored their brain response. They found that just the sound of chuckling, without any humor at all, was enough to trigger neurons in the part of the brain that controls the muscles for smiling and laughing. Scientists have labeled these cells "mirror neurons," since they mirror the behavior being observed. Negative sounds, such as screaming and retching, also activated corresponding mirror neurons, but at a weaker level.[19]

No wonder the crews of professional laughers we auditioned for in Los Angeles are in such high demand to help get sitcom audiences chuckling. Here was more scientific proof that laughter really is contagious.

But when you joke or laugh, you do more than just make those around you prone to laughter, too. Because humor helps you come off as less threatening and more socially attractive, it can help convince others, in an almost voodoo-like way, of all sorts of unreasonable things. In one study, people trying to bargain down the price of a landscape painting were willing to accept a higher cost if the person on the other side of the negotiating table cracked, "I'll throw in my pet frog."[20] In another experiment, people listened to a speech that had been intentionally disorganized, with nearly a third of all sentences rearranged randomly. Those who heard a version that included jokes throughout the discourse rated it more organized than its equally muddled counterpart.[21] So now, if we can use humor to convince people in Nshamba that we, a couple of white guys asking odd questions about some half-forgotten mysterious ailment, aren't up to no good? All the better.

Discussing our options with Rutta, we decide our best bet is to try to track down this woman Amelia. So we pile into the van, which we've renamed the "Hotbox" because of its lack of air-conditioning, and head off into the bush. Deeper and deeper we drive into the backcountry, past verdant stands of banana trees and through rocky, remote valleys. The rain clouds have passed, and the hot African sun beats down on the van. "Welcome to Tanzania," Rutta cracks as we inch down a treacherous series of switchbacks, the rock-strewn dirt road nearly tearing out our transmission. Every now and then, we come across somebody ambling down the road, and Rutta pauses to ask directions. More often than not, these passersby climb into the vehicle to show us the way. Soon we have the equivalent of a small village crammed into the van, all of whom profess to know where Amelia lives.

The dirt roads soon regress to little more than rugged trails, spindly tree branches scraping against the sides of the van. "This is the end of the road," announces Rutta, parking at the end of a dusty footpath flanked by rugged fences of tied-together sticks. At the end of the path, we find an elderly woman in a faded shirt and skirt working in a meager field. She regards us, frowning, and shuffles on bare feet over to a small, mud-walled shack. We follow her inside and sit on the ground in the murky, fragrant interior. Yes, she says, her name is Amelia. Yes, she's from Nshamba. Her dark eyes fix on Rutta alone, hardly acknowledging Pete's and my presence at all. Her white hair frames a rigid grimace.

Then Rutta mentions *omuneepo*. Amelia flinches, startled. "*Omuneepo?*" she asks, leaning forward. But the moment passes. Her poker face returns. "I don't know anything about that," she tells Rutta in Swahili. Rutta doesn't buy it, pushing her to say more. Fine, she relents. Maybe she had the disease once, as a young woman. "But that was 60 years ago," she grumbles. She doesn't remember anything about it.

But what about what happened after? prompts Rutta. Didn't she treat people with *omuneepo*? Yes, she admits, she treated sick people. But she can't recall what she treated them for. We sit there, dumbfounded, as flies buzz about our heads. Beams of sunlight slice through the dusty gloom, radiating from holes in the walls.

She's afraid, Rutta tells us when we step outside for a moment. "In Tanzania, some people are killed if they are practicing witchcraft."

Undaunted, we press on. "I was eight years old when there was war between Uganda and Tanzania, and I still remember it," protests

Rutta. We explain to her that Pete's a university professor, that we've heard the rumors about *omuneepo* and we're eager to hear the truth.

But Amelia just shakes her head, making it clear it's time for us to go. Whatever she knows about *omuneepo*, she's taking it with her to the grave.

Jason Kamala, the principal of the vocational school in Kashasha, recommended we talk to Kroeber Rugeiyamu, Tanzania's first indigenous psychiatrist. He's retired now, Kamala told us, and lives not far from the school. So one warm afternoon, we pull up in front of Rugeiyamu's home, which looks like no other home we've seen in Tanzania—or any other house we've seen anywhere.

A tall, sloping cone of rock, concrete, and corrugated metal rises from the earth, like an industrial-strength igloo. The house is a modernized version of the region's traditional woven-grass huts known as *mushonge*, we learn from Rugeiyamu, a slight, gray-haired man with a wise smile and bright eyes. "My father was content with his *mushonge*, but I am a medical man," says Rugeiyamu, guiding us around his property in a remarkably spry manner, considering he was born in 1928. So, for his *mushonge*, Rugeiyamu mixed the best of both worlds—the traditions of his homeland and the ideas he adopted while studying medicine in Great Britain. The outhouses out back feature subsoil fertilization systems to feed his banana trees and vanilla vines. In the depths of the hut, past the grain storage area and wood-fired ovens, a dusky library overflows with books—the plays of Shakespeare, a biography of Nelson Mandela, a copy of *The Rise and Fall of the Third Reich*. When the tour is over, Rugeiyamu deposits us in the main room of his *mushonge*, where, surrounded by soaring concrete pillars and a cathedral-like ceiling, we sit on the straw-covered ground and pass around a gourd filled with pungent fermented wine made by locals crushing bananas with their bare feet.

From his distinctive perspective, from his fusion of the old and the new, Rugeiyamu offers us his take on *omuneepo*. "It's hysteria, isn't it?" he says with a knowing smile, as though this was obvious all along. More specifically, mass hysteria, the spontaneous communal eruption of hysterical symptoms, often a response to stress. According to Rugeiyamu, the Kashasha pupils and other schoolchildren who came down with the laughing disease had lots to be stressed about. "Life was different for the students before they went to school; They had freedom," he says. "At school, there were strict limits to freedom. And this was a form of expression: the children started laughing. Rather than protesting, they were laughing."

This makes sense from what we've learned. While the Kashasha school sounds far from ghastly, it was clearly not an easy place to go to school, with its windowless dorms and uncomfortable chairs. And since it was one of the first boarding schools of its kind in the region, the schoolgirls were likely unprepared for the religious-based limits on their largely liberated childhoods. As Rugeiyamu suggests, they had reason to protest.

While Rugeiyamu didn't live in this part of the country and didn't witness the *omuneepo* outbreak himself, in later years while working for the ministry of health, he was dispatched to other schools where similar symptoms erupted. And always, he says, he found evidence that something was wrong. Serious overcrowding. Poor food quality. A headmistress who had gone AWOL, leaving the school rudderless. "It's a form of complaint," he concludes. "They have no alternative form of expression."

A few years ago, Christian Hempelmann, a Texas A&M professor of computational linguistics and an avid humor researcher, decided he wasn't sure about the claim in Provine's book *Laughter: A Scientific Investigation* that what happened in Tanganyika in 1962 was an example of the contagiousness of laughter. It just didn't seem to fit into what we knew about laughter, he told me before our trip. So he scoured the psychological literature available and, in a 2007 article published in *HUMOR: The International Journal of Humor Research*, he came up with the same conclusion as Rugeiyamu.[22]

The evidence to support this theory is compelling. Historical surveys of 140-plus outbreaks of mass hysteria between 1872 and 1993 found that half of all cases occurred in schools just like Kashasha, and the majority of the victims were women—young women, in particular.[23]

And laughter, it turns out, has occurred in other cases of mass hysteria, at least the more physical kind known as motor mass hysteria. I learned this when I called Robert Bartholomew, an Australian sociology professor who's an expert on UFO scares, witchcraft terrors, dance manias, headhunting panics, imaginary air raids, and other bizarre human behavior.[24] "With mass motor hysteria, there have long been reports of laughing that go on for long periods of time intermittently," Bartholomew told me. From his extensive computer databases, he called up a variety of those reports: The Klikushestvo shouting manias of the beleaguered later years of imperial Russia. Outbreaks in strict primary schools in turn-of-the-century Europe. Occurrences amid substandard factory conditions in twentieth-century Singapore. Bouts in a down-and-out Canadian sardine packing plant in 1992. Incidents among Nepalese schoolgirls in 2003. In all these cases, said Bartholomew, "the common denominator was they were under, without a doubt, extreme stress."

The fantastical symptoms of *omuneepo* and other communal manias might seem like something from an exotic time and place. And, sure enough, mass motor hysteria is less common in more modern parts of the world. But that doesn't mean what happened in Tanganyika can't still happen right in our own backyard.

"Have you heard about this thing going on right now in Le Roy?" Latif Nasser, a Harvard grad student researching *omuneepo*, asked me when I gave him a call. He's referring to the news that in the New York factory town of Le Roy, high school students were coming down left and right with uncontrollable tics, wild gestures, and crazed outbursts. As in Tanzania, the ailment was primarily striking young women, spreading outward from the most popular in school like some shared secret passing from one girl to the next. Some experts were suggesting mass motor hysteria, possibly due to the stress of growing up in a dead-end town. But many parents rejected the diagnosis, looking for some other cause. Erin Brockovich, the famous environmental legal crusader, even investigated whether the shuttered factories had left behind something horrible in the streams and fields.[25] She didn't find anything.

It's the same way as how people here in Tanzania have shirked our questions, or blamed the strange laughter on witchcraft or dead relatives or the unknowable hand of God. It's sometimes easier to ignore these episodes, or look for a culprit, than to accept them for what they are: a collective cry for help.

On our last day in Tanzania, Rutta remembers something. He's heard rumors that at a nearby school, kids had been acting strangely. He suggests we check it out, hopping in the van with more haste and eagerness than we've seen all trip. Maybe our obsessive-compulsive tendencies are rubbing off.

The school's principal, a matronly woman in a pink pantsuit named Margaret Shilimpaka, greets us when we arrive. She tells us the co-ed school recently updated its curriculum from home economics to more contemporary, practical skills like hospitality training and food services. Looking around the scattering of modern buildings on a grassy knoll, it's hard to conceive anything majorly wrong here. But yes, Shilimpaka tells us, her students have been losing control. "There are many," she declares, eyes widening for emphasis. "They start laughing, crying, 'I like this, I don't like this.'" She shakes her head. The last two years, she says, have been "very, very bad."

We ask to see some of the victims, and she has a teacher fetch the most serious cases. They return with four girls and one boy, all with short-cropped hair and matching gray-and-white school uniforms. They sit quietly, eyeing us curiously, looking like typical high school students. But they're not, they tell us; something's been happening to them: shouting and laughing and convulsing in their sleep. Dreaming that somebody is out to get them. Drinking gallons of water at a time, as if they're dying of thirst. Becoming dizzy and passing out in the middle of the day. Waking up in the night to find they've torn off all their clothes. Screaming and clutching at their throats, as if someone were strangling them. Lashing out at those around them, and causing others to turn violent, too.

In the midst of the students' accounts, I ask each of them how long they'd been at the school when these incidents first occurred. One by one, they respond. One month. Two months. A few weeks. Pete and I exchange glances. A pattern like that is hard to ignore.

Now the students have questions of their own. "Why are you here?" they say, their eyes anxious and pleading. Do we have medicine for them? Can we tell them what, exactly, is wrong with them?

Pete pauses for a moment, collecting his thoughts. "This has been happening for many years in Tanzania. Mostly to girls your age," he says as Rutta translates. "And we think it's because of nervousness. Anxiety. Stress. You have worries and you have symptoms in your bodies. It's normal for being away from home for the first time." This happens all over the world, he tells them—to overworked office workers and nervous mothers and stressed-out cheerleaders. Above all, he says, it's not dangerous. The tense energy in the room dissipates, understanding and relief passing over the students' faces.

Yes, maybe the laughter of *omuneepo* and the laughter of everyday life are inherently different. But it's also true that these expressions share the same fundamental DNA. They're both basic, primal signals, designed to alert, to communicate, to connect, and to disseminate. They tap into the core of what we are as social creatures, verbalizing from one person to another what often cannot be said in any other way: either that everything is in good fun or, in the case of hysteria, that something is wrong. And maybe sometimes we're so busy trying to find reasonable explanations for it all that we miss this underlying message altogether.

No, Pete says to the students, they don't need medicine to get better. They just need time and support. If they're feeling anxious or upset or homesick, I add, they should find someone to talk to—a teacher, a friend, anyone at all who's willing to listen.

Or maybe they just need a good laugh. As we've learned from our time here, laughter is a far more powerful social force than most people realize. It can turn strangers into compatriots, crowds into communities, friends into lovers. And most of all, it signals that everything is going to be all right. If these students can joke and laugh with their colleagues, maybe they won't feel so beleaguered. Maybe they won't feel so alone.

"It will all be okay," Pete continues. "There is nothing at all to worry about."

Or as Rutta would say, "Hakuna matata."

5   JAPAN →   When is comedy
                                                 lost in translation?

What is the Japanese word for "torture"? Whatever it is, Pete and I are experiencing it.

We'd faced the prospect of our fourteen-hour, 6,063-mile flight to Osaka with resolve. We'd pegged Japan as the perfect place to figure out why comedy is so diverse, why what people find funny varies widely depending on their background, gender, and numerous other factors. After all, it was hard for us to imagine a location with a more dissimilar style of hilarity to our own. But we'd heard horror stories about crossing the fifteen time zones between Colorado and Japan, how it can turn an entire trip into one long, unpleasant waking dream. To prepare, we'd watched and re-watched how-to travel videos online and studied journal articles on the roots of jet lag. Pete also studied the film *Lost in Translation* to take pointers from Bill Murray's karaoke routine. Then we'd calibrated the perfect sleep and meal schedule to ensure we'd disembark chipper and alert on the other side of the world. That the entertainment system on our trans-Pacific flight was on the fritz, leaving us with no entertainment other than the GPS sky map updating itself every few minutes? That was no match for the neurotic planning of two anal-retentive geeks like us.

But no amount of groundwork, no possible research or regimen, could have prepared us for what awaited us in Osaka.

We'd been excited to discover that Japan had a thriving academic humor scene. Several top members of the Japanese Humor and

Laughter Society even offered to help us. Before we knew it, the scholars had arranged for us to attend a performance of *rakugo*, a traditional form of comic storytelling, on our first evening in Osaka. Never mind that the show was to begin a few hours after we arrived, with little wiggle room if we had a flight delay. We were told via e-mail the experience was "once in a lifetime," that "you cannot miss it."

So we dashed off the plane, dropped our bags at our hotel, and raced to the performance. And now here we are, sitting in a grand theater filled with several thousand Japanese people, most of whom appear to be past retirement age. On stage, kimono-clad men take turns kneeling on a pillow and reciting long, rambling soliloquys. In Japanese. With no translation. Or helpful props. Or evocative gestures.

We try our best to seem engaged even though we don't understand a word of it. On either side of us, our hosts—humor scholars Heiyo Nagashima and Shinya Morishita—smile and nod, but they aren't much help. "Husband and wife," whispers Nagashima to me, using his broken English to explain the subject of one segment. I try to look illuminated, as if the words "husband and wife" make the hour of unintelligible Japanese I've been listening to clear.

Exhaustion sweeps over us, our bodies giving in to fatigue and monotony. Soon I'm so tired it's painful, my head bobbing up and down as I struggle to focus. "Now I understand sleep deprivation," Pete whispers to me, the color drained from his face. We try to elbow each other awake, but it's no use. I distract myself by writing random thoughts and details into my reporter's notebook, only to look down and discover that halfway through a sentence, I'd started scribbling incoherently all over the page. Pete tries a different tack, composing a haiku in his journal:

Hear but can't listen
Watching kneeling men in robes
Laughter surrounds us

Any oomph it provides him doesn't last long. He's soon staring off into space with half-closed eyes, as if in a Zen-like trance. Glancing around the auditorium, I find we're not the only ones nodding off. Next to Pete, Professor Morishita appears to slumber in his seat.

I give in. As my eyelids slip closed, Pete murmurs a final, half-asleep thought in my ear: "We flew all this way to understand Japanese humor, but how are we going to understand it if we can't speak the language?"

In New York and Los Angeles, we'd hobnobbed with some of the best of the best of the country's joke creators. But even these guys and gals admit that their brand of comedy doesn't travel well. Action films are far more likely to be global blockbusters than comedies. That's because humor appreciation might be even more complex and confounding than humor creation. Sense of humor varies by upbringing and age and gender and political affiliation and other factors. What one person finds hilarious can be boringly dull to a second person, and offensive to a third.

Different cultures even have different forms of "joking relationships," as anthropologists call them, the societal rules about who can joke with whom. Among Ojibwe Native Americans, if you don't joke with your cross-cousin, you're downright rude.[1] In East Africa, the Zaramu tribe can joke with the Sukuma tribe and Sukuma members can rib Zigua tribe members, but when someone from Zigua runs into someone from Zaramu, everybody remains serious.[2]

For many Westerners, there's one particular foreign flavor of humor creation and appreciation that's particularly befuddling. Time and again, we've been asked the same question: "Can you explain Japanese humor?" There's something about Japanese culture, with its sadistic game shows, pornographic anime, intergalactic battle robots, and French-maid-themed restaurants, that triggers serious head scratching on the other side of the Pacific. That goes double for Japanese comedy—especially since there is no wholly accurate Japanese translation for words like "comedy" and "humor."[3]

So maybe the best way to get to the bottom of humor's chameleon-like properties, we'd figured, was to immerse ourselves in Japanese funny business. But we had to make sure Christie Davies hadn't beat us to it.

Christie Davies is the Indiana Jones of hilarity. The British sociologist and past president of the International Society for Humor

Studies has spent decades cataloguing and analyzing jokes from every corner of the globe, from Australia and Bulgaria to Tajikistan and Yugoslavia.

That's why, during a stopover in London, we took a train to Davies's home in the town of Reading, where he teaches at the local university. Davies, a heavyset man with a scraggly gray beard, watery eyes, and a beak of a nose, met us at the train station wearing the sort of khaki, multipocketed vest folks wear on a safari. I imagined it was stuffed with academic keepsakes: a joke-laden papyrus scroll, a Victorian whoopee cushion, a charcoal rubbing of a dirty ditty from an Incan temple wall.

Davies invited us back to his home, a two-story brick duplex that was clearly the home of a man who's spent his career focused on things elsewhere. A mountain of empty de-icer cans littered his front stoop, topped by a dead Christmas wreath. In his sitting room, a sagging couch and a couple of mismatched armchairs threatened to be subsumed by piles of miscellanea rising nearly to the ceiling— assorted foreign-language dictionaries, tangles of power cords, random pieces of clothing. Tacked to the paint-chipped walls were grotesque wooden masks and wrinkled photos from Davies's various adventures: running with the bulls in Pamplona, standing on a frigid ship's deck off Cape Horn. I'll refrain from describing the bathroom.

Clearing space among the clutter and slumping onto the couch, Davies explained that his quasi-nomadic joke-chasing existence began while he was lecturing in India in 1974. When he mentioned that the English liked to joke about the Irish being stupid, his Indian students replied they told the same sort of jokes about Sikhs. For Davies, that was the "aha!" moment, a hint that within comedy's odd connections and quirks lay unmined clues about how different cultures think and operate. As he later put it in one of his many academic humor tomes, for him jokes are "social puzzles, puzzles I have had to try to solve."

And more often than not, he's solved those puzzles. He dug into premarital-sex rates and personal hygiene in pre-revolution France to ascertain the origins of randy-Frenchmen bon mots. He traced the spread of dumb-blonde jokes from their origins in the United States to Croatia, France, Germany, Hungary, Poland, and Brazil, deducing that the zingers emerged as women, long seen as mindless sex objects, shook up gender roles by entering highly skilled professions all over the world. And when the so-called Great American Lawyer Joke Cycle of the 1980s didn't spread anywhere beyond the United States, Davies became an expert in U.S. jurisprudence to figure out why. He concluded that lawyer jokes were a uniquely American phenomenon because no other country is so rooted in the sanctity of law—and in no other country are those who practice it so reviled.[4]

Inspired by Davies's work, Pete would go on to do some academic sleuthing of his own. "What about the idea that the French love Jerry Lewis?" he asked me later. Is the concept real—and if so, what does it mean about the French, not to mention Jerry Lewis? He wasn't the first scholar to ponder this conundrum. In 2002, French literature and culture professor Rae Beth Gordon wrote a whole book on the subject. *Why the French Love Jerry Lewis*, as it was titled, argued that the wild, convulsive physical comedy of cabaret shows and early films in France meshed with Lewis's hysterical mannerisms in movies like *The Bellboy* and *The Nutty Professor*.

Pete wasn't convinced. He enlisted two French speakers, University of Colorado graduate student Bridget Leonard and professor Elise Chandon Ince at Virginia Tech, to design the ultimate *Nutty Professor* experiment. Working with the survey software company Qualtrics, they surveyed 200 people, half from France and half from the States, asking them to rate fourteen things stereotypically associated with France: berets, Brie, mimes, red wine—you get the idea. Included on the list was Jerry Lewis, along with another pseudo-French comedian: *Pink Panther* star Peter Sellers.

As it turned out, Jerry Lewis was a far bigger hit in the States than across the pond, coming in fourth out of the fourteen items among American respondents and eighth among the French. Even when Pete re-ran the study, replacing several items with stuff American respondents might like more—cowboys, apple pie, beer—results didn't change much, with Jerry Lewis still scoring equally high among both nationalities. Other findings? The French *really* like French kissing, but not as much as they like baguettes. Americans, on the other hand, apparently have a thing for scarves. As for Peter Sellers? Nobody liked him anywhere.

But these results are nothing compared to Davies's biggest discovery: inspired by the connection he made between Irish and Sikh put-downs, he started tracking similar examples of humor around the world—and uncovered a universal joke. He's named this the stupidity joke, the sort of barbed zinger that makes fun of outsiders, simpletons, and others on the fringes of society. In America, the obvious version is the Polish joke, but that's just the tip of the mean-spirited iceberg. Take the *Philogelos*, the oldest-known joke book in the world. Of the 265 zingers in the ancient Greek tome, nearly a quarter concern folks from cities renowned for their idiocy, like Cyme in modern-day Turkey and Abdera in Thrace.[5] Later, in medieval England, cracks about the dunces who lived in the village of Gotham were all the rage. (New York's nickname, "Gotham," doesn't sound so impressive once you learn that author Washington Irving coined it to suggest the place was a city of fools.[6])

Since then, stupidity jokes have spread like a healthy fungus. According to Davies's research, Uzbeks get made fun of in Tajikistan, while in France, it's the French-speaking Swiss. The list goes on: Brazilians joke about the Portuguese, Finns knock the Karelians, Nigerians rib the Hausas. The model even extends to the work world: orthopedic surgeons, with their rough-and-tumble musculoskeletal work, are the laughingstock of the medical sphere. ("What's the difference between an orthopedic surgeon and a carpenter? The carpenter knows more than one antibiotic.")

The Irish, it turns out, have a particularly bad lot. Dumb-Irish jokes are equally common in England, Wales, Scotland, and Australia. But it could be worse: if you happen to be an Irishman from County Kerry, you also get made fun of by your fellow Irish.[7]

"Nearly every country has stupidity jokes," Davies told us, pulling a tissue from a bulky vest pocket and loudly blowing his nose. From another pocket he retrieved an inhaler and took a puff. Europe, India, the Middle East, Latin America, Australia—everywhere he looked, the same pattern emerged.

But does the pattern always work? Are there some places that don't fit the mold?

Davies nodded. "East Asia." In Japan, there is no "chucklehead" part of the country. Nor do the Japanese make fun of their neighbors in China or Korea.

"It's a different world," said Davies. Japanese humor, in other words, is a puzzle that still needs to be solved.

In Japan, the history of humor is intimately tied to the samurai, the warrior class that ruled the country for centuries. We learn this from Hiroshi Inoue, president of the Japan Society for Laughter and Humor Studies. The problem, says Inoue, is that samurai aren't funny.

"For samurai, timing was very important," he tells us. There was no time or patience for shameful comedy. "You are laughing at me, so I kill you," says Inoue, pantomiming skewering a wiseass with an imaginary sword.

We're sitting in a conference room overlooking a busy stretch of downtown Osaka, sipping iced green tea and listening to Inoue's lengthy history lesson. To avoid the sort of translation disaster we'd experienced at the *rakugo* performance, we've brought along someone who speaks the language: Bill Reilly. A cheerful 28-year-old from New Jersey, Reilly is the manager of the Pirates of the Dotombori, one of only two bilingual improv groups in the country (the other is the group's sister operation in Tokyo, the Pirates of Tokyo Bay). When he heard we were looking for a translator in Osaka, Reilly volunteered. "Sarcasm doesn't really happen here," Reilly told us when he arrived at our hotel this morning, armed with an umbrella despite the clear skies. (The government had declared that today was the first day of the rainy season. Apparently in Japan, politicians have been granted the power to establish weather patterns.) Reilly welcomed the opportunity to brush up on his sarcasm with us, a couple of fresh-faced *gaijin*—the Japanese word for "foreigners." We are happy to provide him with lots of fodder for sardonic eye-rolling: Pete's constant risk of smacking his head on every low-lying door frame, my inability to extract yen from Japan's bewildering ATMs, our plan to interview one somber-faced Japanese humor researcher after another.

Inoue, in a gray suit and spectacles, tells us we made the right choice by flying into Osaka, a port city on Japan's south-central coast. Osaka is Japan's comedy capital, he tells us through Reilly. Apparently if you go up to strangers in Osaka and point your finger at them, they'll pretend to be shot without missing a beat. (Later, we ask Reilly if we should try this. "No," he says. "You might point your finger at a *yakuza*"—a member of Japan's mafia—"and they might freak the fuck out.") Osaka's brimming with hilarity, says Inoue, because it's long been "the belly of Japan," the country's trade and commercial hub, so the samurai left the city alone, realizing strict hierarchies and customs weren't good for business. That left Osaka's merchants free to haggle and barter and banter as much as they pleased—and a lot of jokes lubricated those transactions.

Osaka isn't just the hub of Japan's comedy business. It's also the focal point for Japanese humor scholarship. The Osaka-based Kansai University even boasts its own humor research department, which we get a tour of one morning with Shinya Morishita, one of our escorts during the disastrous *rakugo* performance. Morishita guides us through a media lab decked out in state-of-the-art video consoles, a full-sized theater with stadium seating, and research labs stocked with gizmos that track diaphragm movements during laughter. "I need to get funded by a Japanese university," grumbles Pete as Morishita escorts us to the final stop on the tour. "Humor science library," he announces, unlocking a door. Inside, we find a spacious room filled with row after row of bookshelves—nearly all of which are empty. In the far corner, a smattering of books fills a single lonely shelf. "Poor library," admits Morishita.

"These guys are wildly optimistic," says Pete. "I like it."

To see if these humor researchers know what they're talking about, we venture out into Japan's comedy capital. American bombers leveled much of Osaka in World War II, and the city that replaced it is a sprawling and modern concrete affair. There's a lively, cosmopolitan feel to the place—elevated trains rumble overhead, illuminated electronic billboards pulse into the night, exotic aromas waft from the food stalls and restaurants that have led the city to be called the food capital of the world. Despite the urban bustle, everyone is incredibly, even disturbingly, well mannered. No one dares disregard "Don't Walk" signals, even when there's not a car for miles around. And whenever Pete or I happen to pause somewhere and look bewildered—something that happens often—a stranger sidles up and inquires in semi-passable English how he or she can be of service.

Friendly, yes. But do Osakans find things funny? On the street, we don't see much evidence of it. Nearly everyone we pass—pedestrians, shopkeepers, businessmen, police officers—remains more or less silent. Riding in packed subway cars, the unnatural hush is so surreal I wonder if something's wrong with my ears. There's none of the steady background noise I associate with city life—no hollering, no hawking, no bickering, no cell-phone babbling, no schoolkid chattering—and most of all, no laughing.

But maybe Pete and I are going about this all wrong. Maybe we need to observe these people removed from the pressures of their everyday lives. We need to see them relaxed. We need to see them in their natural environment.

We need to see them naked.

The idea comes from Reilly. If we're looking for something to do in Osaka, he offers after wrapping up his translation duties, Pete and I *could* visit some of the area's exquisite temples and castles. Or, he added with a wink, we could go to Spa World, where the locals strip down to their birthday suits and, segregated by gender, luxuriate in a seven-story wonderland of hot tubs, steam rooms, swimming pools, and water slides.

No contest. We head to Spa World.

At first, once we've paid our 1,000 yen, or roughly twelve bucks, for all-day spa access (surely the best deal in all of expensive Japan), I'm a bit uncomfortable wandering around among all these naked strangers. But after a few dips in the heated pool and visits to the sauna on the main men's floor of the spa, a steamy Roman baths knockoff the size of a shopping mall, I start to relax. When in Rome—or at least a reasonable facsimile of it—do as the naked Japanese do!

So when Pete decides to investigate other parts of Spa World, I do likewise. While he wanders off to learn firsthand what an "exfoliation scrub" entails, I head to Heaven Spa, a swanky massage-therapy room in the heart of the Roman baths, to find out about a back rub. I stroll through the spa door, naked bits a-dangling, round a bend—and run into a gaggle of mortified Japanese women in masseuse uniforms. Shrieking and gesturing wildly, they herd me back around the corner. That's where I notice the out-of-the-way cubby stocked with cotton shorts.

Ah. In Heaven you wear underpants.

Despite my humiliation, the masseuses don't collapse into hysterics. They just titter. So once again, we've come up empty-handed on Osakan laughter. Why can't we find any of the hilarity these people are known for?

We're not looking in the right places, says Heiyo Nagashima, the other Japanese humor scholar who attended the *rakugo* performance with us. When we meet him at the Osaka headquarters of the Japanese Humor and Laughter Society, he explains that in Japan, comedy is compartmentalized. Nearly every society has developed ways to keep folks' zaniness within safe bounds. In the United States, folks are free to joke with one another in nearly any circumstance, but certain subjects are off limits—scatology, sexual extremes, racist ideas. In Japan, on the other hand, such limitations are geographical rather than topical. Here, nearly anything goes in the name of hilarity, but it is reserved for certain locales like comedy theaters and television. Don't try joking in the office, in the classroom, or—as I'd learned—when you're naked in a classy spa. Take the Laughter Society offices we're sitting in, says Nagashima, sweeping his hand around the unremarkable one-room affair, where two expressionless workers type away at computers. "This is not a laughing place," he says. "We are exchanging ideas about culture."

This idea cracks Pete up. "But this is the Japanese Humor and Laughter Society! If you can't laugh here, where can you laugh?"

We find that place one evening when Reilly and several of his improv colleagues take us to the Dotombori district, the improv group's namesake and the beating, throbbing heart of the city's nightlife scene. Dotombori inspired the setting of the sci-fi classic *Blade*

Runner, and it's easy to see why. The kaleidoscope of flashing neon signs and freakish crab and dragon sculptures that dangle over the bar-lined streets feel like something out of a futuristic metropolis—a metropolis inhabited by folks having the time of their lives.

Gone are the quiet, impassive Osakans we've met. Here is a riotous horde desperate to let loose, screaming for another round of sake over the squeal of Motown hits at a packed bar. Flailing to the unrelenting beat of a video-game dance-off at a busy arcade. Crooning away for hours at one of the area's numerous karaoke cafes. And laughing. Everyone is laughing.

We join in the fun. Late that night, our voices hoarse from one too many Guns N' Roses karaoke tunes, Pete and I wander off down a cramped alleyway—to the smallest bar in the world. In a shallow divot in the side of a building, a space no larger than a cramped closet, a bartender stands behind a thin plank, taking orders. Around him, bottles and drink glasses are fastened to the walls, like he's in a small, one-man space capsule to a thirsty moon. There's no room for clientele, so his half-dozen patrons stand in the alley, huddled around the opening and tossing back drinks. We squeeze our way in.

We don't understand a word of what our companions tell us, nor do they grasp our replies. Even if we did speak Japanese, we wouldn't get the jokes. As Nagashima had explained to us at the offices of the Japanese Humor and Laughter Society, Japan is a high-context society. The country is so homogeneous, so unified in its history and culture, that most zingers don't need set-ups at all. There's no need for explanation or detailed backstories. Folks get right to the punch line. One common joke, about an Olympic gymnast whose leotard was too high, has apparently become so familiar that even the punch line isn't necessary. All you have to do is gesture to your upper thigh.

The United States, on the other hand, is as low context as you can get. All those divergent viewpoints and cultural backgrounds and political opinions make for a lot of great comedy fodder, but it also means that everyone has different kinds of jokes. In 2007, researchers subjected more than 800 people in several parts of the country to a battery of humor questionnaires. They found that Texans were more likely to tell self-defeating jokes than Alaskans, while those from Minnesota go for quips that build bonds with their friends and neighbors. And Texas is so sprawling that it has several different humor regions. Those from the northwest portion of the Lone Star State were the most likely of all to use humor to deal with personal difficulties, while those in the southwest corner were the least likely to do so.[8] No wonder the list of top-grossing U.S. comedians is so wildly diverse, ranging from superstar ventriloquist Jeff Dunham to rock-star comic Dane Cook to late-night darling Chelsea Handler to redneck icon Jeff Foxworthy.

Comedy is so context-dependent that translating jokes from one language to another can be daunting—far trickier than, say, translating a business memo or news report. You can't just translate the words of the jokes. You need to capture and express the totality of shared cultural experiences the original joke builds upon and subverts, an entire universe of beliefs and expectations and taboos at which the zinger itself might only hint.[9] In most Japanese jokes, such context doesn't get mentioned at all. It's why cross-cultural researchers have long seen jokes as a vital window into a given society. As anthropologist Edward Hall put it, "People laugh and tell jokes, and if you can learn the humor of a people and really control it, you know that you are also in control of nearly everything else."[10]

We aren't in control of the jokes flying about the Dotombori district. But that's okay. At the smallest bar in the world, Pete and I get along just fine without knowing any context whatsoever. Arms slung around our new companions and howling into the night, we communicate via sloppy gestures, stupid expressions, and rounds of what might or might not be whiskey. Sure, we don't speak Japanese and they don't speak English, but we all speak Debauchery just fine.

"**Don't move around** the stage so much!"

"Project your voice from your stomach!"

"If you are going to pretend to be a girl, you really have to *sell* it!"

Tomioki Daiku, a tired-looking teacher with graying hair and spectacles, barks criticisms at his 60 pupils. One after another, his young students clamber to their feet in groups of two from where they're sitting along the walls and dash to the center of the parquet-floored classroom, where they banter back and forth with one another in Japanese. Then Daiku picks apart their performance—"Work on your pronunciation!" "Don't make fun of women; most of your live audiences will be ladies!" The pupils listen expressionlessly, bow politely, and hurry back to their seats. There is no laughter here—not from the teacher, not from the performers, not from the other students looking on. Ironic, given that this operation is designed to turn people into comedians.

We're at the New Star Creation comedy school in the heart of Tokyo. The day before, we traveled from Osaka to the Japanese capital via bullet train. When we disembarked—hardly off the train before an army of pastel-clad workers hurried on to scrub every surface clean—it didn't take long for us to realize that folks in Tokyo are even more methodical and meticulous than those in Osaka. When we checked into our hotel, the concierge wouldn't let us be until we'd signed enough forms to adopt an orphan child, had our photos taken ("for security reasons"), and been given exhaustive directions on how to use everything in our room—the light switches, the cabinets, the remote control, the video phone, the three-ring binder of instruction booklets for all the electronics he'd already explained to us. "I think that's everything," he sighs at the end of his monologue.

"Are you *sure*?" cracked Pete. The concierge looked panicked, wondering if he'd forgotten something.

We've come to Tokyo for the same reason that 1,500 would-be comedians from all over Japan come. We've all been lured here by the biggest name in Japanese comedy: Yoshimoto Kogyo. The century-old operation owns the comedy school, which charges 400,000 yen (roughly $5,000) for a twelve-month crash course in comedy, with supplemental lessons in acting, dance, stage presence, and kung fu—but that's not all the company controls. Yoshimoto is essentially Japan's version of Comedy Central . . . if Comedy Central were not only one of the country's largest TV production companies, but also managed 800 Japanese comedians, with several hundred more being groomed in the wings. And owned the comedy clubs. And put on a film festival. And once had its own comedy theme park.

Yoshimoto isn't just Japan's biggest comedy company. It *is* Japanese comedy.

"It's like the old studio system," Aki Yorihiro, CEO of Yoshimoto's U.S. wing of operations, had told me over the phone from his office in Santa Monica, California. "We take care of people throughout their careers and throughout their lives." I'd called Yorihiro to learn about Yoshimoto before our trip, but when he'd heard about what Pete and I were up to, he offered one better: behind-the-scenes access to every aspect of the comedy juggernaut.

That's how we ended up here at Yoshimoto's New Star Creation class, with our own Yoshimoto-employed translator, Takahiro Araki. Thanks to spending a few formative years in Indiana, Araki boasts impeccable English, as well as more than a few American mannerisms. The bespectacled, messenger bag–wearing 26-year-old appears perennially disheveled, has the very un-Japanese tendency to be ten minutes late for appointments and is more interested in gabbing about NBA stars Kobe Bryant and LeBron James over sushi at Tokyo's famous Tsukiji fish market than hammering home talking points about Yoshimoto. We couldn't imagine a better handler.

Watching the New Star Creation students, I notice one routine that's more polished than the others. I turn to Araki: "Were those guys any good?" He shakes his head. "No one is good."

After class, we introduce ourselves to the teacher, Daiku. He looks drained. The students were practicing *manzai*, the two-man comedy style comprised of a straight man, or *tsukkomi*, trading gags with and smacking around a *boke*, his goofball partner, which is the backbone of Japanese comedy. But according to Daiku, all of his pupils have a ways to go until any are *manzai* superstars. If this class is typical, he says, only 3 percent of the students will have a successful job in comedy in five years.

The few who make it through will earn a spot on Yoshimoto's payroll. They'll work their way up the company's hierarchy of theaters and, if all goes well, hit the airwaves on the company's shows. While most comedians' salaries remain meager, a few become superstars and score Hollywood-level windfalls. Sure, it's a long shot, but consider that Downtown, one of the most successful Japanese comedy acts of all time, started as a couple of kids in New Star Creation's first-ever class in 1982.

In Osaka we'd visited Yoshimoto's flagship theater, Namba Grand Kagetsu, a multistage behemoth that's designed to celebrate how far the company has come from its humble beginnings in 1912 as a family-owned Osakan theater company. Yoshimoto cultivates Osaka's comedy-capital reputation, like Jack Daniel's has linked whiskey and its Tennessee origins. All around Namba Grand Kagetsu, colorful shops sell Yoshimoto-branded cookies, golf balls, instant ramen meals, and cell-phone cleaners. In a touristy restaurant, workers grill up aromatic batches of *takoyaki*, the mayonnaise-smothered, ball-shaped nuggets of deep-fried octopus that are the signature snacks of Osaka.

"It's like a Disneyland devoted to Yoshimoto," Pete remarked in amazement. That is, if Mickey Mouse were all about octopus balls and branded toilet paper.

To make it to the main stage of Namba Grand Kagetsu, aspiring comedians should hope they're guys. There are only a couple of women in the entire *manzai* class.

"It's like something out of *Mad Men*," says Spring Day, a U.S. native who performs with the Tokyo Comedy Store, an English-language, ex-pat stand-up troupe. (The operation has no relation to the original Comedy Store in Los Angeles, other than that one of the Tokyo group's founders realized they could mooch off the American icon's name without legal ramifications.) We take Day out for dinner one night, and over barbecued chicken wings and horsemeat sashimi, it becomes clear that nearly everything about Japan disagrees with the blond-haired, feisty comedian (whose real name really is Spring Day—"hippie parents," she explains with a shrug). Her pet peeves about the country include the xenophobia, the outmoded cultural stereotypes, even the cuisine (she's allergic to fish). At the same time, she can't imagine living anywhere else. "It's a messed-up place," she says, "but I love it."

The misogyny is especially frustrating, says Day. Things are especially bad for put-upon housewives. According to Day, if you Google "Japanese husbands," the top results are how-tos on slowly killing your significant other by limiting nutrient intake and encouraging him to smoke. (When I try it, the first result is a news article titled, "Some wives wish their husbands would hurry up and drop dead.")

Gender bias in comedy isn't limited to Japan. Big names ranging from celebrated polemicist Christopher Hitchens to podcast host Adam Carolla have considered the evidence and concluded that women just aren't as funny as men—and they aren't the only ones who believe this. A recent experiment involving *New Yorker* cartoons found that participants of both genders were more likely to attribute funny cartoon captions to men.[11]

Empirically, are women less funny? In the nascent years of humor research, scientists seemed to think so. Researchers found that men were more likely than women to enjoy jokes and cartoons presented to them, and differences were pronounced for sexual or aggressive material. But later reviews of these experiments found the conditions involved were less than pristine. It turned out many of the jokes used were downright sexist, such as this one: "Why did the woman cross the road? Never mind that—what was she doing out of the kitchen?!" So it wasn't necessarily that the female participants didn't enjoy jokes. They just didn't enjoy jokes at their own expense.[12]

More recently, the task of analyzing gender and humor was taken up by University of Western Ontario Psychology professor Rod Martin, whose name should strike fear into the hearts of all comedy dogmatists. Martin is the unofficial dean of humor studies, and with good reason: his textbook, *The Psychology of Humor*, is the bible of the field, 446 lucid pages detailing everything there is to know about academic humor research in eleven tidy chapters. It's proven invaluable to Pete and me, a trusty guidebook to the wild and woolly extremes of humor science. "People have felt that humor is such a difficult thing to study, that it is nebulous and hard to define," Martin told me at a psychology of humor conference we attended in San Antonio, his bespectacled eyes welcoming and kind. "People have shied away from it because of that. I would argue that's all the more reason to put effort into it." But don't let his grandfatherly appearance and genial Canadian demeanor fool you. When Martin gets his academic teeth into any of the comedy world's unsubstantiated ideologies, he doesn't let go until it's torn to shreds.

And that's what he did with the idea that women aren't funny. He examined all the valid experiments on gender and humor, from comedy-appreciation surveys to joke-telling contests to self-report questionnaires to observational experiments, and came to a succinct conclusion, which he relayed at a recent International Society for Humor Studies Conference: "I think Christopher Hitchens is wrong." By nearly every scientific measure, men and women are far more alike than different in how they perceive, enjoy, and create humor. The same goes for naughty stuff: when you do away with sexist material, women go for a good dirty joke just as much as men.[13]

One of the few areas where there are gender distinctions is in dating and mating. These days, that tends to mean Match.com. In 2011 researchers analyzed more than 250 online dating profiles posted by people in London and several Canadian cities. They found that men were nearly two times as likely as women to boast of their humor-production abilities ("I'm an aspiring stand-up comic"), whereas women were nearly two times as likely as men to be looking for a humor producer ("I want someone who can make me giggle").[14]

This discrepancy could tie in to what we learned in Tanzania about humor's evolutionary origins. A sense of humor in men could be seen as a sign of intelligence, social desirability, and overall genetic fitness. In other words, good jokes are a guy's version of colorful peacock plumes. Since women have an evolutionary incentive to find the best possible mate, it helps to be on the lookout for the funniest possible peacock.

All those eons of comedic courting seem to have left a mark. The few studies that have found differences between male and female humor creation do tend to conclude that men might have a small edge over women. But before anyone crowns Adam Carolla the Einstein of comedic gender studies, consider that men might be slightly better at jokes simply because they're more likely to be encouraged to joke around. It's far more acceptable for boys to be class clowns than girls.

This social encouragement gives budding male comics a head start over their female counterparts. But it might come with a disadvantage. For guys, all those overeager humor attempts can have a cost.

Pete asked several of his classes to take part in a joke-writing competition. Working with colleagues Caleb Warren and Kathleen Vohs, as well as HuRL researchers, he found that of the 50 or so zingers submitted, those written by men were rated by a second group of students to be somewhat funnier than those written by women, but the difference was so slight that it wasn't statistically significant. The guys' jokes were far more offensive, however. Take two of the top three funniest-rated jokes, both of which were written by men:

What's the first thing a co-ed does when she wakes up? Walks home.

Penn State football: Go in as a tight end and leave as a wide receiver.

Participants rated both jokes highly distasteful, with the Penn State joke rated the most offensive of all submissions.

The funniest joke of all, on the other hand, was somewhat offensive, but not as much as the two runners-up:

How do you know you've been robbed by an Asian? Your homework is all finished, your computer has been upgraded, and he's still trying to back out of your driveway.

This gem was written by a woman.

In short, men should stop wasting their time calling their better halves the less-funny sex. They'd be far better served working on improving their own jokes. Judging from the guys at the New Star Creation class, they could use the extra effort.

There's something else missing at the New Star Creation classes: political jokes. We've hardly heard any political humor during our time in Japan. "The pillars of American comedy, like politics, are completely off the radar here," we learn from Patrick Harlan, a Colorado-born Harvard graduate who's the *boke* in Pakkun Makkun, one of the few successful *manzai* acts featuring an international duo. The Japanese government is too stable and the elections here too sedate—and the emperor too sacred—for people to crack wise about political affairs.

These days, it's hard to imagine any part of U.S. politics being considered too sedate or sacred for comedic skewering. From the pointed satire of *The Colbert Report* to the snarky rhetoric of Rush Limbaugh to presidential candidates rubbing elbows with their impersonators on *Saturday Night Live*, making fun of politicians has become America's pastime.

But who wins the prize for being funnier—Democrats or Republicans? Judging from the makeup of the comedy industry, it's easy to think the political left has it won hands down. Aside from Dennis Miller, P. J. O'Rourke, and Victoria Jackson, it's not easy to come up with big-name conservative comedians. So why isn't there a Republican version of Jon Stewart? Some people think it's because Republicans tend to have a sunnier disposition on life ("Social inequity? What social inequity?"). Using Pete's terminology, that means they aren't as likely to come across violations that are ripe for making benign.

Speculation aside, are Democrats quantifiably better at being funny? In his book *Debatable Humor: Laughing Matters on the 2008 Presidential Primary Campaign*, University of Arkansas political science professor Patrick Stewart catalogued and analyzed every use of humor in the Republican and Democratic primary debates during the 2008 presidential election. All in all, he says, "I didn't find anything in the last election on which party is funnier."

He did find some differences in how the Democratic and Republican candidates tended to joke. Democrats, for example, often relied on the kind of comedy that was inclusive and convivial. "The Democratic party is a highly egalitarian party," says Stewart. "Anyone can get in or drop out. So you really have to be charismatic like Clinton or Obama to draw people in." Obama was particularly skilled in this area: Stewart found that in the debates he often flashed smiles of genuine amusement and engaged in loose-jawed laughter, the sort of visual signals that suggest, "Join me, I'm here to play."

Republicans, on the other hand, tended to rely on what's called "encrypted humor," says Stewart, the sort of "wink, wink" in-jokes that separate insiders from outsiders. Take Republican candidate Mike Huckabee's 2008 quip that "we've had a Congress that has spent money like [John] Edwards at a beauty shop." By using the term "beauty shop," as opposed to, say "barber shop," Huckabee's joke was "not just an attack on Congress, but also an attack on John Edwards's masculinity," says Stewart.

So Democratic officials don't have a leg up on Republicans in the funny business. But what about how average Democrats and Republicans go about their daily lives? In general, do liberals have a better sense of humor than conservatives? In 2008, Pete's colleague Duke University psychology and behavioral economics professor Dan Ariely and Mount Holyoke College student Elisabeth Malin asked 300 people, half liberal and half conservative, to rate the funniness of 22 jokes on various topics. Not too surprisingly, the conservatives were more apt to enjoy the jokes that reinforced traditional racial and gender stereotypes—including a zinger about a guy choosing a game of golf over his wife's funeral. But conservatives also gave higher ratings to absurdist quips of Jack Handey's "Deep Thoughts." In fact, right-wingers found *all* kinds of jokes funnier than their liberal counterparts.[15] Maybe, then, the concept of humorless Republicans is just a matter of circumstance. After all, the history of American stand-up is littered with hard-core liberals, from Charlie Chaplin to Lenny Bruce to Bill Hicks. It could be that funny conservatives have never been welcomed into the club.

"When you look at a baby, you laugh and smile," says company CEO Hiroshi Osaki. "That's what it's like with Yoshimoto. All you have to do is drop our name and someone might laugh."

We're sitting in a conference room, talking with the Yoshimoto CEO about baby faces, in the company's humble Tokyo headquarters: a retrofitted elementary school near the busy Shinjuku commercial center. The modest surroundings mesh with Osaki's demeanor. While the formal conventions of the meeting unfold around us—assistants whisk in multiple servings of iced tea; a team of media personnel stand at attention in the corner until the CEO gestures for them to sit; a company representative presents us with gift bags overflowing with Yoshimoto-branded paraphernalia—Osaki, in a suit and tie, remains chipper as he smokes a Lucky Strike. Later, when we pose for a photo, the CEO pretends to feel us up to ensure we're all laughing in the shot.

Yoshimoto rose to its place of prominence thanks to savvy decisions the company made decades ago, says Osaki. In the 1920s, executives took note of the slapstick and rapid-fire jokes of American vaudeville and decided it was the perfect way to shake up the stagnant culture of *manzai*. It had remained more or less unchanged since the Middle Ages. According to the scholarly book *Understanding Humor in Japan*, Yoshimoto brass told their performers to wear "'glasses like Lloyd's' and 'a mustache like Chaplin's.'" And later, as Japanese broadcasting came into its own in the wake of World War II, Yoshimoto again borrowed from the comedy industry across the Pacific. Taking inspiration from the skits, bits and banter of *The Bob Hope Show*, the company developed its own, enduringly popular version of the variety show.

What Osaki seems to be telling us is that Japanese comedy is a cultural Galapagos Island. All those bizarre Japanese jokes and gags that leave Americans confused? They're U.S. comedy's bastard stepchildren.

Lately, Yoshimoto has been going global with this unique brand of hilarity. The company has started producing television programs and live shows in China, Taiwan, and Korea. And now, Osaki tells us, Yoshimoto is ready to show America that the student has become the master. The company has announced plans to build a Second City training center in Tokyo, the improv group's first-ever foreign affiliate. And Yoshimoto has inked deals with several U.S. and European TV production companies, among them the operations that created *Survivor* and *The Office*.

There may be a problem with Yoshimoto's plan: could a single kind of comedy ever be popular worldwide? Yes, some examples of comedy have been found to be incredibly, even eerily ubiquitous. The trickster motif, the concept of a wily clown who relies on his wits and ruses to get in and out of trouble, has been found in Native American culture, Ancient Greek myths, Norse legends, African folk tales, Tibetan Buddhist practices, Polynesian religious tales, Islamic fables, and even 17,000-year-old cave paintings in France.[16] But still, these trickster tales vary from culture to culture. There's far from one joke that rules them all.

So is it even possible for a single example of hilarity to achieve global domination? In 2001, a British psychology professor named Richard Wiseman decided to find out. He and his colleagues launched the LaughLab, a website where people uploaded jokes and rated others' submissions using a scale called the "Giggleometer." Over twelve months, the website clocked 40,000 joke submissions and nearly 2 million ratings from people in 40 different countries—the largest-ever scientific humor study, earning a Guinness World Record. And on October 3, 2002, Wiseman announced they'd done it: they'd come up with the world's funniest joke.

During our brief stop in London, we met Wiseman at a busy coffee shop. Since retiring the LaughLab, Wiseman has continued to probe humanity's psychological skeleton closets, deconstructing bad luck, confidence schemes, and ghost hunting. "We deliver, no matter how mad the scientific proposal," he said between sips of cappuccino.

But no proposal was as mad—or as attention-grabbing—as the LaughLab. The world was eagerly watching when Wiseman and his team revealed the winning joke:

Two hunters are out in the woods when one of them collapses. He doesn't seem to be breathing and his eyes are glazed. The other guy whips out his phone and calls emergency services. He gasps, "My friend is dead! What can I do?" The operator says, "Calm down. I can help. First, let's make sure he's dead." There is a silence, then a gunshot. Back on the phone, the guy says, "Okay, now what?"

So what does Wiseman think of his scientific findings? "I think the world's funniest joke isn't very funny," he told us. "It's terrible. I think we found the world's cleanest, blandest, most internationally accepted joke."

In hindsight, the joke's blandness makes sense. The world's funniest-rated joke isn't going to be the zinger that the most people find hilarious, it's going to be the zinger that the least number of people find offensive. Any joke that makes fun of a particular people, religion, occupation, or viewpoint isn't going to fly. It has to be something that's acceptable to everybody—or incredibly ho-hum. And a quip about a couple of bumbling hunters *from Jersey* is as ho-hum as you can get. As Wiseman grumbles, "It's the color beige in joke form."

Pete, ever the competitor, wanted to know if he could use experiments to seek out a funnier variation of the hunter joke without increasing its offensiveness. To do so, he once again partnered with Upright Citizens Brigade LA's "science department." For a control version, one team of UCB participants, using lots of fake blood, made a 30-second web video that stuck as closely as possible to the original hunter joke. Other UCB teams tried to make funnier web versions, and they were given various constraints on how far off script they could go.

A couple of the hunter joke variations—one that turned the scenario into a dubbed kung fu movie, and another that featured a hysterical clown using a squeaking plastic hammer to beat to death a kid choking on a balloon animal—turned out to be no more funny or offensive than the baseline version when Pete submitted them all to a Qualtrics survey panel. But the other two adaptations, one an extreme variation and one a mild variation, were rated significantly funnier while also less offensive. The "less offensive" part is somewhat surprising, considering one of the videos featured an emergency-services operator plagued by all sorts of callers misinterpreting his instructions, leading to a two-minute stretch of death and dismemberment, while the other involved a hunter horribly inept at killing his friend, leading to gunshots, hand-to-hand combat, and a Good Samaritan passerby offering to help by running the guy over with his truck.

But it's all about how the jokes were crafted, Pete pointed out. In the two funniest videos, all the unpleasantness occurred off camera, the violence only hinted at through sound effects. Yes, the hunter joke can be made funnier without becoming more offensive, but it takes some serious work—relying on a subtle medium like video, enlisting comedy masters like those at UCB. "The study illustrates that in some cases, severe violations can be really funny to lots of people if they are done really well," he concludes.

But at Yoshimoto, CEO Osaki concedes he isn't sure severe violations can have international appeal, even when they're being handled by professionals. "I personally don't find American stand-up that funny," he tells us. "Maybe it's lost in translation."

Remember when I called watching the *rakugo* performance akin to torture? Forget I said that. That's nothing compared to what we witness on "Ogata Impossible."

We're on a soundstage in downtown Tokyo, on the set of *Power Purin*, a Yoshimoto variety show that airs late on Wednesday nights on the Japanese station TBS. Most of *Power Purin* is devoted to *Saturday Night Live*–style comedy skits. But every now and then, the comedians engage in a *batsu*, or "penalty," game, a one-off game-show stunt. That's what's happening now.

"Welcome to 'Ogata Impossible!'" shouts the game-show host, who for some reason is dressed up like a demon. "You gamble with your life here!"

The one doing the gambling is Takohiro Ogata, a young Japanese actor with a mop of shaggy brown hair. He tries to look brave as he's presented with a tureen full of scalding hot soup. Ogata, says the demon-host, has 60 seconds to transfer the soup's chunky bits—radish, fish, octopus—onto a plate. Using only his teeth.

At least, that's what we think is happening. Araki, our translator, is trying to explain what is going on, but he looks like he doesn't understand it all himself.

Japanese game shows, with their oddball set-ups and sadistic challenges, have become the most iconic example of Japanese entertainment. And they're intimately tied to Japanese comedy. Yoshimoto produces many of the shows itself. According to Yorihiro, Yoshimoto's U.S.-based CEO, 80 percent of all Japanese game-show contestants are comedians, since the typical Japanese person is too reserved to demonstrate the fear and anguish necessary to sell a bit about diving face-first into a bowl of soup.

An air horn wails, dramatic lights flash and Ogata dunks his head into the tureen. He jerks back up, soup flying, clutching in pain at his face. His mouth is empty. I try to imagine "Ogata Impossible!" going global, with footage like this being a hit in Seattle and Philadelphia, in London and Rio, in Moscow and Dubai.

The soup can't really be hot, Araki assures me. Ogata is just acting. But later, after the shoot, Ogata, his face pink, assures me Araki is wrong. The soup is skin-searing hot. Teeth-aching hot. "Hot!" he tells me, the only English word I've heard him use all day.

A shrill buzzer marks the end of the challenge—with Ogata several soup ingredients short of his goal. The *Power Purin* comedians retire in exhaustion to their messy dressing room. Araki's off somewhere, so we make do without him. The comedians scratch at their dyed, spiky hair and in broken English compare their best comedic horror stories, boasting like they're battle wounds. For a *batsu* game, one had to eat a raw lemon, skin and all. Another was once elbowed so hard by his *manzai* partner that he broke a rib.

One of the comedians nods at Pete and makes a crack about his height. "Big!" he cries, then points at Pete's pants. "Big?" Pete shrugs, smiling mischievously.

"Me small-small," grumbles the diminutive comic, gesturing in disappointment at his groin.

"But you're famous!" I cry.

Sure, he concedes, but he'd rather be "big-big, not famous!"

Soon we've devolved into a shouting match of "Big-big!" "Small-big!" and increasingly obscene hand motions. Araki looks in, drawn by the laughter. "You're missing all the fun!" cries Pete.

Our trip to Japan has proven that humor appreciation is very much culturally mediated. Comedy here is a wholly different entity than it is in the States, with specific social rules about when and where people laugh and what they laugh at. Yoshimoto's global strategy faces some hurdles, since the hijinks of "Ogata Impossible" and other examples of Japanese comedy are very, well, *Japanese*.

But what's going on here in this dressing room isn't professionally crafted, strategically calibrated, big-business comedy. It's humor, in the most organic sense of the word. Humor that occurs without planning or preparation, humor that's all the more hilarious because of it. It's rude-gesture humor, late-night-drinking humor, your-fly-is-down humor, banging-your-head-on-a-door-frame humor. The same sort of stuff that gets us cackling with friends and loved ones back home.

In other words, while Japanese *comedy* may be different from what we're used to in America, the way the Japanese experience *humor* is mostly the same.

And with a realization such as that, maybe we've discovered what makes the Japanese really, truly laugh: the same thing that makes you and me and everyone else bust a gut, too.

What's the key to universal harmony and hilarity? It's simple: peace, love, and dick jokes.

The attack comes out of the blue. First we hear the yelling, an eruption of deranged Danish that shatters Copenhagen's wintry early morning tranquility. We spot a hulking woman across the street from us, eyes blazing as she hollers in our direction. But she's not just yelling. She's on the move, head down and legs pumping in bulky black snow pants. And she's charging at us.

Maybe she believes that Pete, who's been taking pictures of eighteenth-century brick façades and colorful Danish graffiti, snapped a shot of her. Maybe she doesn't like the look of us. All we know is that she's enraged, and we're the cause.

She charges at Pete, arms swinging at his head. At the last moment, she stumbles, pitching forward onto the sidewalk. She lies there, moaning, while we gape. Is she all right? Should we help her? Before we can decide, she pulls herself up, apparently unscathed. We move away, putting some distance between us as she turns her animosity toward whatever else dares cross her—other pedestrians, bicyclists, a passing car or two.

We're stunned. This welcome is not what we've come to expect in Denmark. We're here to explore the dark side of humor, how comedy can divide and degrade. We've learned that humor does all sorts of good, like sell comedy movies and magazines and build lasting bonds and bridge international divides. But comedy isn't all fun and games, insists Pete. Take all the racist, sexist, and homophobic jokes out there, he says. Or how there was something so threatening about the routines of Lenny Bruce and Mae West that those in power censored their jokes. To him, the conclusion is obvious: "Humor comes from a dark place."

To help prove it, Pete ran an experiment with HuRL undergraduate Robert Merrifield Collins that involved one of those newfangled bladeless fans, the kind that seem magically to blow air through an empty ring. When Pete and Merrifield had test subjects place their hands inside the ring while the fan was running, most subjects laughed and found it amusing. On the surface, this reaction doesn't make sense; feeling air running past your fingers isn't funny. But the exercise was humorous to people, believes Pete, because of all those times we were warned growing up of the gory things that would happen if we stuck our stubby little fingers in fan blades. And here they were, *with their hands inside a fan*, under the direction of a paid scientist. It's dark, twisted stuff—and that's where the comedy comes from.

We've been told that Denmark is the perfect place to dissect the dark and twisted side of humor. But so far, we seem to be in the wrong place to do so. Yesterday, when our plane dipped below the ashen cloud cover that stretched from horizon to horizon like a blanket, we gazed down upon picturesque vistas of the Danish countryside: wide expanses of deep-green farmland dotted with quaint, slate-roofed farmhouses. And what we've seen of Copenhagen, the Danish capital, is a model of European elegance, with its stately skyline of church steeples and palace towers, twisting cobblestone alleyways, and bustling pedestrian squares echoing with street performers. Numerous studies have concluded that Denmark is one of the happiest places in the world. Nothing suggests this is the sort of place where you need to be on the lookout for kamikaze hobos.

But then again, people around here have reason to be hostile toward outsiders. Since 2005, hundreds of thousands of people around the world have protested the small, seemingly inconsequential country that pokes into the Baltic Sea north of Germany. Riotous crowds have chanted, "We want Danish blood!" and "Bomb, bomb, bomb Denmark!" Key Danish export markets have collapsed under trade boycotts. Danish newspaper offices have been turned into military bunkers, and private homes have been put under 24-hour armed surveillance in response to death threats and assassination attempts.

Last night, after dropping our luggage at our hotel, we'd gone on the prowl, hoping to take the pulse of the community. We failed. We ended up dining on New York–style slices of pizza, throwing back a pint at an English-style pub full of British ex-pats, and then grabbing late-night snacks from a 7-Eleven.

At the pub, the foreigners admitted that Denmark felt like a damaged shell of its former self. "It used to be a fairy tale here," said a British businessman at the bar, evoking a place of Viking myths, dairy cows, and Hans Christian Andersen tales. "But now," he added, "they screwed up the fairy tale." It's been worse than the hell of World Wars I and II, says another patron. To find any catastrophe that compares, you have to look back to 1864, when Denmark lost a third of its land to Prussia and Austria.

What caused this modern-day disaster? A dozen cartoons.

I thought Pete's academic exploits were weird. Then I learned about Gershon Legman.

Legend has it that Gershon Legman, a self-taught, itinerant scholar who's fabled in the field of folklore, launched author Anaïs Nin's erotica career. (It's true, says University of Illinois folklore professor Susan Davis, who's working on a biography of Legman.) He's also said to have invented the electric vibrator in the 1930s. (Not exactly true, says Davis—it was just some silly device he cooked up with his buddies at the New York Academy of Medicine that nobody used.) And he claimed to have coined the phrase "Make love, not war" at a university lecture in 1963. (Yes, says Davis, though his wording was more along the lines of, "We shouldn't be killing; we should be fucking.")

Here's what is true about Legman: In 1968, after thirty years of work, he published *Rationale of the Dirty Joke*, a scholarly compendium of a thousand filthy zingers he'd spent more than three decades collecting. The subject index alone isn't for the faint of heart:

Sex in the Schoolroom—page 72.
The Fortunate Fart—page 185.
Loves of the Beasts—page 206.
Woman-as-Vagina—page 374.
Incest with the Mother-in-Law—page 471.
Rectal Motherhood—page 596.

And this book focused on the *clean* dirty jokes. Legman saved the *dirty* dirty jokes for his next book, *No Laughing Matter*, published via subscription several years later, as no self-respecting publisher would touch it.

These books weren't shock for shock's sake. For Legman, they were about exposing an uncomfortable but vital part of modern culture too long ignored. "He had this really, really driven quality to collect, print, and expose what no one else was exposing," Davis tells me. As Legman notes at the beginning of *Rationale of the Dirty Joke*, "Under the mark of humor, our society allows infinite aggressions, by everyone and against everyone."

Legman never quit on his mission to catalogue those aggressions. When the obscene research materials he was receiving from all parts of the world raised the hackles of the U.S. Postal Service, he moved to the more laissez-faire French countryside. He went on to produce several anthologies of limericks, dirty and otherwise, edited two volumes on bawdy folk songs titled *Roll Me in Your Arms and Blow the Candle Out*, and worked on his autobiography, *The Peregrine Penis*.

In 1999, before *The Peregrine Penis* could be unleashed on the world, Legman passed away in relative obscurity. His dirty-joke compendiums have been relegated to quirky footnotes, outshone by Norman Cousins's *Anatomy of an Illness as Perceived by the Patient*, the 1979 book that launched the positive-humor movement.

Legman's work likely would have fared much better had he been born a few centuries earlier. For much of recorded history, folks in the know agreed with his belief that jokes were dark and dirty. Plato, in some of the earliest known musings on the subject, argued that people laugh out of malice, delighting in others' pain and misfortune. His "Superiority Theory" proved durable, cornering the market on humor theories for millennia. Church leaders in Christian Europe shared a similar perspective. Displays of hilarity were considered only slightly less repugnant than witchcraft. Of the 29 references to laughter in the Old Testament, only two aren't associated with scorn, mockery, or disdain.[1]

When Lord Chesterfield, the fastidious champion of eighteenth-century manners, noted to his son in one of his famous letters that "there is nothing so illiberal, and so ill-bred, as audible laughter," he was speaking for centuries of thinkers and philosophers. "The threat of anarchy and power structures being undermined is a big reason why comedy has always been seen with a suspicious eye," says John Morreall, College of William and Mary professor and International Society for Humor Studies co-founder. Morreall has spent decades studying humor in history and religion—and how for the most part, the powerful and educated wanted nothing to do with it. "Nobody knows what is going to happen with comedy," he tells me. "It's dangerous stuff."

Humor remained dangerous up until the dawn of the Enlightenment and the rise of benevolent concepts such as democracy and reason. Then philosophers such as Francis Hutcheson began positing that humor wasn't as simple and cruel as just laughing at other people's problems, but was instead born from something as innocuous as noticing incongruities.[2]

Perspectives on humor have changed so thoroughly that these days only one big Superiority Theory holdout remains, a grumpy polar bear on a tiny melting iceberg in a sea of good humor and happy thoughts. His name is Charles Gruner. "Humor is a game," insisted Gruner, a communications professor at the University of Georgia, when I called him. "It is a contest of some sort, and there is always a winner and a loser." That none of his colleagues agree means little to him. "If they accepted it, that means everything is solved," he said. "It makes all other research on humor superfluous."

"Show me a joke that doesn't fit my theory," Gruner demanded. And whatever example you give him, Gruner will find a way to shoehorn it in. Puns to him are a game of wits where the punner proves to the listener his superlative mastery of words. And a cartoon of a plumber plugging a leaky faucet with his finger as water shoots out of his ear isn't funny because it's ridiculous. It's funny because we take pleasure in someone getting brain damage.[3]

Whether or not Gruner is right that *all* humor is a game, there is scientific proof that in many cases, as Jerry Lewis once put it, "Comedy is a man in trouble." In 1983 psychologists ran a series of studies in which subjects rated a variety of cartoons on funniness and aggressiveness. The results revealed that people considered aggressive cartoons funnier than those that were non-hostile.[4] Even more disturbing was a later experiment that revealed that in such aggressive cartoons, it's not the hostility of the protagonist that scores the laughs. Rather, the more pain experienced by the butt of the joke, the funnier folks considered the cartoon until the pain levels involved became downright sadistic.[5]

Some folks are so afraid of experiencing that type of pain that experts have determined it's pathological. In 2004, Willibald Ruch coined the term "gelotophobia" to refer to the fear of being laughed at.[6] There's no known cure for gelotophobes, but for a start, it's best to keep them separated from gelotophiles (those who enjoy being laughed at) and katagelasticists (fans of laughing at others).

So maybe Legman and all those out-of-favor superiority theorists were on to something. The biggest proof of all might be here in Denmark, site of one of the most troubling examples of humor in modern history: the September 30, 2005, publication of a dozen cartoons in the Danish newspaper *Jyllands-Posten* under the headline "The Face of Mohammad." The images unleashed turmoil all over the world, possibly the only cartoons ever to be labeled a human rights violation by the United Nations. As luck would have it, less than a year later, the 2006 International Humor Conference took place in Copenhagen, allowing humor researchers there to deconstruct what's been declared as "the first transnational 'humor scandal'" and "the most powerful anti-joke response in human history."[7]

Despite all the ink spilled over the matter, there are still unanswered questions about Denmark's transnational humor scandal. Why were a bunch of cartoons to blame? Why was the outcry over these drawings so much greater than, say, over the photos of prisoner torture at Abu Ghraib prison in Iraq that had appeared not too long before? And most important, what is it about the things that make people laugh, stuff that's not supposed to be taken seriously, that can trigger so much pain and turmoil?

Still recovering from our run-in with the street lady, we arrive at Zebra, an artist co-op on the top floor of an apartment building off a busy Copenhagen boulevard. Lars Refn, a guy who exudes well-aged coolness, greets us. His gray hair and beard are trimmed, stylish black glasses frame his smiling eyes, and his shirt sports the logo for Carhartt, the street-wear company popular with the hipster crowd thirty years his junior. Refn welcomes us into a wide-open space buzzing with artists hunched over drafting tables, fashion designers flipping through racks of half-finished clothing, and programmers tweaking HTML on jumbo-sized iMacs. We're a bit surprised by Refn's poise and warmth; from what we've heard, he has as much right as anyone to be irritated over what happened to him during the cartoon controversy.

It all started with a letter he received in September 2005, Refn tells us over coffee and Danishes in the studio's conference room. As a member of the Danish union of newspaper illustrators, he was one of 42 cartoonists contacted by the newspaper *Jyllands-Posten* with an unusual request. The paper had learned that a local author hadn't been able to obtain pictures for his children's book about Mohammad because illustrators were afraid of depicting the Prophet of Islam. *Jyllands-Posten*'s editors didn't think much of that sort of self-censorship, so they solicited the union members to "Draw Mohammad as you see him." The paper promised to publish all submissions.[8]

Refn smelled a trap. *Jyllands-Posten*, Denmark's largest newspaper, was known for its right-wing views, and that included its prickly opinions about immigration and Muslims. "It felt like they were making an experiment with Muslims, trying to find a way to make them angry," he tells us. And Refn, a self-described hippie, refused to play along.

As requested, Refn drew a picture of Mohammad, but not Mohammad the Prophet. Instead he drew Mohammad, a seventh-grade boy from a local school district. To drive home his point, Refn dressed the boy in the red-and-blue jersey of a nearby soccer club known for its diversity and socialist leanings. "Mohammad" is pointing to a school blackboard, upon which is written in Persian, "The board of direction of *Jyllands-Posten* are a bunch of right-wing extremists."

As promised, *Jyllands-Posten* published the cartoon, along with the eleven other submissions it received. Refn was thrilled, thinking he'd put one over on the publication, and prepared to put the episode behind him. "I thought that would be it," he told us.

He was wrong.

It started with an ominous phone call from the police. Because he'd poked fun at *Jyllands-Posten* in his drawing, several media accounts of the cartoons focused on Refn. Upset about the images, a young Danish man apparently was planning to murder Refn and the president of the illustrator's union. While police sorted matters out, Refn took his family into hiding. "That is when I realized this is not a laughing matter," the cartoonist tells us. It was just the beginning.

A month later, ambassadors from eleven predominantly Muslim countries requested a meeting with Danish prime minister Anders Fogh Rasmussen to discuss the cartoons and what they saw as anti-Muslim sentiment in the country. When the prime minister refused, Arab countries and organizations ratcheted up anti-Denmark rhetoric. A delegation of Danish Islamic clerics increased tensions by touring the Middle East with a dossier containing the offending cartoons and other inflammatory material. In January 2006, supermarkets across the Middle East began boycotting Danish goods, and on February 3, after dozens of European newspapers reprinted the cartoons in solidarity, a popular Egyptian preacher called for a "Day of Rage."

The Day of Rage stretched into weeks. Around the world, hundreds of thousands took to the streets in protest. Demonstrators damaged and burned Danish embassies in Jakarta, Beirut, and Damascus. Radical Islamist leaders announced rewards for the heads of the editors and cartoonists involved, and police uncovered terrorist plots in Europe. In response, additional newspapers reprinted the cartoons, triggering more turmoil. While no one was killed in Denmark or Europe, violent demonstrations in Afghanistan, Pakistan, and Nigeria left nearly 250 dead and 800 wounded.[9]

"It was really the first international crisis we have had on an issue of culture, and all our conflict-resolution mechanisms failed to stop it," says Jytte Klausen, a Danish-born political science professor at Brandeis University. The title of Klausen's book on the subject sums the crisis up nicely: *The Cartoons that Shook the World*.

But why did the cartoons shake the world? Nowhere in the Koran, for example, does it prohibit depicting the Prophet. Yes, supplemental religious texts do ban the practice to discourage idolatry, but still, Muslim culture is full of pictures of Mohammad, from thirteenth-century Persian manuscripts to colorful postcards sold today in the markets of Tehran and Istanbul.[10] In 2000, the chairman of the Fiqh Council of North America, a Muslim association that interprets Islamic law, pronounced the 60-year-old image of Mohammad inside the U.S. Supreme Court building perfectly fine.

The firestorm surprised Refn, since he hadn't even drawn the Prophet. He wasn't the only one. Of the twelve cartoons published by the newspaper, two didn't portray Mohammad at all, and in three others the depictions are ambiguous at best. Nor did most of the cartoons make fun of Islam. Two of them knocked the children's book author who started the whole mess, suggesting the whole thing was a PR stunt. In a third, the cartoonist satirized himself, scribbling away at a Mohammad stick figure with his blinds drawn and nervous sweat pouring down his brow. And then there's the cartoon that's unintelligible. In a *Harper's Magazine* critique, American cartoonist Art Spiegelman said as best he could tell, it's of five Pac-Men eating stars and crescents.[11] (Despite the cartoons' taboo nature—Klausen's publisher refused to include them in *The Cartoons that Shook the World*, even though the book was all about them—they're easy to find online.)

Part of the problem was that in the parts of the world most incensed over the images, many people never saw the cartoons, just heard bad things about them. A 2006 Pew Research Center survey of thirteen countries around the world found that a staggering 80 percent of respondents had heard about them. But when a Palestinian research organization drilled down into those numbers, it found that while 99.7 percent of Palestinians were aware of the cartoons, only 31 percent had seen them.[12]

And those around the world who did see the cartoons weren't all that likely to understand them. How could a Syrian reader comprehend Refn's drawing of a young boy in an obscure soccer uniform? Or how could anyone, for that matter, figure out what those gobbling Pac-Men meant? And since Refn and most of the other cartoonists followed the Danish police's recommendation not to talk to the press, the artists never had a chance to explain the context of their work.

And comedy, as we learned in Japan, depends on context. Creating humor is a delicate operation built on layers of shared knowledge, assumptions, and innuendo. Remove one piece, and it all falls apart. Maybe a key part of a joke's set-up is forgotten; maybe the delivery is botched, or the wrong tone is used. Whatever the reason, it's easier to fail with humor than succeed. As Pete is demonstrating in HuRL, anything can be made more or less funny depending on what information is provided. In a study he conducted with Caleb Warren and University of Colorado professor Lawrence Williams, he found that a simple violation—having your fly down—was judged by participants in all sorts of different ways depending on the additional information provided. One version of the story was deemed boring (a stranger having his fly down while home alone), a second was funny (a friend having his fly down when talking to a co-worker), and a third was downright upsetting (the study participant having his or her fly down during a big job interview).[13]

It used to be that comedic failures weren't a big deal. Comedy used to be finite and intimate. Folks told jokes to their friends and neighbors, a comedian's routine would reach only as far as the back row of the club, newspaper cartoons would disappear forever once the next issue of the paper hit the stands. Mistakes at this level were small-time, short-lived, contained. But now, thanks to the internet, viral video, and global media conglomerates, comedy can go international with ease. And so when a joke fails, it can fail big.

Refn nods knowingly. He's sick of telling his story, of explaining how his cartoon failed. "If you make a joke and have to explain it, it is not funny," he says flatly. If the cartoonist could do it all again, he would do it differently. "If I had known a billion people would see this," he says with a smile, "I would have made a better drawing."

Refn believes his cartoon bombed. Is he right? Were the Mohammad cartoons a failure—or were they a raging success? It all depends on how you define "failure," and in comedy that's not easy. While a joke has only one shot at being funny, it can fail in one of two ways—it can be too benign, and therefore boring, or it can be too much of a violation, and therefore offensive. But how do you determine whether a joke bores or offends?

Take what seems the most obvious indicator of failed humor: if a joke bombs, people don't laugh at it. But as we discovered in Tanzania, laughter and humor don't always go hand in hand. In 2009, an applied linguist at Washington State University named Nancy Bell subjected nearly 200 people to the blandest, most inoffensive joke she could come up with: "What did the big chimney say to the little chimney? Nothing. Chimneys can't talk." She found that nearly 40 percent of people laughed at the joke, even though it's hard to imagine that all those people found it funny. It seems the social obligation of the joke, the need for people to play the accepted roles of joke teller and joke listener, was too strong for people to groan about it.

Here's another problem with trying to figure out whether a given joke bombed: even successful attempts to be funny can sometimes have dire consequences. Such is the strange case of Alex Mitchell. On March 24, 1975, the 50-year-old British bricklayer found an episode of the sketch-comedy show *The Goodies* so hilarious that he laughed for 25 minutes straight, until he slumped dead onto his sofa, his heart having given out from the strain. His widow took the development with a characteristically British stiff upper lip. She sent *The Goodies* a thank-you note for making her husband's final earthly moments so entertaining.

Now let's take the Mohammad cartoons. At first glance, they seem to fail according to both of Pete's criteria. Everyone agrees that the images in question insulted many, many people. At the same time, it's hard to find anyone who thinks the cartoons were funny. But then again, were these images ever meant to be funny? When *Jyllands-Posten* published the cartoons, the newspaper framed them in a serious, almost confrontational manner. According to an essay that accompanied the images penned by Flemming Rose, the editor who'd commissioned them, the effort was all about freedom of speech and self-censorship.

It's hard to know for sure what *Jyllands-Posten* meant by publishing the cartoons. For a paper that's all about free speech, no one from the operation is eager to talk to us. Neither the paper's editor in chief nor its press liaison responded to repeated e-mails and phone messages. Before we left for Denmark, I'd been able to reach Rose, the guy who'd collected the cartoons, but he was less than thrilled by the prospect of meeting with us. "I've tried to move on," he told me.

Anders Jerichow, head of the Danish writers union, is less reluctant to talk. He tells us to meet him at the Copenhagen offices of his employer—*Politiken*, the country's second-biggest newspaper and *Jyllands-Posten*'s chief rival. The offices also house the Copenhagen branch of *Jyllands-Posten*. The same company owns the two competing periodicals.

The offices stand at one corner of Copenhagen's sprawling City Hall Square. Since Pete is a few minutes behind me, I wait out front and pass the time by taking photos. I snap shots of neon advertising sprouting from redbrick buildings, yellow double-decker buses cruising by, the monumental city hall that stands at one end of the plaza, the electronic security gates and surveillance cameras installed in front of the newspaper building. An armed security guard is soon at my side, asking what I am doing.

It's a good question. What am I doing standing out here in full public view, photographing the security measures of an organization besieged by death threats? Clearly, I am either a terrorist or an idiot. I stammer out an apologetic explanation, offering to delete the offending photo from my camera. When he's satisfied, he thanks me for understanding. "Normally we'd have to take you to the police station for questioning," he says before returning to his post, "but I'll let this go."

Pete shows up. "Did I miss anything?" he asks.

Soon Jerichow arrives to escort us in. "To get to my office, I have to use my clearance card five times," he tells us as, one at a time, we step into a closet-like body scanner, sliding glass doors locking us into place as unseen mechanisms scrutinize us for devious devices. It's been this way ever since *Jyllands-Posten* began getting targeted with murder threats and assassination plots. Since the two papers share the same building, everyone at *Politiken* lives with the same sort of security lockdown, even though the publication had nothing to do with the cartoons.

Jerichow, a silver-haired guy in a gray sweater, with the look of a kindly professor, has the dubious distinction of being the first to see the problems coming. He tells us this over a lunch of lasagna and pickled herring in the sleek cafeteria the two newspapers share, with abstract artwork on the walls and trendy light fixtures dangling from the ceiling. During a radio interview the day *Jyllands-Posten* published the cartoons, Jerichow predicted the issue might spiral into an international controversy. He knew what he was talking about. He's written, edited, or contributed to nearly two dozen books on human rights and international relations in the Middle East.

From his perspective, *Jyllands-Posten*'s cartoons were little more than a publicity stunt. "To me it had the smell of childish manifestation," he tells us. "It had the smell of someone trying to show how big he was by being willing to use forbidden words."

Still, insists Jerichow, the paper can't bear full blame for what happened. "Just as we can call on cartoonists and editors to accept a certain responsibility, you can call on readers to show a responsibility in how they react to it and abstain from violence," he says. In Denmark, Muslims by and large demonstrated that responsibility. Only a small fraction of the country's 200,000-plus Muslims expressed public displeasure at the cartoons, and they did so through petitions and peaceful protests.

The reaction was far different in places such as Syria, Saudi Arabia, and Pakistan. Jerichow, for one, believes there were political reasons behind it. For four months after they were published, there was little outcry over the cartoons. Only after diplomatic channels collapsed did the Middle East erupt. And in Syria, was it really possible that thousands were able to organize, publicize, and pull off a demonstration that culminated in the razing of the Danish embassy without attracting the attention of the country's pervasive intelligence operations?

In Jerichow's opinion, politicians and insurgents in Syria and several other Middle Eastern countries encouraged the anti-Danish protests for their own gain. It was a way to distract people from their own internal problems, a way to exert their authority on an international stage, a way to prove that they were the true defenders of Islam.

It helped that picking on Denmark was like bullying the smallest kid on the playground, says Jerichow: "Denmark is a small country; it has no international weight, no profile in the Middle East. Denmark is not important to them, but it is a wonderful tool for them."

And in the middle of it all lay a bunch of cartoons that lots of people hadn't seen and those who did likely didn't completely understand? All the better.

Maybe, then, the cartoons weren't a failure after all. Maybe the folks who came up with the assignment knew what they were doing all along: stoking controversy for publicity purposes. Just as those in power half a world away were more than happy to play along for political gain. They *wanted* the cartoons' humor to fail—and they succeeded beyond all expectations.

The two serious-looking men with weather-beaten faces and translucent transmitters in their ears are expecting us. "Come," they demand, taking us around the back of a building where their colleagues, a couple of Danish police officers, are waiting. "We have to check your passports and do a quick frisk," one of them says. A bomb-sniffing dog noses through our bags, slobber flying. "I am mentally prepared for this," Pete quips, stepping forward and raising his arms in anticipation of a pat down. The guy doesn't crack a smile.

We're in Aarhus, Denmark's second-largest city, located halfway up Jutland, the long, curving peninsula that comprises the western half of the country. We'd spent the morning driving here from Copenhagen, through muddy, rolling farmland, and hopscotching from one island to the next via thin suspension bridges arcing over the

Baltic Sea. An endless, dreary cloud cover blotted out the sky, as it had since the moment we arrived in Denmark. We've taken to coming up with names for the different flavors of gray overhead: "dawn gray," "midday gray," "dusk gray," "gravy gray," "grey gray," "soul-crushing gray."

We're not that surprised by the hard, serious men who've greeted us at our destination in Aarhus, a single-level, middle-class bungalow in the city's suburban outskirts. After all, we're here to meet with Kurt Westergaard, the most famous and reviled of the twelve Mohammad cartoonists. He's someone many people would like to see dead.

Of the Mohammad cartoons published by *Jyllands-Posten*, Westergaard's is the most iconic, not to mention the most incendiary. For the assignment, he drew a bushy-browed, bearded Mohammad wearing a sizzling bomb for a turban. That likely would have been enough to make him a target, but Westergaard, who was on staff at *Jyllands-Posten*, made matters worse by continuing to talk to the press when the other cartoonists decided to keep mum, stirring up more trouble even as threats to his life—and those of others—began to mount.

In Copenhagen, Refn had turned pensive when we'd asked about Westergaard. "He is not very popular with our group of people, and he's forced to live in a fortress. I almost feel sorry for him."

When Westergaard's security detail escorts us to the cartoonist's front door, we expect to come face-to-face with some media-hungry, xenophobic lunatic. Instead, we're met by Santa Claus dressed for a leather convention.

"Please excuse my pets," says a smiling, jovial Westergaard, sporting a shaggy white beard, black leather vest, studded belt, and red pants. He's referring to the officers of PET, Denmark's intelligence service, the ones who'd patted us down and watch over him, day and night, on the government's dime. "There are two things they are happy about," he tells us. "One, that I am not a winter swimmer, and two, that I am not a nudist." He ushers us into his dining room, where he's prepared a spread of coffee, tea, and baked goods. "You should try my wife's beer cake," he says. "It is the PET's favorite."

Westergaard doesn't seem like the kind of guy to inspire rage all over the world. Since he retired from *Jyllands-Posten* a couple of years ago, he's spent his days painting fantastical watercolors of mermaids and trolls and fishermen on toadstools. But when we wander about his house, the drawings that line his walls from his newspaper days tell a different story. Naked women getting ravaged. A concentration-camp inmate with barbed wire threaded through his ears. Jesus Christ in a business suit coming down off the cross, leaving behind a sign reading "Back on Sunday."

For Westergaard, incendiary imagery was all in a day's work at *Jyllands-Posten*. It didn't matter whether Westergaard, who considers himself socially liberal, agreed or not with a particular newspaper assignment. "I have to be loyal to the author of the story, to the editor, even if it's not my opinion," he says.

That's why, when he heard about the Mohammad assignment, he didn't hesitate. For him, it wasn't about drawing something funny; it was about making his point as evocatively as possible. He claims he wanted to evoke how Muslim terrorists have essentially taken Islam hostage; that's why he stuck the bomb in Mohammad's turban. He says he can't imagine anyone interpreting his cartoon any other way—even though millions of outraged Muslims all over the world clearly had no problem doing so.

"Is there anything you wouldn't draw?" asks Pete, scrutinizing the evocative images on the walls.

"No," says Westergaard, "but if you satirize, there must be a reason. Satire is a way in which you can vent frustrations in ways that can be very vicious and very accurate."

Westergaard has a point. One of the most compelling explanations for the existence of sick jokes, comedy that seems designed to insult wide swaths of people, is that as despicable as they may be, they're a way for folks to deal with forbidden frustrations and hang-ups. A society-wide version of Freud's idea that jokes are our personal safety valve.

No one was better at deconstructing these dirty one-liners to expose society's deepest, darkest secrets than Alan Dundes, a Berkeley folklore professor who had two passions in life: elevating jokes to a serious discipline and courting controversy. He received death threats from football fans over a seminar he gave on the homoerotic undertones of the NFL called "Into the End Zone, Trying to Get a Touchdown." When his cataloguing of jokes about Auschwitz victims for a 1983 issue of *Western Folklore* triggered an uproar, he set to work penning a follow-up, "More on Auschwitz Jokes."

"We are not reporting these jokes because we think they are amusing or funny," wrote Dundes. "We are reporting them because we believe it is important to document all aspects of the human experience, even those aspects which most might agree reflect the darker side of humanity." His efforts to document the human experience, dark side and all, led to the creation of the Folklore Archive at the University of California, Berkeley, a small, cluttered room in an out-of-the-way building that I spent a day exploring on a trip to San Francisco, rifling through filing cabinets filled with thousands of jokes and witticisms and superstitions and folktales and urban legends and myriad other examples of verbal folklore collected by Dundes and his students. There are American jokes about the French ("Why do the French smell? So blind people can hate them, too") and French jokes about Americans ("What's the difference between yogurt and Americans? Yogurt has culture") and everything else in between.

Dundes saw these jokes, especially the upsetting ones, as a code that he could use to understand humanity's secrets. Take the dead-baby joke cycle of the 1960s and '70s, when Americans shared quips like "What's red and sits in a corner? A baby chewing razor blades." According to Dundes, the zingers were born from a fusion of trauma over the Vietnam War, fear of newfangled conveniences, and modern-day ambivalences about pregnancy.[14] Then there were the homophobic AIDS one-liners of the late 1980s, truly sick stuff like, "Do you know what 'gay' means? 'Got AIDS yet?'" Dundes saw them as a way for the public to distance themselves from—as well as express their fears of—HIV and homosexuality.[15] He spent so long mining mean-spirited comedy that he even claimed to have discovered the missing link between one cruel joke cycle and another. According to his research, Polish jokes had been in vogue for a while when somebody in the 1960s or '70s came up with this one: "How many Polacks does it take to screw in a lightbulb? Five: One to hold the bulb and four to turn the chair." That, according to Dundes, was the genesis of the lightbulb joke.[16]

So what might Westergaard and the others' Mohammad cartoons say about the secret side of Denmark? Maybe shattering taboos is a Danish pastime. Denmark, one of the least religious places in the world, was the first country to legalize pornography and, later, same-sex marriage. One of the country's biggest cultural hits is *Klovn*, Danish for "Clown," a popular TV comedy show that spawned a hit film that grafted sodomy, murder, and child endangerment onto a family canoe trip. Everywhere we go in the country, we run into racy posters advertising a show called *Paradise Island*, each featuring two bikini-clad, surgically enhanced women. Compared to past public images that have gone up around the country, these pictures are tame. Before the cartoon controversy broke in 2005, the big news in Denmark was how saboteurs had posted around Copenhagen explicit pictures of mayoral candidate Louise Frevert made up like a porn star. The photos weren't doctored. Frevert made it no secret that she'd formerly starred in hardcore films using the name "Miss Lulu."[17]

So Westergaard was doing his duty as a Danish cartoonist: slaughtering a couple more sacred cows. In return, he's nearly been slaughtered himself. He's been the target of many of the death threats triggered by the cartoons, and in 2008, after authorities uncovered a murder plot targeting him, police began escorting him to and from work. The worst came on New Year's Day 2010, in an incident that caused him to be placed under 24-hour security, likely for the rest of his life. Westergaard was home alone with a five-year-old girl, the daughter of an Albanian woman he'd taken under his wing, when a man smashed through his back door with an ax.

Westergaard ran into his bathroom, which had been retrofitted as a panic room with a steel door and bulletproof glass on the windows. That left the little girl, who happened to have a broken leg, out in the open with the man with the ax. Fortunately, the man seemed to have no interest in harming the girl, and five minutes later, with Wester-gaard still hiding in the bathroom, police arrived and shot the intruder.

"It was good that I did as I did," says Westergaard, looking down at the dining room table and tracing one of his wrinkled hands along its grain. He's 77 years old, he explains. If he'd tried to confront the intruder, the little girl would have witnessed his grisly demise, if not suffered a worse fate. "I was able to think very rationally, and do the right thing," he says. It seems like he's trying to convince himself, not us.

Despite the threats and attacks and never-ending police surveillance, Westergaard has also received benefits from his notoriety. He's found success selling copies of his Mohammad cartoon. Folks have even tried to buy the original. One $5,000 offer came from Martin J. McNally, a former American sailor who spent several decades in prison for hijacking a Boeing 727 in 1972. A more lucrative bid of about $150,000 came from a man in Texas, but at the last minute the guy backed out, explaining to Westergaard that the purchase might not be politically expedient for him, considering he worked at the Danish consulate.

So for now, the cartoon that launched a jihad sits in a vault somewhere. For the right price, Westergaard might give it up. "As my very practical wife puts it," he says with a grin, "'first there was Mohammad the Prophet. Now there is Mohammad the profit.'"

We think we've found the solution to the great Mohammad cartoon conundrum. It was one part mischievous cartoonists, one part attention-hungry journalists, one part manipulative politicians, and one part global misunderstanding. If there's a victim in the whole ordeal, it's likely poor little put-upon Denmark. Mystery solved, case closed.

So we think. Until we meet Rune Larsen.

Anders Jerichow at *Politiken* had recommended we talk to Larsen, a fellow reporter who lives in Aarhus. On our last morning in the city, we arrange to meet him at a café along the city's bustling river walk. We arrive a bit early and take in the atmosphere. While Aarhus has long been a victim of the "stupidity joke" phenomenon, with its residents the butt of many a Danish joke, we find the city and the people here pleasant. We've grown accustomed to the Danish method of doing things, the way folks on the street hurry about in a determined yet cheerful manner, the way they all drive in a courteous fashion in diminutive German cars, the way their cities intermingle half-timbered buildings with modern edifices of translucent glass and soaring steel. No wonder Denmark is the birthplace of LEGO bricks. Everything fits together tidily.

The LEGO façade comes tumbling down when Larsen shows up, late and out of breath. He doesn't waste time with pleasantries. Stumbling over his words, the boyish-faced journalist is desperate to get his story out. We don't know the whole story of the Mohammad cartoon controversy, he insists, eyes blazing as his iced coffee sits untouched.

The joke at the heart of the matter wasn't the cartoons, says Larsen; it was the joke the Danish government played on the world. It was a "caricature of diplomacy," as he calls it, carried out by the prime minister and his colleagues in the months leading up to the violent protests. As Larsen claims in his Danish book *The Caricature Crisis*, the situation might never have gotten so out of hand if only Prime Minister Rasmussen had met with the Muslim ambassadors when they first approached him. But he refused.

The decision does seem a bit odd. Everyone we've talked to in this country has welcomed us warmly, happily sitting us down for a chat over coffee and pastries. To do otherwise seems downright un-Danish. So why would the prime minister decline to do so with high-ranking ambassadors, especially if it had a potential to defuse the growing controversy?

Larsen believes it's because of Denmark's growing undercurrent of xenophobia. Until the 1960s, the country remained homogenous and culturally insular. That changed when workers started emigrating here from Turkey, Pakistan, and the former Yugoslavia. While today Muslims account for only about 4 percent of the country's population, for many it was still a major demographic shift, and not a welcome one. In 1997, a *Jyllands-Posten* survey found that nearly half of all Danes saw Muslims as a threat to Danish culture.[18]

It was fertile ground for the rise of the Danish People's Party, a far-right, anti-immigrant group that burst onto the scene in the 1990s. By 2002, it had become the third-largest party in the Danish parliament. The DPP, as it's known, takes a hard stance on Islam. Its chairperson has claimed parts of the country are being "populated by people who are at a lower stage of civilization."[19] While just a fraction of Danes support the DPP and its rhetoric, it's still large enough to exert influence in Denmark's multiparty system.

"The only reason Rasmussen could govern was that he had the People's Party's backing," Larsen tells us while catching his breath. "So when this controversy came along, it was right up the alley of the People's Party, and he couldn't do anything else but ignore the ambassadors."

Larsen doesn't come off as a loony conspiracy theorist. Because everyone we've met has been so friendly, it's been easy for us to overlook the moments when folks haven't been as open-minded as we'd expected. Take Westergaard. For all his claims of being socially liberal, the cartoonist had grown circumspect when we'd brought up immigration. "These people came to this country, and we welcomed them,'" he tells us. "So people might ask, 'Why can they not show a little gratitude and respect for our culture, of our way of making satire and criticizing people or gods?'"

To talk with these so-called ungrateful Danish Muslims, we head to Bazaar Vest, a shopping center on the outskirts of Aarhus that caters to the large Muslim community in the area. The bunker-like mall is surrounded by dreary, monolithic apartment buildings, and through its front doors, Arabic music filters from a sound system. Around here, the ubiquitous *Paradise Island* billboards have been painted over so the women's bikini-clad chests are cloaked in red paint.

"This is what's known as a ghetto in Denmark," says Nihad Hodzic, political chairman for the Danish organization Muslims in Dialogue, who's met us here for lunch. We'd expected Hodzic to be an older man, possibly an immigrant from Pakistan or Turkey. Instead, we're soon eating shawarma with a light-skinned 21-year-old who'd blend right into the general Danish population if not for the neck beard curving under his chin. An Ethnic Bosnian, Hodzic admits he doesn't fit into the narrow Danish stereotype of a backward Muslim. That's his point: as demonstrated by the diversity of clothing shops and hair salons and restaurants here in the shopping center, Denmark's Muslims are far from homogeneous. Bosnians, Serbs, Syrians, Somalis, Pakistanis, Turks . . . the list goes on. "Muslims in Denmark are actually very divided," says Hodzic.

The one thing they did agree on was that they didn't like the Mohammad cartoons. While only a tiny fraction expressed public displeasure about them, a 2006 survey found that 81 percent of Danish Muslims found the images offensive. For most of them, the problem wasn't Muslim prohibitions against depicting Mohammad, explains Hodzic. It was how cartoonists like Westergaard depicted him. "It would have had a totally different outcome if this had been a nice painting of Mohammad. I would not be angry," he says. "But this was clearly something that was made to mock." The image of Mohammad in the United States Supreme Court wasn't divisive because it placed the Prophet in a place of honor. The cartoons, however, were about making fun of him.

"If the point of these cartoons was to make people laugh, they failed," concludes Hodzic. "If they were to mock people and offend people, they succeeded."

As we found in Tanzania, humor can be a powerful social adhesive, building bonds and increasing positive vibes. Even teasing, which gets a bad rap in classrooms and schoolyards, can be helpful in establishing group morals, testing relationships, and conveying provocative concepts. Just ask University of California, Berkeley, psychologist Dacher Keltner, who's been studying teasing for years. In one experiment, Keltner and colleagues invited fraternity brothers and their pledges to their lab and had them tease one another. They found that while the frat brothers' teasing of the pledges was at times quite pointed, everyone involved became better friends because of the playful back-and-forth. The more the target of the tease showed signs of embarrassment—blushing, averting his gaze, smiling nervously—the more the teasers ended up liking him.[20]

But there's a difference between lighthearted teasing, which gently guides behavior, and bullying, which imposes social distinctions. Take the concept of pranks, which most people consider fun and fairly harmless. In reality, pranks are all about social boundaries—not bridging them, but highlighting them. Moira Smith, an anthropology librarian at Indiana University, has spent several decades researching practical jokes. She's tracked down historical pranks, such as the time in 1809 when Theodore Hook, a renowned British practical joker, sent thousands of fictitious letters to people all over London, convincing a small army—chimney sweeps, fishmongers, doctors, cake bakers, vicars, even the Duke of York and the Lord Mayor—to all appear at the same date and time at the Berners Street address of a baffled woman named Mrs. Tottenham.

We laugh about such stories now, but think about all the consternation and confusion suffered by poor Mrs. Tottenham, said Smith when we spoke. "Pranks accentuate the difference between the jokers and those whom the joke is on," she said. If you're the victim of one, the joke is very much on you.

And practical jokes aren't the only type of humor that underscores differences between people. All too often jokes divide and conquer, separate the haves from the have-nots. Yes, humor creates in-groups, but also out-groups. Racist jokes, sexist jokes, homophobic jokes—they're all about confirming stereotypes, and since they're couched within the confines of comedy, they can be harsher and more insulting than would otherwise be allowed. After all, "it's just a joke."

But for folks like Hodzic at Muslims in Dialogue, the Mohammad cartoons weren't just a joke. They had a serious undertone, one possibly even more troubling than the Abu Ghraib photos: they hammered home that in Denmark and beyond, Muslims were still outsiders.

There's another problem with disparaging humor and practical jokes, one that helps explain why, once the cartoon crisis erupted, it was nearly impossible to resolve it. If you're the butt of a joke, it's difficult to respond without making the situation worse. The majority of Muslims offended by the Mohammad cartoons went on with their lives, quietly accepting the insult. It was the most conciliatory route to go, but also the most frustrating. By doing so, they signaled that their dignity is fair game. That's why others refused to accept the slight sitting down, instead deciding to protest. But they ended up looking violent, uncivilized, and—most degrading of all—like they couldn't take a joke.

Maybe Charles Gruner, the last remaining superiority theorist, is right: maybe joking is a game, and in this particular contest, Muslims were bound to lose.

It gets worse. Cartoons like these don't just highlight social divisions; they have the potential to further the divide. Thomas Ford, a psychology professor at Western Carolina University, has developed the "prejudiced norm theory," the idea that disparaging jokes can increase tolerance of discrimination. In one experiment, Ford asked undergraduate males to watch a variety of comedy videos. Then he gave them what they thought was a real assignment: cut funding for different student groups such as a study-abroad club, a Jewish organization, a black student union, and a women's council. Not all that surprisingly, the students who'd previously scored high for hostile sexism were the most gung-ho about slashing the funding for the women's group. But among all the men who rated high for hostile sexism, only those who'd first seen funny videos degrading women, such as a skit from the *Man Show* television program about sending annoying spouses to "wife school," were willing to slight the women's organization. The similarly sexist guys who had instead watched an innocuous clip, such as one of the E-Trade talking-baby commercials, were no more willing to downsize the women's group than those who scored low for hostile sexism.[21]

Ford explained that the limits of what society deems acceptable is like a rubber band. Derogatory jokes, by allowing people to goof around with taboo subjects in a non-critical manner, tend to stretch the band of acceptability into areas hitherto off limits—racism, homophobia, anti-Muslim sentiment. Once it's stretched, it's hard to go back.

Perhaps Mohammad cartoons were so catastrophic because they threw the country's racial divisions into stark relief, leaving those involved with little opportunity to find common ground. Plus they had the potential to make the divisions worse. At the time of the cartoons, Denmark was a powder keg of tense cultural relations. Maybe those little doodles of Mohammad were the spark that set it off. The aftershocks stretched far and wide in a post-9/11 world already anxious and fragmented.

It's hard to know for sure without a counterexample, another country where an incendiary Mohammad cartoon popped up that had the potential to trigger international controversy.

We have one in mind.

"Now I have to get used to a new language I don't understand," cracks Pete as the GPS device on our dashboard announces that we're entering a new country. We're halfway across the Öresund Bridge, the five-mile span that connects the easternmost part of Denmark with the southern tip of Sweden. Powerful winds gusting off the Baltic send our rental car veering across the roadway. When we're safely across, Sweden stretches out before us . . . and it looks just like Denmark. The same rolling green fields, same puffing smokestacks and churning windmills, same desolate, ashen sky.

We're here to see Lars Vilks, Sweden's counterpart to Kurt Westergaard. In 2007, Lars drew an image every bit as provocative as the Danish cartoonist's, a ragged sketch featuring the Prophet Mohammad's head on the body of a dog, an animal considered unclean by many Muslims. But there was a difference: when Westergaard made his drawing, he had no idea of the mayhem he was about to unleash. When Vilks depicted the Prophet two years after the cartoon controversy had shocked the world, he knew what he was getting himself into. He did it anyway.

Southern Sweden is a local vacation destination. In the summer it's downright balmy around here, at least compared to up north, where the country stretches into the Arctic Circle. But now, in the grip of winter, the area is largely deserted. The roads are empty and the expensive shops and restaurants in the resort towns are boarded up. We've had no choice but to book a room at the only hotel we could find open, a romantic couples retreat that advertises special "love weekend" packages on its website.

To get to Vilks's house, the GPS device directs us to pull off the highway and crisscross a maze of country roads. As light drizzle patters the windshield, we pass rural hamlets and half-timbered barns. We pull up at a small yellow house surrounded by muddy fields. As we get out of the car, four muscle-bound men with gun bulges under their jackets emerge from a camper out back. Without a word, we hand over our passports and assume the position for pat-downs. We know the drill.

"We met your counterparts in Denmark," Pete mentions to a

member of the security team whose face resembles weather-beaten granite. "We know," he replies, before clearing us to enter the house.

An older man with tousled gray hair, thick plastic-rimmed glasses, and a bulky, fraying sweater, welcomes us out of the cold. Vilks gestures for us to take a seat in his small living room. It's hard to know where to do so. Drawings and art tomes and old notebooks are strewn across every surface. On a coffee table, between empty tomato cans sprouting paintbrushes and paper plates smeared with hues of paint, Vilks has been hard at work re-creating Rembrandt's iconic self-portrait on a sheet of card stock, but with an added element: the Mohammad dog image is nestled under Rembrandt's chin.

Vilks explains he's been working on a series in which his notorious Prophet image crops up in all manner of celebrated artwork: Mohammad appearing as the face of one of the cheetahs in Titian's *Bacchus and Ariadne*. Mohammad being worn like a pendant of a necklace in Mary Cassatt's *Lydia at the Theatre*. Mohammad substituted for the central seal in Andy Warhol's Campbell's Soup can. While some might consider it tacky, if not blasphemous, it's the way Vilks operates. As a conceptual artist and theorist, he's not one to play by the rules. One time, he submitted his car to an art exhibit. For another show, he turned in himself. For Vilks, it's all about how people interpret and react to what he creates. The more agitated the reaction, the better.

"Risk is very important in art," Vilks tells us, lounging in an arm chair. He sports a perpetual look of surprised bemusement, as if life is one long, unexpected joke. "Most critics say this or that artist is taking risks, but it is mostly just rhetoric."

Vilks decided to take a real risk in July 2007, when a small gallery in a town up north asked him to submit something for its exhibition on "the dog in art." It was the sort of cutesy exhibit where visitors were encouraged to bring their pets, explains Vilks. "I suppose they invited me because they thought I could put a bit of salt in the exhibition," says Vilks. They got what they were asking for.

Echoing the rationale of *Jyllands-Posten*'s editors, Vilks says the three Mohammad-dog drawings he submitted were all about freedom of expression, about proving that "freedom to insult religious symbols should not be a problem." He insists he didn't believe his statement would go any further than the exhibit, but it's hard to believe he wasn't expecting what happened next. The gallery decided not to show his drawings. Then the media got involved. Soon enough, word of a scandalous Scandinavian Mohammad drawing was once again spreading internationally.

But this time, the cartoon didn't shake the world. Maybe officials had learned a thing or two from the Denmark quagmire; maybe Sweden wasn't as entangled in anti-Muslim attitudes. Or maybe everyone was burned out from the first time around. In Sweden, the prime minister met with Muslim ambassadors and emphasized the importance of respecting Islam. Politicians in the Middle East were prudent, and even Mahmoud Ahmadinejad, the antagonistic president of Iran, waved Vilks's drawing off as some sort of vague Zionist plot. Yes, a flag or two went up in flames, but all things considered, part two of the Mohammad cartoon controversy was far milder than part one.

That is, except for the guy who started it. An Iraqi insurgency group put a $100,000 bounty on Vilks's head, with a bonus of $50,000 if he was "slaughtered like a lamb." In the years that followed, multiple groups of people have tried to take a shot at the reward. That includes Colleen Renee LaRose, an American caught planning an attack. She became known as "Jihad Jane."

The closest anyone came to succeeding was in May 2010. While Vilks was giving a lecture on free speech at a Swedish university, protestors stormed the stage. Security guards pulled Vilks out of the fracas, with shattered glasses but otherwise unharmed. A few days later, assassins tried to burn his house down. He wasn't home, and the attackers succeeded only in briefly lighting themselves on fire. When the bumbling arsonists retreated, they left behind a driver's license for the benefit of the police.

Vilks recounts it all with a heavy dose of droll humor. Of everyone we've talked to, he's the only who's willing to laugh about the cartoon controversies. "You have to look at it in an absurd way," he says. Like all good conceptual artists, he's determined to accept wherever his incendiary art leads him. "There will probably be more chapters in this story," he says, speaking more quietly, suggesting that those chapters might not have a happy ending. Still, he adds, "You have to accept the story."

It's similar to how he's accepted the strange story that's emerged from his other famous artistic escapade: *Nimis*, a driftwood sculpture he started building in a local nature preserve in 1980. When the local council caught wind of the creation, they ordered it dismantled. But Vilks, never one to duck a fight, refused to do so, launching years of bureaucratic hand-wringing and bizarre legal battles.

In 1996, in an effort to protect the monument, Vilks and his supporters proclaimed the one square kilometer surrounding the sculpture to be the independent micronation of Ladonia. While it's not recognized by the local council, Ladonia now has its own flag (a blank green rectangle), a national anthem ("Ladonia for Thee I Fling"), and a citizenry of more than 15,000, courtesy of www .ladonia.net, where people from all over the world apply to become Ladonians free of charge. Before her arrest, Jihad Jane was welcomed as a Ladonian citizen, something that caused the CIA agents tracking her no end of confusion, says Vilks.

Ladonia has become the area's biggest tourist attraction. Each year, 40,000 people visit the sculpture, says Vilks, entering the odd little micronation from a path not too far from here.

Pete and I look at each other. It's time for a trek into Ladonia.

We're soon tramping through the snowy woods, our breath freezing in front of our faces as we stumble across muddy streambeds and down slippery cliff sides. We've been following a series of yellow "N"s painted on tree trunks, supposedly pointing the way to *Nimis*. But we've gone too long without any sign of the monumental sculpture, and the late-afternoon sky is growing dark. At any moment now it seems an assassin is going to step out from behind a tree, raise a pistol, and put us out of our misery.

Vilks had offered to show us to the path to Ladonia, so we followed behind him in our rental car as his handlers drove him to an out-of-the-way assortment of thatched-roof farm buildings. Here's where the trail starts, Vilks told us, pointing out a muddy pathway leading into the woods.

We headed down the trail, then turned back to wave good-bye. That was when we saw one of Vilks's security team sprinting off into the forest in the opposite direction. What was he doing? Had nature called? Did Vilks ask him to shadow us, to make sure we didn't go tumbling off a precipice? Or had these Scandinavians decided to rid themselves of our meddling once and for all, thanks to a backwoods assassination?

We round a bend and find a strange freestanding gateway bridging the path, a spindly arch fashioned out of twisted planks and branches. Stepping through it, we come upon *Nimis*, larger and grander and stranger than anything we've imagined. Passageways and bridges and towers spill down the cliffside like a tree house on acid, a riot of driftwood and wood scraps that stretches all the way down to where the Baltic laps against a rocky shore.

We're silent as we scramble through the maze of corridors and tunnels, awestruck at what one solitary, obstinate man has constructed. Scrambling up a boulder near the shore to get a better look, Pete shakes his head in wonder. "This is really something," he says. "Why the hell does the local council give a hoot about this?"

As Vilks would be the first to tell us, beauty is in the eye of the beholder. While one person might see a stunning sculpture, another might see a bureaucratic headache and a willful flaunting of local laws. It's the same with the Mohammad cartoons. To one person, the controversy was a great big misunderstanding. To another, the images presented the perfect opportunity to launch some politically expedient turmoil. To a third, the cartoons were visual cruelty, racism writ large. And to a fourth, the hullaballoo was a wondrously strange, artistic experiment, a global performance art piece built from dog exhibitions and angry headlines and bloody fatwas.

And here's the thing about creating humor: just like, as Vilks believes, the best art comes with risk, so, too, does the best comedy. We laugh loudest at the most arousing humor attempts, the stuff that's laced with a bit of danger. To come up with the best comedy, we have to skirt ever closer to the realm of tragedy, hurt, and pain. For some people, the result will hit that perfect, hilarious sweet spot. For others, it goes over the line.

Humor, we've learned, is malleable. Comedy can mask infinite aggressions, but it can also hold infinite opportunities for healthy camaraderie and innocent amusement. A joke's intentions, good and bad, don't lie within the joke itself. They come from the people who tell it, and the people who hear it. That way, even the most innocent joke can have a hint of darkness in it, just like the darkest, most troubling joke can have a spark of light, too.

The spark of light in the middle of the Mohammad cartoon controversy might be growing. The Muslim community in Denmark has become stronger and more unified because of the controversy, reports Hodzic: "I think if it happened today, we would handle it better than we did before." The general Danish population might handle it better, too. Recent reports suggest Danes are becoming more tolerant of immigrants, despite the fiery rhetoric of some of their elected officials.

The cartoonists have also learned a thing or two along the way. Refn and several of his colleagues used copyright money they earned from Mohammad cartoon reproductions to start their own cartoon website called caricature.dk. They have complete control over their distribution and positioning, and it won't be so easy for folks to use them for their own devices. While Westergaard, ever the black sheep, has declined to be a part of it, he's found other ways to be helpful, donating nearly $50,000 of what he's earned to disaster relief in Haiti.

As for Vilks? He's likely to continue doing what he's doing, building fairy castles and causing trouble, waiting to see what the next chapter of his story will bring.

We hope the Swedish commando watching from the woods makes sure it has a happy ending.

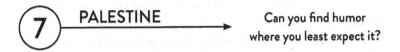

Everyone thought we were crazy. "You're going *where*?" they asked incredulously.

"To Palestine," we'd reply. Our time in Denmark and Sweden put an idea in our heads. Lots of folks had taken the Mohammad cartoon controversy to mean that Islam isn't funny. We think they're wrong. To prove it, we were off to one of the most historically unstable regions on the planet, a place synonymous with violence and suffering, suicide bombers and grieving mothers, deep hatreds and lost hope. "We're going to find humor there," we'd explained to people. "Lots of it."

"Oh, sure," they'd responded. "Palestine is going to be *hilarious*."

Now, as we're speeding down an Israeli highway toward the West Bank, I'm starting to think everyone was right.

Our problems began the day before, when we touched down at Israel's Ben Gurion International Airport. Neither the Gaza Strip nor the West Bank, together known as the Palestinian territories, has a commercial airstrip. (It's why typing "Palestine" into a flight search engine won't get you anywhere. Trust me. I tried.) One of the few ways to get to Palestine is to fly into Israel, then head for one of the security checkpoints. But since Israelis consider both Gaza and the West Bank occupied territories, they decide who comes and goes. It's why the Gaza Strip, the small patch of turmoil at the southwest tip of Israel, is pretty much off limits unless you are part of an NGO or are skilled at digging tunnels. And while Israel does allow folks into the West Bank, a more stable area the size of Delaware, the stern security guards at Israeli passport control weren't too keen on letting us do so when we told them we were in search of what makes things funny.

After the airport, things got worse. Our Tel Aviv cabdriver plowed into a parked car as he deposited us at our hotel. He took one look at the damage he'd caused, gestured for payment, and sped off. Apparently Jewish guilt doesn't have the same oomph here as it does in the States.

The kicker was in Pete's inbox when he logged on at the hotel. Months earlier, Pete had discovered Palestine's one and only televised comedy show, a satire called *Watan ala Watar*. The creators had invited us to visit them in the West Bank for a taping. It was to be the centerpiece of our trip to Palestine. But they'd just e-mailed to say they wouldn't be taping during our visit after all.

We'd just traveled 6,861 miles to have all of our careful arrangements fall apart. In a place like the West Bank, even the best-laid plans don't typically end well.

"It's American. It's the best," says Leore, our Israeli cabdriver, distracting me from my worries as he points to the state-of-the-art police scanner mounted overhead. Leore is dressed in a tight black T-shirt and pants, accentuated by stylish black shades. Not the sort of outfit most folks would choose to wear to a heavily armed security barrier between two warring lands. "Are we going to a club?" Pete wonders.

Leore scoffs as he turns up the volume on the video screen flashing Lady Gaga videos from his dashboard. And no need to worry about road mishaps; a blaring warning signal alerts Leore if he drifts off course. All that's missing is an Israeli version of KITT, the Knight Rider computer, offering instructions in bossy Hebrew.

Leore and his souped-up Mercedes sum up the audacity and industriousness we've witnessed in Israel, a country willed into being by the chutzpah of its people. Since our arrival, I'd been struck by how different this world is from the sort of Jews I grew up around. I'm the son of a New York–born Jewish mother; my people are a neurotic, shlubby bunch who play bridge and watch PBS fund drives and whose weapon of choice is a sharply worded "Oy vey." Here, however, was an entire nation of Jews the likes of which I had never seen. Jews dining on tomato-and-cucumber salads at ritzy Jewish-owned cafes overlooking a tranquil harbor dotted with Jewish-helmed fishing boats. Jews rushing to work in Jewish-driven taxis to Jewish businesses in gleaming skyscrapers built and owned by Jews. Jews sunning their noticeably non-shlubby bodies along the eastern edge of the Mediterranean Sea. Young Jews marching about in army uniforms, brandishing large assault rifles. Oy vey.

The Israelis have clearly moved on from the whole "suffering through millennia-long exodus" thing with determination and style. In 1948, they carved out a piece of Palestine roughly the size of New Jersey, and then, once they'd fended off the resulting incursion of Egyptian, Syrian, Transjordan, and Iraqi forces, moved forward with establishing an independent state. Since then, they've fended off attacks from one Arab neighbor after another and taken the land they'd claimed—a rugged backwater region that Mark Twain described as "desolate and unlovely"—and built one of the most developed countries in the world. As a side project, they took the ancient literary language of Hebrew, at the time not spoken by anybody, and turned it into the mother tongue of Israel's 5.8 million Jews.

There was just one problem in the Zionist plan to reclaim their ancient homeland: there were a lot of Arabs living there who weren't keen on the arrangement. Hence the violent fracturing of the region into the Jewish-controlled state of Israel and the Palestinian territories.

Although Israel has thrived, Palestine has not. Palestine's per capita GDP is just $2,900, about the same as Ghana's. Life expectancy is only 66 years, compared to 80 in Israel. In most financial and social benchmarks, Palestine falls far down the list of country-by-country rankings—that is, if Palestine were a country and not an amalgamation of occupied territories without a unified government, a standing army, or even an agreed-upon border.

And right now it's in the middle of summer, and Palestine and the rest of the Muslim world is in the midst of Ramadan, the holy month in which many Muslims refrain from eating or drinking all day. It's the sort of arrangement that would make anybody less than chipper, let alone someone living in a struggling, war-torn region in the midst of the sweltering Middle Eastern summer.

Outside the taxi, an increasingly parched and hilly landscape rolls by. As we move farther inland, away from the Mediterranean, grass and trees give way to dusty knolls and valleys of scrub brush. Watchtowers top hilltops, and along one stretch of the highway, a shorn-off Israeli fighter jet wing is propped up like a macabre roadside attraction. I ask Leore how often he drives foreigners to the Qalandia checkpoint, which connects Jerusalem to the West Bank. It used to be fairly common, he says, but not so much since an Israeli tank gunned down an Italian journalist a few months back. I change the subject.

Most cabbies refused to take us to the main checkpoint into the West Bank because of the rocks that sometimes come hurtling over the wall and do a number on their paint jobs. But Leore didn't hesitate. He understands the Palestinian situation, he says, noting, "It's like Bruce Springsteen, when he's singing about the lowest of the low."

Encouraged, we broach the subject of Israeli settlements, the Jewish communities encroaching onto the West Bank to claim more land for Israel. The settlements have triggered protests and violence and have been condemned by the International Court of Justice and the United Nations. "What do you think of those settlers?" Pete asks Leore, his tone suggesting we should all be able to agree they're a tad bit excessive.

"Why does everyone call them settlers?" Leore snaps back. "It is our land!" We scrap our plan to usher in a peace plan to the strains of "Born to Run." Leore elaborates: "I don't hate Palestinians, but I don't like them."

So there you have it: we're about to enter a region scarred by decades of violence and suffering, a place controlled by cocksure and annoyed Israelis holding big guns and Palestinians going about in the sweltering heat with hunger headaches.

Leore drops us off at the checkpoint, an imposing conglomeration of barracks and fences and 26-foot-high concrete walls. Beyond lies Palestine. Gesturing with his assault rifle, a gruff-looking Israeli soldier directs us toward a cheerless one-story building. Inside, we pass through a series of floor-to-ceiling turnstiles. I glance around to figure out what's next in the security process, steeling myself for a gauntlet of questions and paperwork. But then I notice through a sunlit doorway a line of dingy Palestinian cabs idling at a curbside, eager to take us on our way.

"That's it?" I ask. We had just entered one of the most turbulent places on earth, and it was easier than navigating a New York City subway station.

"Yeah," says Pete. "But just remember: it's a lot easier getting in than getting out."

The incident began on an overcast January day in 1968, just off the coast of North Korea. Patrolling the area, North Korean naval vessels spotted a suspicious cargo ship and moved in to investigate. The crew on the ship raised an American flag, and the North Koreans ordered it to stand down. Upon boarding their prize, North Korean officers found a trove of classified documents in various stages of hurried destruction.

North Korea had captured a U.S. spy boat, the USS *Pueblo*.

As news of the capture spread to the States, the USS *Pueblo*'s 82 crew members were locked away in a POW camp in Pyongyang. North Korean guards tortured the American officers, holding loaded guns to their heads and demanding confessions. At first, most of the prisoners assumed the situation wouldn't last long. But with the Vietnam War escalating, the administration decided one international quagmire was enough. There would be no ultimatum, no rescue mission. The 82 crew members were being left behind.

But then something strange happened. Things got funny.

The North Koreans demanded the prisoners write letters back to the States renouncing their evil capitalist ways. Instead, the crew members scribbled out comedy routines. "Say hi to Howdy Doody for me," one prisoner wrote to his mother. Lloyd Bucher, the USS *Pueblo*'s commander, admitted to having been given spying orders "in the TOP SECRET Japanese lair of the CIA's evil genius, Sol

Loxfinger," a name he borrowed from a James Bond lampoon in *Playboy* magazine.[1] In his final confession, Bucher wrote it was his "fervent desire to paean the Korean People's Army Navy, and their government." Apparently nobody noticed that he'd stated he wanted to pee on his captors.

Then there was "the digit affair." In staged photos taken of the prisoners, crew members began flipping off the camera. Soon nearly all the propaganda photos of the captives showed the crewmen giving North Koreans the bird. Eventually, North Korean brass demanded to know what the middle finger meant. Bucher, on behalf of his crew, explained, "Why, that's the Hawaiian good luck sign."

"The whole ordeal was one big humorous thing," said Alvin Plucker of the eleven months he and his crew members spent in captivity, which ended on December 23, 1968, when the North Koreans released them. Plucker, a friendly fellow with thin gray hair and piercing blue eyes, is the vice president of the USS *Pueblo* Veterans Association and the group's unofficial historian. He lives just an hour from me in Colorado, and so I visited the makeshift USS *Pueblo* museum he's fashioned in his basement. The small, windowless room is crammed with memorabilia—a copy of *The Pyongyang Times* announcing the capture of an "Armed Spy Ship," the gray rice-straw prisoner's uniform he wore in captivity. On one wall there's a photo of Commander Bucher, taken a month before he died in 2004, beaming and flashing the Hawaiian good luck sign.

Stories like the *Pueblo* incident and the digit affair suggest humor is far more durable than most people realize. Pete connects it to the benign violation theory: you need to start with a bunch of violations, he explains, if you want to come up with great benign violations. He's not the first person to suggest that laughter and pain go hand in hand. As Mark Twain wrote, "The secret source of humor is not joy but sorrow. There is no humor in Heaven."[2]

But here's what's puzzling about suffering and humor: people in desperate situations seem *compelled* to be humorous, even when it might get them in trouble. Flipping off their captors wasn't in USS *Pueblo* crew members' best interest. Just like telling taboo *anekdoty*, or jokes, in the USSR was a big no-no. But that didn't discourage the

Soviet citizenry from developing one of the richest joke collections the world over. There were even Soviet jokes about jokers busted for their jokes:

Who dug the White Sea Canal?
The right bank was dug by those who related anecdotes.
And the left bank?
Those who listened.[3]

It's almost as if making people laugh during dark and troubling times is so vital, so crucial, that it overrides common sense, and maybe even self-preservation.

Maybe we'll find this same against-all-odds humor in Palestine. But for our own self-preservation, we won't be flashing the Hawaiian good luck sign at anybody.

In the Palestinian city of Ramallah, we are off the map.

Ramallah is the administrative capital of the territory, the seat of power for the Palestinian Authority, the political apparatus that controls the West Bank. The city is also experiencing something of a building boom, thanks to the loosening military restrictions in the area and increased foreign aid and investment.

But still, there is no map of Ramallah. That's according to the concierge at our accommodations at the Mövenpick Ramallah—a brand-new, $40 million operation that's the city's first five-star hotel. He tells us, "We are still growing. We don't need maps yet."

He's confused about why we'd want to walk around Ramallah. "The old city?" he responds when we ask about historical parts of town. "There is an old city, but you can't use it."

We discover the concierge is wrong: we do need a map of Ramallah. The city is modern and Mediterranean, filled with mid-level high-rises topped with terracotta roofs and mosque minarets piercing the hazy turquoise sky. But it's also confusing. A perplexing tangle of streets roll up and down Ramallah's rocky hills, and spending too much time wandering them would be a surefire detriment to our health. The narrow, undulating sidewalks are pockmarked by gaping holes and cracks, with streetlights few and far between.

"One thing you can say about Palestine is there are lot of rocks," says Pete as we wilt beneath the noonday sun. "For a population that isn't armed, that's useful."

Everywhere we look, there are cafés and restaurants where we could seek shade and directions. But because it's Ramadan, most are shuttered. Two upscale coffee shops are open, we are told: Zamen, a café on one side of town, and Zaman, a different operation on the other side. When we ask a taxi driver to take us to one, he typically will deposit us at the other.

After failing to find anything of interest in the city on our own, we flag down one of Ramallah's ubiquitous yellow cabs. The drivers seem to operate with one hand affixed to their horn. "Can you take us to the old city?" we ask, to a look of incomprehension. "The old town?" we try. "The place where there are old buildings?" Stumped, the driver calls his taxi dispatch—who apparently hasn't heard of the old city, either. We give up and decide to head back to our hotel. "How about the Mövenpick?"

"Ah, the Mövenpick!" replies the driver triumphantly, and deposits us back where we started.

But we're not going to give up that easily. After all, we know comedy is no stranger to the Middle East. Islam has long embraced humanity's funny bone, just like every other successful faith.

"Humor is part of the human experience. If a religion does not fully embrace the scope of the human experience, it is not going to make sense to a lot of people," says Father James Martin, a Jesuit priest who's been named the "*Colbert Report* Chaplain," as well as author of the book *Between Heaven and Mirth*. "From a practical point of view, if you were starting a religion on your own, who would want to come to your services if it were just a gloomy group of people?" Maybe that's why the origin story for Judaism, Christianity, and Islam begins with a chuckle. In the book of Genesis, when the 100-year-old Abraham, the forefather of all three religions, learns from God that he will bear a child with his 90-year-old wife Sarah, he falls on his face laughing. No wonder they name this child Isaac, Hebrew for "he laughs."

The Koran, too, insists humor is divinely inspired. As the Islamic holy book notes, God is the one "Who makes (men) laugh and makes (them) weep."[4] And while Europe was bumbling through the Dark Ages, the Arabs kept the high art of hilarity alive. In the eleventh century, Iranian scholar Al-Abi took up that mantle with "Scattered Pearls," an unparalleled seven-volume encyclopedia of jokes and anecdotes that begins by cracking wise about Muslim traditions, then digresses into chapters on lunatics, transvestites, noisy (and silent) farting, and a treatise on those considered the worst of the worst: canal sweepers.[5]

Have Palestine's tribulations wiped away that comedic tradition or fostered its growth? Since all of our official plans have fallen through, we go about our research the old-fashioned way: we approach random strangers around Ramallah and ask if they are funny.

Pete waylays a stylish young woman smoking a cigarette at one of the Zamen cafés. "I don't think we're funny," she says. But her equally chic female companion scoffs. "Tell them what your name is," she says.

"Hurriyah Ziada."

"In Arabic, that means 'Extra Freedom,'" says her friend. "Her name is 'Extra Freedom' and she lives in Palestine. Now, *that's* funny."

The French philosopher Henri Bergson argued that comedy arose from "something mechanical encrusted on the living," awkward attempts to restrict the manner folks go about their lives. It may be why the Soviet Union was such a gold mine of punch lines, since Communist leaders tried to mechanize every aspect of daily existence. The results were awkward, to put it mildly.

In Palestine, too, life is defined by restriction. Arbitrary checkpoints hamper commutes. Where you can travel is limited by what color identification card you have in your wallet. And since 2007, when Palestine fractured into warring factions, with the hard-line Hamas party taking power in the Gaza Strip and the more moderate Fatah party controlling the Palestinian Authority in the West Bank, there's not even much harmony between the two isolated territories.

In other words, there are plenty of violations around here to make benign.

Later, after evening prayers echo from the minarets to mark the end of the day's fasting, Ramallah comes alive. The shops and eateries throw open their doors, and the streets throng with people hungry for food and social interaction. Overlooking a taxi-clogged traffic circle that doubles as the city's central square, young people drink espresso at the "Stars and Bucks Cafe," which flaunts its copyright-violating name and logo. Down the street, techno music pulses out of the provocatively named "911 Cafe," where waiters deliver drinks in faux bulletproof vests.

On an open-air patio, we join in with a group of middle-aged men sharing a bubbling hookah pipe. They ask if we've heard about the unofficial Arab comedy ladder. On one end, the funniest of the funny, there is Egypt, a place so chock-full of jokesters that during the presidency of Gamal Abdel Nasser, a special intelligence unit monitored wisecracks about the government.[6] On the other end of the comedy scale is Jordan. One of our companions cracks: "Have you heard the one about the Jordanian businessman? Every morning before work he puts on his shirt, tie, and angry face."

So where does Palestine fall on the Arab comedy ladder?

The best person to ask is Sharif Kanaana, professor of anthropology and folklore at Berzeit University in Ramallah, since he's spent his career collecting Palestinian jokes. But to go along with our bad luck, he's not in the West Bank. He's in the States, visiting his son in California. "Despite all of the pain and agony, there is a lot of humor in Palestine," says Kanaana over the phone. Much more, in fact, than he ever expected. Israeli-Palestinian relations over the last few decades have been marked by a cycle of intifadas, periods of intensified conflict. In 1989, the midst of the First Intifada, Kanaana was struck by all of the wisecracks and laughter he witnessed among the revolutionary youths, even as they returned bruised and bloodied from confrontations with Israeli soldiers.

To explain all that laughing, Kanaana began collecting the jokes he heard—and he never stopped. Now he has an archive of thousands of Palestinian jokes, all written down on index cards and arranged chronologically in his office.

And according to Kanaana, among all those boxes and binders of jokes, he found a pattern. During the First Intifada, when unity and energy swept the occupied territories, the jokes depicted the

Palestinians as champions. Many involved canny street kids getting the better of Israeli soldiers. But then, in the disillusioned low in between the First Intifada and the Second Intifada in the early 2000s, the jokes turned dark and pessimistic. One post-intifada joke describes several heads of state meeting with God and making requests for their people. To each, God says, "Not in your lifetime." Then Yasser Arafat, the former Palestinian leader, asks for his people's freedom and God says, "Not in my lifetime."

"The humor follows a curve," says Kanaana. "In retrospect, you can see the uprising coming from the humor you find. The morale gets very low, the jokes turn very dark, and people start to demand something be done. Then the uprising comes."

So, I ask him, what do the jokes he's found lately say about Palestine's future?

Kanaana's voice darkens. "For the last year and a half or so, there hasn't been anything new," he says. "What it means to me is that the Palestinian people cannot see where things are going. They cannot see a way out of the present situation. Therefore, they have no humor."

The sketch comedy program with no plans to tape while we're in town haunts us wherever we go. Every evening after the breaking of the Ramadan fast, televisions are switched on in restaurants, cafés, and homes all over the city in time to catch the intro music for *Watan ala Watar*, Arabic for "Homeland on a String." Usually the fifteen-minute show airs once a week, but during Ramadan, it airs nightly. The holy month is apparently akin to the U.S. "sweeps" period, since after the big post-sundown meal, everybody crashes in front of the TV.

On one of our first nights in Ramallah, we convince the hotel staff in the Mövenpick's lounge to switch on the show and ask a local businessman we've been chatting with to translate. The first sketch opens with angry locals besieging the Palestinian attorney general. They all want to file lawsuits over *Watan ala Watar* making fun of them, says the businessman, translating from Arabic. One woman in the sketch says the TV show hasn't parodied her yet, but she wants to file suit preemptively. During the commotion, the frazzled attorney general gets a call. It turns out the show just made fun of him, too.

A couple days later, we meet with the woman from the sketch, Manal Awad, at one of the two Zamen cafés. Even here, among the city's elite, her Western appearance—trendy jeans, a stylish shirt—is striking. "Before we started, there had never been stand-up comedy in Palestine," she says with a British accent, courtesy of her time in London pursuing a master's degree in theater directing. Every time she puffs on her cigarette, a tiny tattoo flashes below her right wrist. It's hard to imagine the thirtysomething's dark curly hair ever hidden under a hijab, unless it's for the purpose of a comedy skit.

While Israel has a long history of popular satirical television shows like *Eretz Nehederet*, Yiddish for "It's a Wonderful Country," Palestine's airwaves were satire-free. That changed thanks to Awad and her two colleagues, Imad Farajin and Khalid Massou, a trio that first began developing a comedy act in 2008. Their resulting theatrical show was a huge hit, drawing the likes of Mahmoud Abbas, president of the Palestinian Authority. Then came the offer of a show on state-run television, which Manal says they accepted on one condition: "No censorship."

Palestinian officialdom agreed, even allowing them to air a sketch in which President Mahmoud Abbas announces a peace deal—that is, Mahmoud Abbas the thirteenth, at a time 500 years in the future. Hamas, too, has received its fair share of knocks. One skit featured an Islamist judge in Gaza making eyes at a male courtroom reporter. No one is off limits: Israeli negotiators, Osama bin Laden, Barack Obama. While the shenanigans have angered Hamas—its Ministry of Information in Gaza called the show "an example of black propaganda"—it has long enjoyed the blessing of the Palestinian Authority. Yasser Abed Rabbo, one of President Abbas's closest advisers, even played himself on the show.

In 2010, a polling organization found that 60 percent of those in the West Bank and Gaza who'd seen *Watan ala Watar* liked it, far higher approval ratings than either of Palestine's two major political parties. With a mandate like that, Awad and her colleagues have diversified, turning their satirical gaze upon Palestinian society:

outdated medical practices, shabby police operations, backward cultural traditions. They also have plans to start a comedy training program, maybe someday open Palestine's first-ever stand-up club.

While the everyday jokes Professor Sharif Kanaana has long collected may be stagnant, in Ramallah the comedy business seems to be booming.

That's because folks around here are desperate for something—anything—fun to do, says Rami Mehdawi, a local journalist and social activist we meet one afternoon in Ramallah. "There has long been no space for any kind of entertainment here," says Mehdawi, who sports a tightly cropped beard and a rakish smile. "I am 32 years old, and all I can do is go to the gym if I want to do something." He points out that Ramallah is essentially park-free. There are no leafy promenades, no stretches of grass. With so little in the way of diversion, Palestinians are eager to embrace comedy or anything else to pass the time.

To prove his point, Rami offers to become our unofficial guide to what little nightlife Ramallah offers. Pete's all in, declaring, "Let's go break some cultural norms!"

Rami is happy to oblige. He takes us to an open-air club in the hills over the city where student revolutionaries practice their pickup lines rather than debate rebel tactics. He introduces us to the pleasures of Arak, the traditional anise-flavored liquor, and Taybeh, the celebrated local beer. And he invites us to a bar to watch the big soccer match between Barcelona and Real Madrid, a rivalry Palestinians follow religiously. "The young generation needs something to believe in," says Rami between handfuls of bar pretzels. "The new generation loves Barca and Real Madrid more than any leader, more than any nationality."

After the game, Rami insists on checking out the late-night scene in the center of the city. Soon, we're swept up in a maelstrom of honking cars and flag-waving young men. Everywhere, people are yelling and chanting, while Palestinian Authority soldiers fidget with assault rifles and attempt to maintain order. Is this noise the rumblings of a new uprising, the dawning of a new intifada?

Nope. Just jubilee over Barca's game-winning goal.

Awad calls with good news: *Watan ala Watar* will be taping a show while we're in town after all.

She offers to pick us up at the Mövenpick and take us to the shoot, but when the day comes, she stands us up. Half an hour passes, then an hour. Pete calls her cell.

Something terrible has happened, she tells us. The Palestinian attorney general has shut down the show, citing recent grievances filed over it. It's reminiscent of the *Watan ala Watar* sketch we'd watched several days earlier—maybe too reminiscent. It seems the attorney general can't take a joke.

We jump into action. We reach out to a contact we've landed in the Palestinian Authority, and soon we've finagled the personal number of the attorney general. Pete, in full investigative-reporter mode, wastes no time making use of it. "Hello, this is Peter McGraw," he declares into his phone when he gets through. "Hello? Hello? Hello?" He goes on like this for a while, then puts his phone away. "I got in eight hellos, then he hung up," he says. So much for that Pulitzer.

Disheartened, we take a taxi to the security checkpoint back into Israel. We're scheduled to meet with a Holocaust survivor named Gizelle Cycowycz in Jerusalem. But as Pete predicted, getting out from the Palestinian side, where the graffiti-covered barrier walls are blackened from Molotov cocktails, is more complicated than getting in. At the checkpoint, we join a line of Palestinians lucky enough to have the right permits in a dirty, corral-like hallway, waiting for an electric turnstile to let us through. The gateway seems to start and stop arbitrarily, severing husbands from wives, mothers from children. In the corridor beyond, Palestinians run belongings through a metal detector and flash their identification to young Israeli soldiers peering through thick glass panels. It's a tense experience—not just for those of us moving through, but also for those on the other side of the glass. All in all, the process takes us twenty minutes, but we consider ourselves lucky. We've heard the waiting times at checkpoints can sometimes be hours long.

We take a crowded bus into the city, riding through East Jerusalem, the largely Arab, holy site–rich neighborhood that both Israelis and Palestinians claim as their own. After our time in Ramallah, it's striking to notice what we'd been missing. Clean streets. Traffic lights. Trees.

Cycowycz lives on a quiet, tree-lined street not far from Jerusalem's old city. She welcomes us into her spacious apartment, brimming with artwork and book-laden shelves. Like all good Jewish grandmothers, she offers us massive amounts of food. Once we've had our fill of tea and cookies and chocolate, we want to hear her story.

For the next several hours, Cycowycz tells us her tale: the Nazis taking over her native Czech Republic when she was a young girl, forcing her out of school and her father out of his job. Getting sent to the Auschwitz concentration camp as a teenager, where she was shorn of all hair and crammed into a barrack with a thousand other women. Watching as those deemed too elderly, too infirm, or too young were shuffled off to the gas chamber. Eventually making it home with her mother and sisters after the war to find their house ransacked and desecrated—and learning that her father had been sent to Auschwitz's crematorium on the last possible day.

It's a horrible story, one all too common among survivors of the Holocaust. The sheer enormity of the "Shoah," as Jews refer to it, is such that it's hardly ever referred to in anything other than solemn or sacred tones. But while Holocaust humor is still off limits (aside from a few successful outliers like Mel Brooks's *The Producers*), that doesn't mean there wasn't humor during the Holocaust. "We laughed under the worst circumstances," says Cycowycz, a psychologist who now runs support groups for other Holocaust survivors. At night in her barracks, Cycowycz says the dirty jokes traded by former prostitutes who slept nearby fascinated her. When sent to a work camp, she and other girls on the production line giggled over funny songs and stories. And at times she laughed to herself over the hardships of those around her, something she's not proud of today. "We were hungry like hell, but we laughed," she says. "It had to be a release."

A release, a salve, a moment of respite—that's the explanation most people ascribe to the humor found during horrific ordeals such as the Holocaust. "Holocaust humor was about affirming life, not giving life," says Steve Lipman, author of *Laughter in Hell: The Use of*

Humor During the Holocaust. "It was a coping tool, an escape, a way to step back and take control of the situation in some small way." The same goes for gallows humor, the idea of laughing at your fate when all hope seems lost. As Sigmund Freud put it, "The ego refuses to be distressed by the provocations of reality, to let itself be compelled to suffer. It insists that it cannot be affected by the traumas of the external world; it shows, in fact, that such traumas are no more than occasions for it to gain pleasure."[7]

Such humor was survival humor. And that may be why the sort of Holocaust jokes Gizelle describes to us—dark, witty, self-deprecating—sound familiar. We found the same brand of funny in Palestine. The beleaguered quips tracked by Sharif Kanaana after the intifadas, the put-upon snark of *Watan ala Watar*—this is humor as self-defense, a way for the tellers to inoculate themselves from further despair. It is, in other words, what many people consider "Jewish humor."

It could be one more bit of ammunition in humor scholar Elliot Oring's ongoing scholarly battle to dismantle the misnomer that is "Jewish humor," the idea that Jews have long held a monopoly on self-deprecating underdog jokes. "People presume that Jewish humor is in some ways special, but no one has been able to say with evidence whether that is really the case," Oring says. As he points out, there's no proof, no Talmudic comedic passages or ancient Israelite joke books that suggest the Jews' reputation as jokers is anything but a modern creation. For another, to suggest that Jews alone employ underdog humor ignores a rich variety of Jewish comedy, including the cutting satire and sometimes militaristic jokes of Israel. And lots of different people use humor as a psychological buffer zone, a way to put themselves down before their enemies have a chance to do so—and that includes the folks we've met in Ramallah. While most people on either side of the security barrier aren't likely to admit it, Israelis and Palestinians share a comedic sense of self-preservation.

But while self-preservation may account for some of the jokes we find in Palestine, it can't explain all of them. The assertive anti-Israeli jokes

Sharif found during the height of the intifadas weren't about surviving. And if the satirical humor of *Watan ala Watar* was just about helping people get by, government officials wouldn't have been so eager to censor it. Instead, Awad and her colleagues had the same aim as all satirists who came before them, from Aristophanes to Jonathan Swift to Jon Stewart: mocking folly and vices to expose them.

Humor like this is a tool of subversion, proof that wit can be wielded like a weapon. But in Palestine, a place of flying projectiles, assault rifles, and explosives, does funny firepower stand a chance? We figure the best place to find out is at the Freedom Theatre.

Israeli-born artist and activist Juliano Mer-Khamis founded the Freedom Theatre in 2006 in the West Bank city of Jenin. The idea was to serve the city's large population of refugees who'd fled Israel during the 1948 Palestine War. Mer-Khamis's decision to launch the theater with the help of Zakaria Zubeidi, the former leader of Jenin's martyr brigades, did little to endear his fellow Israeli countrymen to his endeavor; neither did his tendency to slam the occupation. But he had detractors in Palestine, too. The first play staged at the Freedom Theatre was a Palestinian version of *Animal Farm*, George Orwell's satire of revolutionaries. On stage, boys and girls acted together while wearing pig masks. It didn't go over too well with conservative Muslim nationalists.

It seemed only a matter of time until somebody somewhere lashed out. It happened one night a few months before we arrived in Palestine.

That evening, a masked assailant opened fire on Mer-Khamis as he was leaving the theater, killing him. The murder rocked both Israel and Palestine. We'd heard that in the wake of the tragedy, Mer-Khamis's colleagues were attempting to carry on his mission at the theater. So we take a taxi to Jenin.

The hour-and-a-half cab ride, corkscrewing up and down rolling, arid hills, leaves Pete wracked by carsickness. I consider asking our driver to ease off on the breakneck speed, but then remember he hasn't had a smoke, a drink, or a bite to eat all day.

When we get to the Freedom Theatre, a colorful building wedged into a dingy street on the outskirts of Jenin's refugee camp, we find a world awash in chaos. Young children from the camp scream and run about the theater's cramped offices, here to watch *Dora the Explorer* and *Teletubbies* with Arabic subtitles. Outside the 200-seat theater, signs still hang for *Alice in Wonderland*, the last play Mer-Khamis put on before he was killed.

In a side office, Jacob Gough, the theater's acting general manager, hunches over a MacBook as he answers a stream of urgent phone calls. Gough, a wry, scraggly haired Welsh production manager who's spent years living in Palestine, offered to help hold the Freedom Theatre together after Mer-Khamis's death. He had no idea the level of bureaucratic absurdity he'd be up against.

The absurdity extends to Mer-Khamis's murder investigation, he says. The Palestinian Authority tried to look into the matter, but since Israelis confiscated Mer-Khamis's body, car, and personal belongings, there was little for local detectives to go on. And while the Israeli army has been conducting its own investigation, its strategy seems to involve little more than harassing members of Freedom Theatre in hopes that one of them would confess. The man arrested for Mer-Khamis's murder has been released because of a lack of evidence. "The situation is absurd," says Gough, shaking his head.

Since Gough is behind in his work, Pete and I venture off into the refugee camp. We expect it to resemble a scene from the nightly news, a sea of tents and thrown-together structures. Instead, the camp is a full-blown village—a town, even—crisscrossed with power lines and packed with concrete and cinderblock multistory buildings. Nearly 60 years old, it's a camp in name only. The people here refuse to give up hope that they will one day return to their family land in Israel, even though most of them were born here.

Everywhere, there are signs of a community wracked by poverty and violence: empty lots piled high with dusty skeletons of desiccated cars. Cement walls pockmarked by bullet holes and covered in graffiti. A grim martyr's cemetery housing many of those killed when the Israeli army occupied the camp in 2002. There's little hope of a better life for these people anytime soon. What to do about the hundreds of thousands of refugees displaced from Israel is one of the most intractable subjects in peace negotiations.

Pete, per usual, is eager to make everybody feel better. He borrowed a Barcelona soccer flag he found in our taxi driver's glove compartment, and he waves it at any young children who pass our way. "BARCELONA!" he shouts at them like a deranged hooligan. The kids scream and try to snatch the flag, to Pete's delight. "Let's find more kids," he says. Considering that Americans aren't popular here, much less Americans who taunt small children, I suggest a little more discretion.

Moving through these labyrinthine streets, seeing the destitution and ruin, it's easy to wonder if any of Mer-Khamis's and his colleagues' work makes a difference. That's especially true of the satire Freedom Theatre uses to critique both Israel and Palestine. After all, some humor experts claim subversive humor doesn't have any practical use whatsoever.

Show me an insurrection launched by joking, these skeptics say. Show me a despot overthrown, oppression overcome, because of the right punch line. Some people go further, arguing that not only is comedy incapable of launching revolutions, but it might have stopped a few from happening. Just as Pete's PSA study suggested that funny sex-ed ads led people to take birth control less seriously, it's possible that joking among the discontented masses might act as a safety valve, allowing folks to let off steam and view their plight in a less threatening manner instead of rising up in rebellion.

Even the great Soviet Union comedy boom, the upwell of political jokes just before the fall of the Berlin Wall, is suspect. International joke expert Christie Davies spent decades tracking USSR humor, and he concluded that among all the things that led to the Soviet Union's spectacular collapse, joking didn't even crack the top twenty.[8] At best, the explosion of Soviet jokes was an indication of a rising fervor already under way among the populace, not the spark that turned up the heat. Or as Davies put it, "Jokes are a thermometer, not a thermostat."[9]

Revolutionary humor, conclude Davies and other cynics, is a misnomer. There's never been a case of jokes changing the world.

For Pete, this is a "black swan" argument, and it's his favorite kind of reasoning to dismantle. All you have to do to disprove a statement like "There are no black swans," he says, is find a single swan with black feathers.

In this case, we think we found a whole country of black swans.

Flash back to Serbia in 1999. The small Balkan state was in its tenth year in the autocratic grip of President Slobodan Milošević. Four recent wars with neighboring republics of the former Yugoslavia had left Serbia isolated, financially ravaged, and aggressively nationalistic. No one expected the situation to change any time soon.

A year later, everything was different. A half-million people had taken to the streets in protest, and Milošević resigned in disgrace. What happened in between? A whole lot of jokes.

It came at the hands of Otpor!, a Serbian youth movement. On Milošević's birthday, Otpor! baked the president a giant cake, only to carve it up just as he'd disastrously carved up Yugoslavia. Another time, Otpor! leaked word to police that their main office in Belgrade was receiving a big delivery of important materials. The authorities showed up at the appropriate time to confiscate the heavy-looking crates, with the media standing by. Only the crates were empty, so when the police went to hoist them up and carry them away, they accidentally tossed them all in the air, looking like a *Looney Tunes* cartoon as the cameras rolled.

It was all about "laughtivism," injecting humor into protest movements. That's what I learn from former Otpor! leader Srđa Popović, a man who calls himself a disciple of both Martin Luther King Jr. and Monty Python. According to Popović, who met with me while he was staying in Colorado, teaching a class in nonviolent action, humor added three key elements to the movement. First, it allowed the protestors to break through the "fear barrier" that kept much of the population immobilized. It's harder to be afraid of someone once you've laughed at him. Second, the young, laughing activists wearing hip Otpor! T-shirts and engaging in goofy street theater made protests seem cool and fun. Or as Popović put it to me with a wink, "If you weren't arrested in Serbia in 2000, you couldn't get laid."

Finally, humor was integral to Otpor!'s signature "dilemma actions"—protests designed so that however Milošević responded, he looked stupid. One example involved Otpor! painting Milošević's face on a barrel and letting folks on the street take a whack at it. Since Milošević wasn't about to let citizens smack him in the face, police confiscated the prop, allowing Otpor! to report that the authorities had arrested a barrel. In Denmark and Sweden, we'd learned how derogatory jokes and pranks often put the powerless in a lose-lose situation. Otpor! figured out a way to turn that phenomenon around and use it against the most powerful people of all.

"The age of laughtivism is coming," promised Popović. As part of their new organization, the Center for Applied Nonviolent Action and Strategies, or CANVAS, he and former Otpor! colleagues are now teaching laughtivism techniques to activists all over the world.

Maybe next can be a stint in Jenin. Despite its recent setbacks, Gough remains convinced that the operation Mer-Khamis built at the Freedom Theatre remains a potent weapon against intolerance and oppression. But the Freedom Theater performers need to polish their comedy routines. According to Gough, the jokes around here are rough stuff. Theater members once decided to play a prank on a new volunteer. Before the new guy left the theater one night, his colleagues warned that Israeli soldiers might be out and about. As he walked home, the former freedom fighter Zakaria Zubeidi snuck up behind him and put an assault rifle to his head. "Take me to Zakaria!" he shouted to the volunteer, impersonating an Israeli commando. "I want to kill him!"

The ruse continued, with Zakaria threatening to shoot the volunteer all the way back to his house. Only when the guy seemed on the verge of a nervous breakdown did Zakaria reveal that—surprise!—it had all been a joke.

"Everyone thought it was funny," says Gough, chuckling at the memory. Then he notices our stricken looks. On second thought, he says, "maybe the joke went a little too far."

We've found humor in Palestine—a lot of it. But is it everywhere? Is there a point where circumstances become so difficult, so trying, that it's hard to keep laughing? Is there a point where joking dies away?

Alvin Plucker, survivor of the USS *Pueblo* incident, reached that point—though it wasn't while he was locked away in North Korea. It was after he returned home, in the subsequent decades as he struggled with post-traumatic stress disorder because of what he'd been through. "It changed you," he told me. "There was no more laugh in you."

Gizelle experienced that moment during the Holocaust. For her, the laughter came when there were flashes of relief—the time she spent at a work camp, the moments she spent with her sisters. But often, she says, the oppressive doom of Auschwitz killed all potential for humor. The thousands of gaunt faces, the omnipresent aura of dread, the terrible cold and hunger—it was too much for humor to survive.

Pete has found this comedic point of no return in his research. When Hurricane Sandy first developed in the western Caribbean in late October 2012, he and his collaborators, Lawrence Williams and Caleb Warren, collected potentially humorous tweets from the Twitter account @AHurricaneSandy, such as "It's RAINING men. Literally. I just picked up a bunch of dudes and threw them" and "OH SHIT JUST DESTROYED A STARBUCKS. NOW I'M A PUMPKIN SPICE HURRICANE." Then, at various points as the hurricane approached the East Coast of the United States, came ashore, and subsided, online study participants rated the funniness of these tweets. The resulting humor ratings followed a curvilinear pattern. The day before the storm hit, participants scored the tweets the funniest. Humor ratings peaked again 36 days later, then dwindled as the catastrophe faded from memory. But in between these two comedic high points, as the hurricane made landfall and left millions without power, the nation reeling from billions of dollars in damages, and communities in mourning for the hundreds killed? Far fewer people found @AHurricaneSandy funny.[10]

While our circumstances in Ramallah are far less dire than those in Hurricanes and POW camps, Pete and I seem to be approaching some sort of laughter-free zone, too. When we first arrived in Palestine, the quirks of our travel arrangements were entertaining, even comical. Like how every taxi driver insists his meter is broken, charging us a flat fee of twenty Israeli shekels, whether our destination is clear across town or just a few blocks away. Or how in our hotel room, the transparent glass wall separating the bathroom and the bedroom makes it all too easy for one of us to play "guess the body part" while the other is showering.

It doesn't help that we have a lot on our minds. We have been traveling a lot, and the time away from my family is getting to me. Juggling his research and teaching hasn't been easy on Pete, either. For the first few days, we chuckled about our difficulties. These days, not so much.

In Palestine, there seems to be at least one subject that's off limits for comedy: Israeli settlers. The settlers are seen as usurpers, evicting Palestinians from their land; the situation is too troubling, too upsetting, to make light of. In all his years of Palestinian joke collecting, Kanaana insists, "I never came across jokes about Israeli settlers."

If that's the case, there may be one place in the West Bank where the line has been crossed, where there is little to joke about. That place is Hebron, a city where Palestinians and Israeli settlers live side by troubled side.

"You will never see anything like you see in Hebron," Mehdawi, our nightlife guide, tells us during one of our evening excursions. "I am Palestinian, and I don't understand it."

"Hebron?" adds Jacob Gough, amid the turmoil of the Freedom Theatre. "Oh, yeah. That place is really fucking crazy."

When we get to Hebron, after another long, stomach-churning taxi ride, Bashar Farashat is waiting for us. Farashat, who'd been recommended to us by a contact in Ramallah, flashes us a boyish smile and hands us his card. "International Trainer," it reads. "Life skills and human development." Business is surely going well for a professional problem-solver like Farashat. These days, Hebronites have a lot of problems that need solving.

Hebron, the biggest city in the West Bank, has long been a center for trade and commerce. It's also a spiritual hub. At the heart of the city lies the Cave of the Patriarchs, the supposed burial place of Abraham, the forefather of Judaism, Christianity, and Islam. That makes Hebron one of the holiest places on earth. It would make sense, therefore, for Hebron to be a beacon of industry and unity, a place where people could come together in recognition of their shared spiritual roots. Unfortunately, little in Hebron makes sense.

Farashat offers to take us to the 2,000-year-old structure enclosing the Cave of the Patriarchs, which Muslims call the Ibrahimi Mosque. As he guides us through narrow, twisting alleyways that snake through Hebron's old city, we pass underneath metal latticework overhead, a mesh ceiling littered from above with trash and bricks. Settlers who live in the buildings that line the alleyways toss detritus down upon those heading to the mosque, explains Farashat. The mesh stops litter, but not the dishwater, bleach, and other unpleasant liquids that sometimes rain down.

Farashat's tour of discord and sorrow continues. Here is where Palestinians were forced out of their homes to make room for Israeli settlers. The settlers said they were reclaiming land lost when they fled the city during the 1929 Hebron massacre, in which Arab rioters killed nearly 70 Jews. Here is the part of Hebron under Israeli military control, where thousands of soldiers protect 400 settlers. Here are the narrow passageways where Palestinian merchants hawk their wares—fresh spices and squirt guns and fragrant, de-skinned goat heads—ever since the settlers have shut down the city's big central market.

We reach the entrance to the Ibrahimi Mosque, where we're greeted not by a majestic ancient gateway, but instead the somber turnstiles of a security checkpoint. Increased safety measures have been in place here since 1994, when an Israeli settler opened fire on Muslims praying at the mosque, killing 29 people.

Past the checkpoint, we enter a sweltering courtyard. All around us, a sea of kneeling Muslims bow their heads in prayer toward rough-hewn temple walls dating back to the Roman king Herod. Helmeted Israeli soldiers brandish assault rifles and meander through the crowd. From stone minarets overhead, speakers boom out Arabic prayers. But then the prayers are drowned out by the sound of up-tempo Hasidic music pumping from a building across the way. It's a Jewish event hall, and someone inside has decided that right now, in the middle of Ramadan prayers, is the perfect time to blast local Top 40 hits.

While Farashat prays at the mosque, we procure a patch of shade beneath a nearby Palestinian shop awning and struggle to get our bearings. We notice on the street in front of us an approaching Israeli police officer, gun strapped to his belt. He makes a beeline for the Palestinian who owns the shop where we are. Pete and I brace for trouble.

Instead, something unexpected happens. The two clasp hands and begin chatting in Arabic, yammering back and forth like old friends. Amazed, Pete snaps a photo of them together. Gesturing at Pete and his camera, the shopkeeper says something to the officer. "He says he's going to post your photo on Facebook so all the officer's colleagues can see it," translates Farashat, who's returned from prayer.

"Oh, yeah?" retorts the policeman. "Then I'm going to print out a copy and fasten it above your shop and invite everybody from Fatah and Hamas to come see it!"

The two double over in laughter. The Palestinian puts his hand around the Israeli and turns to us. "He is Palestinian in his heart, not in his uniform," he says in English.

We're flabbergasted. Then we join in, laughing with relief. Everyone said we were nuts, looking for laughter in Palestine. But we proved them wrong. We found humor designed to ease people's pain, a laughter shared by Palestinian street kids and Israeli Holocaust survivors alike. And we found humor that's subversive, a way for people to stick it to their oppressors, whether they be gun-toting soldiers, hardline Islamists, or blundering officials.

And, most incredibly, we've found humor in Hebron, like shoots of grass sprouting from scorched earth. And this humor is different. It's not a weapon or a tool, a balm or a bludgeon for times of need or turmoil. It's simpler, more elemental—and possibly most resilient of all.

It's the basic, everyday laughter shared by policemen and shopkeepers, people bumping into each other as they go about their daily lives. Despite the years of discord, Israelis and Palestinians still inhabit the same world. And if they're around each other enough, whether they like it or not, they're going to laugh at many of the same things.

Is it enough laughter to solve the Israeli-Palestinian crisis once and for all? No, but it's a start—and in a place like Palestine, a little laughter goes a long way.

THE AMAZON ⟶

The cargo plane we're sitting in lurches and bucks as it hits a patch of turbulence somewhere above the Andes Mountains. Mechanical whistles and squeals unlike any we've ever heard fill the long, hollow cargo hold. I tighten the safety belt strapping me to the cargo netting and distract myself by focusing on the tiny circle of sky I can see through one of the few windows in the fuselage. Pete slips on a sleeping mask and earphones to try to nap. I consider passing the time by chatting with my seatmates, but the deafening roar of the aircraft's four propellers makes conversation difficult. Plus, I don't know what to say to them. They're all clowns.

Next to me, a lady dressed as a giant bee fiddles with her red clown nose. Across the aisle, a young woman weaves rainbow-colored pipe cleaners into her dreadlocks. Bubbles float through the cargo hold, and a bright yellow smiley-face balloon bops here and there like we're at a birthday party. Someone starts up a round of "Oh! Susanna," and others join in on kazoos. Pete's nap is a lost cause.

We're in a Peruvian Air Force cargo plane headed into the heart of the Amazon with 100 clowns, to answer a simple question: is laughter the best medicine? Yes, humor can tear nations apart and help inspire revolutions—but can it heal? Across the globe, careers have been launched, fortunes have been made, and medical practices have been transformed based on this idea—that laughter cures. To find out if that's true, Pete and I are tagging along with the hospital-clown version of a biohazard team—an elite group of buffoons and pranksters who are planning to romp, frolic, and mime through one of the most beleaguered and destitute places on earth. They're happy to have us along, on one condition: we have to become clowns ourselves.

I cross my arms and huddle down in my seat, trying to keep warm. The Peruvian Air Force, as a gesture of goodwill, arranged transportation for us. But their method of transport leaves something to be desired. Sitting on the runway back in Lima, the plane's cargo hold had been airless and stifling. Once airborne, the unheated cabin turns frigid, freezing our sweat-damp clothes. Around me, people pull out jackets and wool hats and huddle under swim towels. Shivering, I think about what my wife, Emily, said when I told her about this trip. She'd patted my arm and said, "You're not going to be a good clown." I haven't mentioned her prediction to Pete. He's been a bit distracted. Ever since we arrived in Peru a few days ago, he's been focused on inserting the words "Lake Titicaca" into as many conversations as possible.

With a stomach-roiling dip, the cargo plane begins its descent. The clowns begin to clap in unison. With a jolt and a cheer, the aircraft touches down. We've arrived in Iquitos, a city in the Peruvian rain forest. Upon landing, the cargo hold reverts to a sweltering oven. Stripping off sweaters and jackets, everyone piles out of the plane and into the Amazonian heat, the air thick with humidity. Waiting for our luggage in Iquitos's bare-bones airport, our colleagues use the baggage carts as bobsleds, pushing each other across the concourse. Others are strumming on banjos and washboards. One clown takes a rubber pig he's been pulling around on a leash and places it on the baggage carousel. Others coo and pet it lovingly as it glides by.

"I'm really having fun," exclaims Pete. I'm inclined to agree—but then again, we haven't had to put on our clown suits yet.

Our journey into the Amazon began several months earlier, when we were sitting in a grand hotel conference room in Chicago, Illinois, listening to a welcome speech presented by a sock puppet.

"Welcome to the Annual Association for Applied and Therapeutic Humor Conference," said the sock puppet, attached to the hand of AATH president Chip Lutz, sweeping its googly eyes around the several hundred people in attendance—men in loud Hawaiian shirts, women in sparkly flapper dresses. "The sock puppet has good eye contact," noted Pete.

Shenanigans like this are par for the course at the AATH conference, one of the oldest and largest gatherings associated with the therapeutic humor movement. At an evening cocktail reception, where we mingled with social workers, nurses, doctors, and professional speakers from all over the world, a typical icebreaker was, "Are you a Certified Laughter Leader?" Perusing the AATH conference store, we found table upon table covered with books like *Laughter: The Drug of Choice, This Is Your Brain on Joy*, and *What's So Funny about . . . Diabetes?* Nearby stalls offered up water balloon launchers, light-up detachable ears, and bumper stickers that read, "Clowning for Jesus." One afternoon, I stepped into a hotel elevator with a woman who had what looked like a butterfly sprouting from her head. "Nice wings," I said. She looked at me like I was a pervert.

Considering the current enthusiasm for therapeutic humor, it's easy to forget that for most of recorded history, humor and health were considered to have nothing to do with one another. The ancient Greek founders of Western medicine had a whole lot to say about all sorts of therapeutic concepts, but were noticeably silent on laughter's role in health, other than a stern warning that those plagued by too much mirth should take up a steady diet of boring lectures.[1]

Everything changed, however, with the publication in 1979 of *Anatomy of an Illness as Perceived by the Patient*, journalist Norman Cousins's account of laughing away a possibly fatal degenerative disease of the joints with a steady diet of *Candid Camera* and Marx Brothers films. As Cousins wrote in his bestseller, "I was greatly elated by the discovery that there is a physiologic basis for the ancient theory that laughter is good medicine."[2]

He wasn't the only one excited about his discovery. Since then, a booming industry has sprung up around the idea of healthy humor. Clown programs, comedy carts, and humor rooms have become common hospital elements. A variety of therapeutic humor conferences and consulting businesses compete with AATH in the business of teaching people how to infuse trauma and tragedy with humor.

And then there's laughter yoga, a movement that now involves 16,000 laughter clubs in 72 countries, offering people the world over a chance to chuckle their way to physical and mental health. To experience laughter yoga for ourselves, Pete and I had stopped by one of the weekly meetings of the Denver Laughter Club. In a downtown Unitarian church, we joined a dozen or so club members being led by two so-called laughter leaders ("Jovial Jeff" and "Crazy Karen") through a surreal chain of exercises. We began with "greeting laughter," moving around the room and shaking each other's hands with a hearty, forced chuckle. Then we carried on extended conversations in nothing but gibberish, and imitated lawn sprinklers while others pretended to run through our spray. Other drills followed—"bumper-car laughter," "happy pills," "laughter bombs"— each designed to encourage so much fake laughter that everyone broke down for real. At one point, I passed an imaginary laughter bong to a gray-haired grandmother, from which she took a deep drag and burst out cackling.

"I do feel more energized than I did an hour ago," admitted Pete when it was over. I, on the other hand, felt like I'd gone through a trial run for living in a loony bin. Still, the regulars, a welcoming and normal-seeming bunch, seemed to be getting a lot out of it. "You don't need stand-up comedy or movies or plays," one of them told us. "You can just laugh."

That's the point, said Madan Kataria, the doctor who developed laughter yoga in 1995 and is now recognized internationally as the "Guru of Giggling." When I reached him via Skype in his home base of Mumbai, India, he told me, "Laughter was always conditional and dependent on jokes, comedy, life happenings. For the first time, in laughter yoga, laughter has been disconnected from our daily lives, because there are often not enough reasons to laugh. My discovery was that laughing without reason was enough to give people benefits."

According to Kataria, those benefits include decreased stress, better immune-system function, improved cardiovascular health, enhanced mental states, stronger social ties, and a more spiritual approach to life. Those are far from humor's only purported medical benefits, which have expanded far beyond anything ever suggested by Cousins, who passed away in 1990. These days, you can find claims that laughter and humor relieve headaches, provide good exercise, ward off coughs and colds, lower blood pressure, prevent heart disease, mitigate arthritis pain, ameliorate ulcers, vanquish insomnia, combat allergies and asthma, prolong life spans, protect against AIDS, and help cure cancer.[3] Some go so far as to suggest that clowning improves pregnancy rates for in vitro fertilization—although fair warning: if you try wearing a clown nose to bed, there might not be any fertilization.[4]

As humor has become increasingly "healthy," it's also become increasingly lucrative. While Kataria stipulates that all laughter yoga clubs must be free, he makes money from laughter leader trainings and other related enterprises, and in Bangalore, India, he's now building the first of what he hopes are many Laughter Universities. At the AATH conference in Chicago, the schedule was packed not just with seminars titled "How to Establish an Intergenerational Laughter Club" and "Holy Hysterics: Laughter and Joy in Your Community of Faith," but also "How to Turn Laughter into Revenue." Many of the attendees had figured out how to do that. At the conference's ritzy awards dinner, a signed portrait of comedian Red Skelton—which resembled one of those bad clown paintings you find at the back of a thrift store—was auctioned off for more than $1,600.

Is all this attention and investment worth it? For his book *The Psychology of Humor*, Rod Martin looked into the matter, reviewing the dozens of scientific studies dealing with humor and physical health. What he found was far from encouraging. As he puts it, "Those who advocate humor and laughter as a pathway to better health seem to have moved too quickly to promote their views on the basis of rather flimsy research evidence." So far, none of the most common claims about humor and laughter—that they boost immune-system function, stave off various illnesses, and decrease heart-disease risk—have been substantiated by rock-solid research findings. Some studies have found the opposite—that laughter and humor appeared to decrease empirical indicators of good health.[5]

Ten years ago, to settle the matter once and for all, a professor from the Norwegian University of Science and Technology named Sven Svebak included a brief sense-of-humor questionnaire in one of the largest public-health studies ever performed: the HUNT-2 study, in which members of the entire adult population of the county of Nord-Trøndelag in central Norway were surveyed about their blood pressure, body-mass index, various illness symptoms, and overall health satisfaction. According to Martin, it was "the largest correlational study of senses of humor and health ever conducted." In 2004, Svebak and his colleagues unveiled the results: there was no connection at all between sense of humor and any objective health measures.[6]

"Well, we have anecdotal evidence that humor helps with cancer patients," argued one nurse at the AATH conference when confronted about such research. Sure, replied Pete, "But we also have anecdotal evidence that supports the existence of ESP."

Still, Pete wasn't willing to write off humor's healing effects just yet. That likely had something to do with his relationship with psychologist and "joyologist" Steve Wilson. Founder of the Ohio-based World Laughter Tour therapeutic laughter program, Wilson has been working in humor and health for more than 25 years, and he held court at the Chicago conference in his polka-dot clown hat like a wise old Jedi master. He was eager to welcome us into the fold, since he's known Pete for years. When Pete was pursuing his PhD from Ohio State University, Wilson and his wife, Pam, welcomed him into their family.

Understanding humor and its therapeutic benefits, Steve Wilson told us, isn't as simple as taking saliva samples and comparing blood-pressure readings. "We don't claim any cures," he said. "If we have to claim anything, it is adjunctive therapy. It is something that a person can engage in to help a primary treatment work better. The secret to a happy life is balance. If you are running away from humor and laughter all the time, you are going to miss the balance."

Maybe Wilson was right. But we weren't going to take his word for it. To find out for ourselves, we decided to track down the most famous hospital clown of all.

At the end of the 1998 Hollywood blockbuster *Patch Adams*, in which Robin Williams portrays real-life clown-doctor Hunter "Patch" Adams and his attempt to inject compassion and humor into the American medical system, the audience is told that Patch ends up launching a medical practice that treats patients without payment, malpractice insurance, or conventional health facilities, just as he always dreamed, and that construction of his world-changing "Gesundheit! Hospital" is under way.

What the movie never says is that after twelve years of operation, Patch's medical practice shut down because of doctor burnout and lack of resources. Raising the millions needed to complete the Gesundheit! Hospital in West Virginia has proven next to impossible. To help raise attention to his cause, Patch and his colleagues launched Gesundheit Global Outreach, an international service organization that has sent clown brigades to 60 countries on six continents. Since 2005, Gesundheit Global Outreach has focused much of its attention on one venture in particular: an annual, multiweek project involving international clown groups, government organizations, and NGOs, all focused on helping the community of Belén, a slum on the edge of the Peruvian city of Iquitos that's one of the most impoverished communities in the Amazon. The Belén project is one of the largest and most ambitious international clown endeavors anywhere.

Which is why we're standing in the lobby of our hotel in Iquitos, a building that has been overrun by clowns. The building has become the Belén project's makeshift headquarters. All around us, folks are in their clown costumes, ready for the first activity of this year's endeavor: a celebratory parade into the heart of Belén. Meanwhile, Patch Adams is standing at the front of the crowd, lecturing on the dangers of sunburn.

"Put on sunblock!" demands Patch, gesturing for emphasis with the rubber fish in his hand. "Here's what happens if you don't: 'Ow, ow, ow!'" He cringes in mock agony, rubbing at a make-believe sunburn all over his body.

This is the latest in a long list of instructions Pete and I have been given about joining the Amazonian clown brigade. John Glick, one of

Patch's closest friends and the calm-and-composed director of Gesundheit Global Outreach, was happy to have us along when I first
contacted him. But he warned me, "Organizing clowns is like herding
kittens." That meant we were in for a lot of organizing. Soon we were
receiving e-mail after e-mail detailing all the things we'd have to do
to get ready for the trip. Make sure your vaccinations are up to date
for all third-world communicable diseases, we were told, which led
me to spend a colorful morning at my local travel health clinic, learning all the unpleasant yet fascinating ways my body could implode in
the middle of the Amazon. ("You don't want any diseases that end
with 'osis,'" I was instructed. "'Osis' means 'worm.'") Then we were
schooled in the basics of Amazonian "clown fashion," the more colorful, garish, and humidity-friendly the outfit, the better. For starters,
Pete and I raided thrift-store racks of their most outlandish Hawaiian shirts. Then my five-year-old son, Gabriel, decided to contribute
one of his prized possessions: He offered up his extra-large polka-dot
dress-up tie, solemnly handing it over like it was one of the Crown
Jewels.

Last but not least, we were told to get clown noses. "The nose
is your most important feature," noted one of the organizers in an
e-mail. "Your magic. Your power. Your passport into the world. It
opens doors for you and allows you to do things you never imagined
yourself doing."

I had no idea what the organizer meant, but I was referred to
someone who would: Jeff Semmerling, a Chicago-based mask maker
who crafts noses by hand for Gesundheit and similar organizations.
Semmerling, I was told, is the Ralph Lauren of red schnozzes.

"Some say the clown nose is the most evolved mask," said Semmerling when I called him in Chicago a few weeks before our trip.
It's so simple and elegant—slip a red bulb over your nose, and people
the world over know you're a clown. Semmerling offers a catalogue
of nearly two dozen varieties in neoprene and leather, from rotund
bulbs to diminutive nose caps to elongated missiles. Since I couldn't
choose, I sent Semmerling photos of Pete and myself and asked him
to do the honors. He selected a big round nose for me and a large
button cap for Pete, then sent them along with a warning: "Don't be

surprised what you might find yourself doing or becoming when you release your clown."

And now here we are, at the start of the parade into Belén, red noses on and ready to release our clowns. Everyone is far too hot and sweaty here to bother with clown makeup, although many never paint their faces at all. "The face is more open without the paint, thus allowing more intimacy," Glick tells us. "Plus it tends to freak out the clown-phobes less." Patch is nearby, and he seems to notice my apprehension. He catches my eye and grins like a maniac. "Are you ready to go nuts?"

With a cacophonous eruption of drums, whistles, and the blaring horns of a Peruvian Navy marching band that's volunteered to lead the parade, we're off. A rainbow-colored river of tutus, suspenders, and baggy tie-dyed pants streams through Iquitos—a city whose existence here doesn't make a whole lot of sense. While Peru is most commonly associated with llamas, mountaintop ruins, and other images of the Andes, a good 60 percent of the country is taken up by the jungle fed by the gargantuan Amazon River system. And here, in the heart of this vast, nearly uninhabited wilderness, lies a city of half a million people where no city of half a million people should be. Iquitos is the largest community in the world that doesn't have any roads to it. The only way to get here is the way we did, via aircraft. Or you can take a long, slow boat ride.

The city blossomed here because it was an epicenter for the rubber boom of the late nineteenth and early twentieth centuries. But that golden age has come and gone. Now grimy three-wheeled motor taxis clog the streets, and the city's grand European-style river promenade is decorated with billboards demanding "No child sex tourism." The rubber barons' once-opulent, porticoed mansions have been gutted, their interiors filled with grocery stores and curio shops.

But the shabbiness of downtown Iquitos resembles Beverly Hills compared to what comes next. The parade route makes a left at an intersection, snakes past a fragrant open market, and slopes downhill toward the river. The street becomes a packed-earth lane lined with open-air sewage ditches, and the brick and cement buildings shift to thatch-roofed wooden shanties perched on ten-foot-tall stilts or resting on horizontal logs lashed together like rafts. We've reached the slums of Belén. The 60,000 inhabitants, we've been told, live in destitution. Rampant unemployment. Minimal electricity and no sanitation system. Spotty health care and extensive malnutrition. Widespread alcoholism and drug use. Wide-ranging family violence and crime, with no official police presence.

Each year, during the rainy season between January and June, the river here rises several meters, which is why the houses are built on stilts and rafts. But this year, the area experienced 100-year floods. Marching past the stilt-legged homes of Belén, we can see water stains and washed-away paint reaching halfway up the houses' walls, marking where a few months earlier, the buildings were half-submerged. Scores were killed, and hundreds more were forced out of the area, relocated to schools and shelters. When they returned, they found new disease epidemics taking hold, including dengue fever and leptospirosis.

In other words, we're in the poorest part of the poorest part of a country that's fairly poor to begin with. And right now, this situation is worse than ever.

Stomping down these dusty streets, something happens to me. Maybe it's the beat of the parade music, or the infectious glee of 100 marching fools. Maybe it's the delighted smiles of the barefoot children who flock to us, or the shy grins and waves from the adults who peer down from the porches of their homes. Maybe it's just heatstroke. For whatever the reason, I begin to clown.

I traipse past throngs of onlookers, slapping high fives left and right. I chase children beneath the buildings, leaping over the sewage ditches and weaving through support beams. In the hazy afternoon light, I dance with other clowns as a loudspeaker jerry-rigged to a motor taxi blasts the clown expedition's theme song: an up-tempo tune about washing your hands to prevent dying from dengue fever. At one point, a little girl in a purple shirt takes my hand, and she never lets go. We march through Belén, side by side, and eventually I'm carrying her in my arms.

When it's all over, when the parade music wraps up and the purple-shirted girl scampers away with a smile and a wave, Pete looks at me and grins. "Your dad training is coming out." Pete, in his goofy floppy hat and shiny red nose, didn't do too badly himself.

"That place came alive," he says as we trudge back to the hotel. "You see the difference, with all the smiles and laughter." On the other hand, he adds, "What a monumental problem this is. You need millions of dollars to help Belén. You essentially have to move the whole city."

"It's worse than I ever expected," he concludes. How can a bunch of clowns ever hope to make a difference?

Clowning in the Amazon, it turns out, is like summer camp—if summer camp came with a moderate risk of malaria.

There are "clownings" all over Belén and other spots around the city, including an old-folks' home, a shelter for abandoned children, even a local prison (don't bring your "stabby" toys, prison-bound clowns are warned). Some activities involve teaching kids how to hula-hoop, make shadow puppets, and bang out rhythms on plastic-bucket drums. Others take the form of door-to-door clown interventions, hammering the importance of throwing away trash and tossing out stagnant water through pratfalls and squirt-gun gags. Many clownings are just about gathering up a group of street kids and having fun.

While most of the 100-clown squad are in their twenties, many among this assortment of college students, social workers, nurses, and professional circus performers are still relative old-timers, coolly reminiscing about Belén escapades from years past. ("Remember that time Levi and David had stolen earrings planted in their luggage in El Salvador and had to spend a week in prison before paying off the right officials? Those were the days!") Others are newcomers, timid and awkward, trying to find their standing among the clown pecking order.

Complicating matters are the different clown styles among the group, far more than we knew existed. The South American clowns, from professional squads in Peru and Argentina, are practiced and polished, with carefully tailored jester costumes and refined routines.

They're the New York Yankees of clowns. And then there's us, the ragtag Americans under Patch Adams.

For the Gesundheit clowns, many of whom have never clowned before, there are no crash courses in buffooning, no how-to handbooks or ironclad rules. Patch doesn't believe in it. "It's too restricting," he says. "I don't want any mystique about it. I want everybody to be a love revolutionary." He's less like the group's leader and more like a very bad influence, delegating logistics to others so he can focus on the work of play. After growing up as a troubled, bullied kid, Patch says that one day in high school, "I decided to serve humanity and be happy the rest of my life." He's been clowning every day since then—clowning through med school, clowning during the twelve-year operation of the Gesundheit! Clinic, and now clowning all over the world.

He's doing so in Iquitos and Belén, clowning everywhere we look. One moment, he's eating lunch at a ceviche restaurant wearing underpants on his head. The next, he's sauntering down the street sporting a face-distorting set of false teeth beneath his handlebar mustache. Later, he's chasing after squealing children with his half-gray, half-blue ponytail flapping in the wind, stopping only to wrap up elderly ladies in big, sweaty hugs.

During what turns out to be one of many long, rambling conversations I have with Patch, I discover formal clown training isn't the only thing he doesn't believe in. He doesn't believe in the cold, corporate machinations of Western medicine, or much else about capitalism. He doesn't believe in computers, instead responding to each of the hundreds of monthly letters he gets by hand. He doesn't believe in organized religion, preferring the more basic spirituality of love and compassion. He doesn't believe in traditional family structures, figuring we'd all be better off living in communes. And he doesn't believe that humanity has much chance of long-term survival. "Nothing I've studied suggests we will stop our extinction soon," he tells me, scratching at the underpants he's wearing on his head. "Humans are an embarrassment."

There's one other thing Patch doesn't believe in. "I never said laughter is the best medicine," he declares the first time we talk. Instead, he believes the key to a healthy life is connected, loving relationships with anyone and everyone, and he sees humor as the perfect tool to break down the social mores, boundaries, and anxieties that often get in the way. After all, he points out, clowns are all about shaking things up: "The jester is the only person in the king's court who can call the king an asshole."

It's true. Clowns, like comedians, are outsiders and rebels. All over the world and through most of civilization, clowns, jesters, tricksters, and picaros have stood apart from the crowd, with full license to break all the rules. They can spit in the face of conformity. They can say what no one else dares to say.

Maybe that's why in the United States, the image of the clown is now often associated with the dark and the scary, a staple of haunted-house rides and serial killer stories. After all, the chaotic and disorderly nature of clowns can be frightening. (It doesn't help that in the 1970s, two different amateur clown performers—Paul Kelly, aka "Weary Willie," and John Wayne Gacy, aka "Pogo the Clown"— killed multiple people.)[7] A few years ago, a study at the University of Sheffield in England found that 250 children, aged four to sixteen, all believed clown images were too scary for hospital décor.[8] Of course, there's a difference between a clown painting on the wall when you're trying to sleep in a hospital ward and a real clown face peeking around your door during visiting hours, wanting to know if you want to play. Maybe that's why a follow-up study at a British children's hospital found that children, their parents, doctors, and nurses all agreed that clown interventions at the facility were beneficial.[9]

The rebellious nature of clowning is likely why, maybe for the first time ever, my wife is wrong. I'm not a bad clown. I throw myself into games of hide-and-seek and jump-rope contests, play peeka-boo with giggling babies, and chase rumbling taxis down the street like a maniac. After one of the clownings, Gesundheit director John Glick approaches me. "You've got it, man," he says with a grin. "You are a regular Patch." I soak up the compliment, not minding that I'm drenched in sweat and probably sewage, that my mouth feels like it's been sandblasted, that I look like a fool. Jeff Semmerling was right: the red nose gave license to my clown, stripping away all the hang-ups I've accumulated over the years.

The best part of my clown costume, the biggest hit among the youth of Belén, is the clown tie loaned to me by my son Gabriel. The children never tire of tugging on it, of using it to lead me around like I'm a pet buffoon on a leash. Their love of this game makes sense. These children are some of the most put-upon, least-powerful people in the world. And thanks to a clown costume, they have complete power over a grown white American man. Their world is turned upside down.

Pete gets into the action, too, albeit from a different direction. Because these projects are all about clowns letting loose their inner child in environments that are none too hospitable to any kind of children, someone has to be there to look out for them, to make sure they don't fall into sewage pits or pass out from dehydration or get kidnapped by Amazonian gangsters. Someone who thrives on responsibility and order, someone who's always thinking about what might go wrong. So Pete retires his red nose and becomes one of the civilian guides assigned to watch over the clowns.

Pete comes along as one of the civilian guides when we travel to a mental hospital on the outskirts of Iquitos one afternoon. While most of us clown around in a tree-dotted courtyard, dancing and playing catch with giggling patients, Pete shadows a blue-haired Argentinian clown named Ramiro as he explores the hospital's rudimentary living quarters. In a bare, dingy room, Ramiro finds an old woman cowering in her bed, covers drawn over her face. As Pete watches from a window, Ramiro sits on the edge of her bed and begins playing his harmonica. After a while, he stops. "Move your foot if you like the music," he says in Spanish. A foot wiggles beneath the blanket. He continues to play.

This continues for 30, 40 minutes—Pete watching from the window, Ramiro playing his harmonica, the woman lying in her bed. As time passes, a face emerges from beneath the blanket. Finally, when it's time to go, the woman rises from the bed and clasps Ramiro in a long, silent hug.

Later, when we all meet for a debriefing session at an open-air bar near our hotel, Pete raises his hand to speak. "I didn't know a lot about clowns before I came here. But I saw a lot of beautiful things today." His voice cracks with emotion. "What you're doing is really important."

A big, matronly Argentinian clown named Lorena leaps from her seat and wraps Pete in her arms. *"Bienvenidos al grupo de payasos,"* she says as she squeezes him tight. "Welcome to our clown family."

About halfway through the trip, Pete and I realize we're having a lot of fun. And that doesn't make any sense.

We're not grumbling about the lack of fresh vegetables in our repetitive meals of fried fish and hamburgers. Or the *National Geographic*–worthy world of critters that infest our beds each night. Or that our hotel room is draped with sweat-damp clothes that never fully dry in the sticky heat.

"If this were just the two of us . . ." I say to Pete one morning.

". . . we'd be freakin' miserable," he replies, finishing my sentence.

But it's not just the two of us—we're surrounded by people even more crazily upbeat than we are. The clowns here are not at all like the hammy, squirting-flower bozos we'd imagined, the sort of clock-punching performers who transform into beaten-down old men once their clown shifts are over. Instead, they're as energetic and loving and generous as a company of young evangelicals, never ceasing to clown around with everyone they see. So why aren't we all miserable? Maybe it's because we're too busy clowning around to focus on how miserable we should be. Humor and coping, after all, seem to go hand in hand. Successful humor inspires all sorts of positive feelings and emotions, which can act as a psychological buffer when things go wrong. Not only that, but as we've learned, humor is all about shifting one's perspective, reassessing situations, and, as Pete would say, transforming violations into benign violations. So by cracking jokes about our Peruvian bedbugs and gross clown clothes, we'd found the perfect way to keep our spirits up, not to mention defuse what would otherwise be a total bummer.

Over the years, several compelling studies have suggested that these theories aren't just theories, that humor and coping really are intertwined. In one especially touching experiment, researchers interviewed a group of widowers six months after the death of their spouses. Those able to smile and laugh about their marriage during this time of lingering sadness had fewer problems with grief and depression in the years that followed.[10]

There's also evidence connecting humor and coping from the USS *Pueblo* incident in North Korea, courtesy of all those POWs flashing Hawaiian peace signs at their captors. When researchers examined the 82 survivors once they'd been released from captivity, they found that those who best handled the ordeal relied on a variety of defense mechanisms such as faith, denial, and, yes, humor.[11]

This research is a step in the right direction, says Pete, but when it comes to data like this from the real world, there's a hitch: none of it proves that humor is a coping mechanism. These studies are correlational. It's unclear whether the humor helped people cope with their hardships, or whether the people who were already better equipped to cope with adversity had an easier time joking about their problems.

That's why psychology researchers are turning to wonderfully devious lab experiments to untangle the relationship between humor and coping. In one study, researchers had participants narrate a thirteen-minute safety video featuring dramatized versions of grisly wood-mill accidents. Those asked to come up with a humorous narration reported less stress afterward than those who described it seriously, and readings of skin conductance, heart rate, and skin temperature suggested the comic narrators were less physiologically stressed, too. (Unfortunately, the subsequent paper didn't include examples of how the narrators came up with quips about industrial ripsaws.)[12]

Not surprisingly, sadistic research like this appeals to Pete. He's especially interested in what he calls humorous complaining. As we know, tragedies big and small can lead to comedy, so humor can be a common outcome of stuff worth grumbling about—a missed flight, an unfair parking ticket, a crummy meal at a high-priced restaurant. Pete, in collaboration with graduate students Christina Kan and Caleb Warren, scrutinized hundreds of business ratings on Yelp.com. They found that negative reviews, especially those accompanying one-star ratings, were rated by other consumers to be significantly funnier than positive reviews. But Pete believes griping in a humorous way is not only natural, it's beneficial. It makes the complainer feel better than if they just grumbled negatively, and it makes other people feel better about the complainer, too. Pete is hoping to prove this by subjecting people to painful situations and having them complain humorously about it. While research is still in progress, all I know is that when Pete had me stick my hand in a bucket of ice water for five minutes, all the going-down-with-the-*Titanic* jokes I cracked didn't stop my right pinkie from feeling numb for weeks.[13]

We don't need any buckets of ice water here in Peru to appreciate the connection between humor and coping. We see it everywhere thanks to all the clowns. Their shenanigans don't just help the residents of Belén deal with their problems. They help the clowns cope, too.

Gesundheit Global Outreach director Glick is the yin to Patch Adams's yang. While Patch is rowdy and provocative, Glick is gentle and serene. There's always a peaceful smile below his well-worn clown nose, always a few supportive words to pass along. He's so full of bliss that we're surprised when Patch summons everyone to the hotel lobby one night for a special "clown healing" for Glick. It's only once everyone has arranged themselves in a wide circle in the lobby and Glick stands in the center that I notice that Glick's right hand is trembling. The problems started four years ago, he tells us, his smile never fading. "Something funny happened with my hand," he says, gazing at his shaking fingers. He asked a neurologist friend what was going on. The man looked him in the eyes and said, "This is Parkinson's disease."

As a physician and acupuncturist, Glick had worked with people with Parkinson's, people who couldn't keep still, who couldn't talk, couldn't swallow. "What is it like in there?" he wonders out loud. "Trapped inside this body that won't let you do what you want it to do?" I look over at Patch and realize he's weeping, wiping his eyes on the sleeve of his fluorescent-colored shirt.

"There are two of me now," continues Glick. "My ego is on this side," he says, pointing to his left side, the side that doesn't shake. "I am in control here. I like to be in control. I've spent my whole life wanting to be in more control." But, he adds with a smile, "My shaking side has a different agenda. My shaking side tells me to let go. My shaking side says, 'This is my soul.' And what happens when I let go is Patch comes to me." He looks at his old friend. "And Santiago comes to me." He glances at another clown in the circle. "And Paula and Kelly and Anya and David and Shlomo and Levi . . ." He looks in turn at each clown. There's hardly a dry eye in the room.

Patch enters the circle and places his arms on Glick's shoulders. "I think clowning is special healing magic," he says. And he wants us to give Glick some of that magic all at once. "Like electrocution."

Patch has Glick lie on the floor and asks everyone to crowd in close, resting their hands on his arms, legs, head, all over his body. Then Patch and others begin to sing: "Amazing grace, how sweet the sound . . ." Here's Patch Adams, a guy who doesn't believe in religion, belting out one of the most impassioned versions of "Amazing Grace" I've ever heard.

When the song is over, there's one last procedure to perform. "Wiggle your fingers at Glick," Patch commands. "Boogiewoogiewoogie!" holler 100 clowns, waggling away.

"That," concludes Patch, "is clown healing."

I **don't see** it coming. No one does. On our last day in the Amazon, there's a full-fledged clown emergency. And I'm stuck in the middle of it.

In the world of Gesundheit, Carl Hammerschlag looms large. Two decades ago, Hammerschlag, a six-foot-six Yale-trained psychiatrist, heard Patch speak at a dental conference, and he's been clowning with the man ever since. Here in the Amazon, the 73-year-old Hammerschlag, who's more often than not wearing a pink tutu and tights, has assumed the role of "street psychiatrist." He's assembled a rag-tag group of clowns who in their normal lives work in therapy, nursing, chiropractic, and other health professions, and he's staging medical clinics in various neighborhoods devastated by the flooding.

That morning in Iquitos, I tag along with Hammerschlag's clinic, dressed in my now-well-worn clown outfit. A squadron of motor taxis deposits us at our location for the day: Punchana, a poor neighborhood at the edge of Iquitos hard hit by the floods. As a gray, overcast sky looms overhead, we make our way down rutted, muddy streets strewn with trash and debris, past houses bowing precariously on waterlogged stilts. In some places, homes have collapsed altogether. The scene resembles a war zone.

We set up shop in Punchana's central plaza: a bedraggled, puddle-strewn square of dirt with rough-hewn soccer goals at each end. Another organization is working here, too, a grassroots veterinary clinic. Families begin to wander in—far more than expected. Crowds press in tightly around the volunteers handing out free vitamins. Therapists struggle to find a quiet corner to host ten-minute, one-on-one therapy sessions with residents. The air is filled with the howls of local dogs being spayed and neutered in full view in the veterinary tent. The situation is spiraling out of control, and it's made worse by the dozens upon dozens of children lured to the plaza by the commotion, running about and getting in everyone's way.

"Somebody's gotta do something about the kids," says Hammerschlag in his deep, commanding voice. He looks to the only two clowns who aren't working at the clinic: me, and an older guy named Mark. We know what we have to do.

On the far side of the plaza, we get to work. As nearly 100 children gather about, I pull out every gag, game, and prank from my limited bag of clown tricks. I dash about the square, splashing through the mud as I grab squealing tykes around the waist and lug them under my arm like I'm running a football play down the field. I stage bullfights with my ratty handkerchief, hollering, *"Toro! Toro!"* as I twirl about the charging tykes. I borrow another clown's face-painting crayons and begin decorating forearms, the children crushing around me and demanding in Spanish for their tattoo of choice: *"Flor!" "Mariposa!" "Anaconda!" "Corazón!"*

Eventually, Mark and I scramble onto a nearby porch and begin fashioning rudimentary balloon animals. We assemble endless flowers, swords, and poodles and toss them to the screaming horde below, working until our bag of 100-plus balloons is empty. And still, the children keep coming. And coming. And coming.

Three hours later, as the clinic winds down and the tidal wave of kids subsides, my clown clothes are in tatters. My Hawaiian shirt is ripped beyond repair; my polka-dot tie dangles from my neck, having been yanked far too many times. I should be exhausted, but I'm also elated.

Hammerschlag comes up to me. "That was a stroke of clown genius," he exclaims, beaming. We kept the kids occupied, but we also did something else: "You presented the message that in the middle of all this trauma, we can still find a way to play."

Just as my clowning in Punchana worked in conjunction with the efforts of the medical clinic, Pete's come to believe that humor is most helpful when it's combined with other approaches to health. Maybe it's a doctor working a few jokes into a checkup routine, or a hospital integrating a clown program into its children's ward, or people weaving a good sense of humor into a lifestyle geared toward happiness and well-being. It's like how physicians recommend exercise and a nutritious diet as part of a healthy daily routine. Maybe it's time they start telling their patients to have a little more fun in their lives.

"Humor is not the only tool," concludes Pete, "but it is an important tool in the tool kit." It's a lesson we'll take home with us from the Amazon—along with potentially something else.

Not long after we depart Peru, we receive a message from John Rock, one of the Gesundheit organizers. Apparently right after we left, skin rashes and excessive itching broke out among the clowns who remained, causing dozens to be quarantined.

"You probably have scabies," Rock tells us. "Clowns are the best!"

A week after we return from the Amazon, Pete gets a call from the police. His mother, Kathleen, has been found dead in her home in New Jersey.

The news is sudden, but not unexpected. Pete's mom had been in and out of hospitals for years, struggling with pain and health problems, and rejected nearly all attempts at help. As Pete would put it in her obituary, "Kathy lived life the way she wanted, with determination and spirit." As a single mother, that tenacity helped her survive and rubbed off on her only son, inspiring him to pursue his own idiosyncratic route in life. But it also made her increasingly difficult to get along with. By the time of her death, Pete had become her primary caregiver, as no one else in his family maintained regular contact with her.

"Taking care of my mom has been one of my biggest challenges, and it's also one of the things I'm most proud of," Pete tells me. Even though she lived nearly 2,000 miles away, she was always in the back of his mind, like a stereo speaker that always has a slight, constant hum, whether or not music is playing. That hum could be concerns that surfaced at night as he lay in bed, or a voice mail message from her on his phone that might or might not be bad news. "And now," he tells me, "for better and worse, that hum is gone."

In lieu of a funeral, Pete flies to New Jersey to scatter his mother's ashes at her favorite beach, accompanied by his sister Shannon. Pete shares a similar and sometimes twisted sense of humor with his sister, which came in handy during a childhood that wasn't always easy. And it comes in handy now. During their drive from their mother's house to the Jersey Shore, the two crack up over shared memories, like how for family trips to the beach, their mother would pack their Ford Pinto so full of coolers, umbrellas, and boogie boards it was a wonder there was any space left for the three of them. Or how, to save money, their mother often wouldn't buy admission tags for her kids to play at the shore, which meant that whenever she'd spot beach employees wandering down the sand, she'd send Pete and Shannon into the ocean and tell them to stay there until the workers were out of sight.

When Pete and Shannon arrive at the beach that day, they stand at the water's edge on a quiet stretch of sand, taking turns sprinkling ashes into the waves. Pete also tosses in a colorful bracelet he purchased in Peru, a present he was unable to give his mom. It's a quiet, tearful moment, but then Pete gets a sudden urge to lighten the mood.

"Make sure you get everything," he tells his sister as she scatters the remaining ashes. "Don't leave behind a toe."

"That was wrong, but it was funny," Pete tells me later. They both needed the levity, and it helped make for what turned out to be a touching and pleasant afternoon.

Pete doesn't feel bad about using jokes to help him deal with his grief. If there's one thing our time in the Amazon with a bunch of clowns has taught us, it's that in difficult situations, humor can help.

No, laughter can't live up to all the claims put forward by Norman Cousins and his disciples. It's not going to reverse a degenerative disease, stop a heart attack, or cure cancer. But while science doesn't yet support the idea that humor improves people's physical health, there is evidence that it improves emotional health. As we've found, it helps people cope with their problems, it distracts from dispiriting thoughts, it creates an escape from what ails you, whether that be the loss of a loved one, a diagnosis of Parkinson's, a lifetime of suffering in a place like Belén, or just a crummy day. While that's not the same as lowering blood pressure or jump-starting the immune system, improving your outlook can be a good thing.

Yes, says Pete, Patch is right: laughter is not the best medicine. But he's convinced that laughter *is* medicine, even if it's not the best.

That's why I plan to keep my clown nose handy. Just in case of emergencies.

Backstage at the Comedy Nest, an upscale comedy club in downtown Montreal, we're a world away from the Denver dive bar where we launched our adventure more than a year ago. But everything about this place feels strangely similar. There's the same sort of audience filling in around the stage, ready to cheer on those who make them laugh—and skewer those who don't. Around back in the cramped greenroom, there's the same sort of nervy pre-show energy. Comedians pace back and forth, saying little, while others slouch on a well-worn couch, sipping coffee and rehashing their routines. No one touches the meager basket of tortilla chips and plastic cup of salsa the club's manager has placed on a counter.

I can hardly sit still. I meander about the club, trying to gauge the vibe of the crowd, then wander backstage. Pete sits alone at the far end of the greenroom, illuminated by the harsh white bulbs of a row of makeup mirrors. He's staring off into space as he prepares to go up on stage—his second official attempt at stand-up. Once again, he's wearing a sweater vest.

As we'd planned, we'd finagled our way onto the lineup for the Montreal's Just For Laughs comedy festival, the largest comedy event in the world. So far, no one has given us interlopers much notice—but that might soon change. The month-long festival involves hundreds of comedy shows, seminars, live podcast tapings, and film screenings at venues big and small all across Montreal. Tonight, the last night of the festival, the theme at the Comedy Nest is "As Seen on TV." According to a sign on the wall, the comics who'll be performing have all appeared on programs such as the *Late Show with David Letterman*, *The Tonight Show with Jay Leno*, and *Conan*. On the shuttle ride over from our hotel, a sitcom casting director tagging along to scope out the talent asked Pete what he'd been on. He had to think about it. "I was once on Channel 9 in Denver!" She wasn't impressed.

Pete has spent much of the day by himself, going through his routine in our hotel room while I explored Montreal. Later, as we got ready for the night's big event, he said to me, "If someone had told me two years ago that one of my biggest talks ever would be at the Comedy Nest at the Just For Laughs festival, I wouldn't have believed them." He's taught hundreds of classes and presented in front of conference audiences numbering in the thousands. But something about the 80 or so people who can fit into the Comedy Nest feels so much more intimidating, so much more difficult.

"I've been thinking about the clown noses we wore in Peru," Pete had told me, looking at the outfit he'd laid out for himself on his hotel bed. "When you put on the clown nose, you are the clown. When I put on this sweater vest, I'll be a moderately funny professor."

And now the professor's here in the Comedy Nest greenroom, sweater vest on, minutes away from determining just how humorous he is. A Just For Laughs staffer armed with a clipboard approaches. "When do you want the red light?"

"Red light?" Pete looks bewildered.

The red light is the signal that your time on stage is almost up, explains Debra DiGiovanni, a bubbly comic who's the night's MC. A veteran of *Last Comic Standing* and one of Canada's top female comedians, DiGiovanni takes one look at Pete and out come her maternal instincts. "Have you done any other shows?" she asks him.

"No."

"Really, no other shows here in Montreal?"

Pete clarifies himself. "No other shows, *period*."

The show soon gets under way. DiGiovanni takes the stage to warm up the audience before the first comic. A few minutes later, she's back in the greenroom. "This is what you call a bad crowd," she says, chuckling. Later, after she's introduced the next comedian, she revises her assessment: "They're terrible."

It's Pete's turn. "Need me to do any set-up?" asks DiGiovanni as she heads out to introduce him.

"Just make them like me," pleads Pete.

As Pete starts to follow her, I offer one last piece of advice. "This time," I say, "try not to unplug the microphone."

A couple of months earlier, Pete and I had begun preparing his routine. If our time studying what makes things funny had taught us anything, it's that good stand-up requires practice. We knew that if we'd spent the whole year honing a few choice jokes, we would have ended up with some good material. But we hadn't done that, because that wasn't the point. People already know that in comedy, hard work pays off. We wanted to prove there's another way—a method that involves a little less sweat and a little more science.

We started by making a list of all our expeditions, and what we'd learned from each about how to make things funny:

Los Angeles: Who is funny?

- → It's not whether or not you're funny, it's what kind of funny you are. Be honest and authentic.
- → It helps to be an outsider. Be skeptical, analytical, rebellious.
- → Stand-up is experimentation. Write, test, repeat.

New York: How do you make funny?

- → Since most things aren't funny, come up with a lot of ideas.
- → If solo comedy creation gets you nowhere, try the team-based approach. Two minds are better than one.
- → If you can't be "ha-ha" funny, at least be "aha!" funny. Cleverness is sometimes good enough.

Tanzania: Why do we laugh?

- → Don't be afraid to chuckle at yourself. It signals everything is okay and lets others laugh, too.

- ➤ Good comedy is a conspiracy. Create an in-group with those you want to get the joke.
- ➤ Laughter has momentum. Get the guffaws going as quickly as you can.

Japan: When is comedy lost in translation?

- ➤ Complicated comedy is subjective, but bare-bones humor is universal. In other words, keep it simple.
- ➤ Context matters. No one is going to laugh if they don't know what you're talking about.
- ➤ Know your audience. Making something broadly appealing often kills the funny.

Scandinavia: Does humor have a dark side?

- ➤ It's easier to fail than to succeed—especially as comedy goes global. Tread carefully.
- ➤ Making things funny means nearly going over the line. Learn to be a comedic tightrope artist so you don't go too far.
- ➤ Who's the butt of the joke? Comedy can victimize, so be sure it's not the person who's supposed to laugh.

Palestine: Can you find humor where you least expect it?

- ➤ Humor is hardy stuff, so no topic is off limits. It's just a matter of finding the right way to make the violations benign.
- ➤ The best comedy turns the world upside down. Make fun of yourself before others get a chance to do so.
- ➤ Laughter is disarming. Make light of the stuff everyone's worried about and you'll negate its power—not to mention win over the crowd.

The Amazon: Is laughter the best medicine?

- ➤ Comedy signals an escape from the world. Create a safe, playful space where folks are free to laugh.
- ➤ Jokes can be a coping mechanism. Don't be afraid to kid around about the harsh realities of life—people need it.
- ➤ Humor is as important to the humorist as it is to the audience. If you don't enjoy your comedy, no one else will, either.

Some of these takeaways were easy to put into action. Considering our travels, Pete and I had a lot of comedy fodder from which to choose. And as a professor scrutinizing the world of comedy, Pete was very much an outsider looking in. Plus, thanks to all we'd been through together, it was clear we had no problem coming up with material as a team.

Other rules were harder for us to implement. With our hectic schedules, it was difficult to find the time to generate joke after joke, knowing the vast majority would be nixed. Nor was it easy coming up with material dealing with taboo topics and harsh realities—stuff that toed the line—while finding a way to make it honest and authentic coming from a university professor. We also knew that to set the tone and win over the crowd, Pete would have to be confident and congenial, plus score a laugh right away. And if we hoped to play to the audience and keep things simple, both of us would have to dial back our bad habits, such as Pete's tendency to want to explain everything, and my predilection to use abstruse words.

Finally, to make sure nobody got offended, it would be best to make Pete the butt of the joke. That, we knew from experience, would be easy.

Since our checklist suggested that the best material often comes from collaborating with other humorists, once we'd pulled together a rough routine we asked a few of our comedy contacts how we could punch up our material. Be spontaneous, suggested *Last Comic Standing* winner Alonzo Bodden. As Bodden put it, "One of the illusions we project is that we just thought of the joke." Meanwhile, Jordy Ellner, director of talent and digital at Comedy Central, took all his years working with comics and distilled what he'd learned into a single word: "Smile."

Los Angeles–based comic Shane Mauss offered his own advice. "The benign violation theory might explain the basic mechanics of how a joke is done, but delivery is the practiced sleight-of-hand that makes the joke surprise and wow," he pointed out. Take our punch lines, said Mauss—the "punch," the funniest part of the joke, should always be at the end of a zinger, so Pete won't step on potential laughs.

We decided to put the routine through a test run. A week before our trip to Montreal, Pete signed up for another Denver open mike, but this event wasn't on the cutthroat stage of the Squire Lounge. Instead it was a low-key affair on the back patio of a scruffy Polish restaurant, a place known for letting comics try out material.

Surrounded by potted plants and dangling strings of all-year Christmas lights, Pete ran through his routine as a small crowd looked on. And you know what? He got laughs. A lot of laughs—significantly more than a few folks that night who'd performed at this open mike before.

A buddy of Pete's named Terry came out for the performance, just as he'd attended Pete's first stand-up attempt at the Squire Lounge. After Pete's run-through on the patio, Terry came up to me. "At the Squire, I saw a professor trying to do stand-up," he said. "But this time? I saw a comedian up there, not a professor."

Pete and I were elated. We'd done it, we believed—we'd used science to build a better comedy act. From here on out, we figured, everything would be easy.

Then we got to Montreal.

Athletics have the Olympics. Film has Cannes. Music has South by Southwest. Comedy? It has the Just For Laughs.

The night before we arrived at the festival, I had a disturbing dream. When we touched down in Montreal, even though it was July, snow was everywhere. Everyone was in parkas, sitting around roaring fires in frosted ski chalets. And here I was, freezing in my lightweight summer clothes.

"Oh, my God," I thought. "I've made a terrible mistake."

While there wasn't a snowflake at the festival, that didn't make it any less intimidating.

In the heart of Montreal, a large swath of downtown had been fenced off from cars and transformed into an open-air bacchanalia. Colossal stages showcased free dance concerts and magic shows all hours of the day and night. Quirky parades of huge pickle puppets snaked through the crowds. Giant balloon incarnations of Victor,

Just For Laugh's red-horned, green-snouted mascot, hovered over the revelry like Canadian castoffs from the Macy's Thanksgiving Day Parade. And aromatic food trucks lined the streets, offering up various international delicacies—including, I was surprised to discover, *takoyaki*, the balls of deep-fried octopus that were so huge in Osaka.

The next day, we forced ourselves awake just in time for a catered festival luncheon. "We're turning into comedians," cracked Pete. "Out of bed at noon for free food." As we prepared to leave, we discovered a letter from hotel management by our door. Don't expect much in terms of housecleaning, warned the note: labor negotiations with the city's hospitality workers had just broken down. The city was packed with a thousand comedians with something to prove, and everywhere the hotel staff was on strike. Things would get messy.

So how did Pete and I gain access to this red-carpet hoopla? Did I use my crack reportorial skills to pull the right strings behind the scenes? Did Pete score VIP passes through sheer force of personality? Neither.

A few weeks after we first came up with our plan to storm the Just For Laughs festival, Pete received an e-mail. "I heard about your research," wrote the author. "We gotta become connected." It was signed Andy Nulman—president of Festivals and Television for Just For Laughs.

Nulman, a suave character who's always the best-dressed person in the room, was just the sort of guy we wanted to be connected with. In 1985, Nulman joined the nascent Just For Laughs festival, then a small-time francophone event. By the time he departed, fourteen years later, Just For Laughs was an international powerhouse. Then, after founding the tech company Airborne Mobile and selling it for millions, Nulman came back. Now, as part of Just For Laughs' thirtieth anniversary celebration, he wanted to innovate—and that included inviting as his guests two outsiders trying to deconstruct all of comedy. As he put it to Pete, "Our event is the playground for your research."

Access to that playground came with a price. Nulman wanted us to present our findings at the Just For Laughs Comedy Conference. To keep it interesting, we'd be facing off against Kenny Hotz. Hotz is famous in Canada for his shock-and-awe brand of comedy. On one television series, he made a go at cannibalism and tried to convince a Jewish community to build a mosque. In another stunt, he ran afoul of the British Columbia Human Rights Commission by flying a banner over Toronto that read "Jesus Sucks." But speaking to us over the phone before the festival, Hotz seemed like a reasonable guy. There was nothing to worry about, he told us; everything was going to go fine.

We believed him—right up until we got on stage with him at the conference. Pete hardly had time to go over his benign violation theory before Hotz pulled out the heavy artillery. On a video screen, he flicked on a comedy clip he'd put together linking the Pope and pedophilia. "Is that funny, and why?" probed Hotz over the mixture of groans and chortles in the packed conference hall. "Is that a benign enough violation?" Continuing on, he played a real-life video of horribly misguided New Age do-gooders crooning "You're the Sweetest Thing" to a suffering denizen of an Indian leper colony. Hotz, for one, found this hilarious. So, he grilled Pete, how do you explain why, Professor?

"Yeah, um . . ." started Pete. The usually gregarious academic was at a loss for words.

But then Pete caught a break, courtesy of a video clip Hotz played of a neighborhood fireworks show gone horribly wrong. The seminar audience was mostly silent as the man filming the scene hollered in terror as his video camera captured fireworks exploding all around him. Then, halfway through, the cameraman exclaimed, "That was awesome!" In response, the crowd erupted in applause and laughter. Afterward, Pete seized his chance. "I don't know if you noticed this, but one of the biggest laughs was when the gentleman recording this said, 'That was awesome,'" he said. "I put this to the audience. Why did that moment in time get the biggest laughs?"

Immediately, people saw where he was going. "That's when it became benign!" someone exclaimed.

The rest of the seminar went well, and conference organizers seemed excited and appreciative for our involvement. ("What are you thanking them for?" cracked Hotz. "I did everything!") It's not the first time in our adventures that the benign violation theory has come through in a clutch. If anything, Pete's journey with me beyond the ivory tower have made him ever more confident in the theory.

Take the "violation" half of the theory, says Pete, the idea that humor is born from situations that are wrong, threatening, or disruptive. We witnessed this concept all over the world, from the Japanese *manzai* duos, where the dim-witted *boke* always started the joke by doing something incorrectly, to the clown mission in the Amazon, which was all about turning the world upside down and breaking social norms. And let's not forget the comedy we found in Palestine: if that isn't proof that humor arises amid threats and violations, we don't know what is. Find something wrong, and you're likely to find somebody joking about it.

Of course, our findings weren't all doom and gloom. For Pete, it was clear from our travels that the "benign" half of his theory was just as essential as the violation, that humor can only take root when situations are seen as playful, safe, or otherwise okay. In New York, we'd learned from Todd Hanson of *The Onion* that even something as terrible as the 9/11 terrorist attacks can be joked about, just as long as the butt of the joke deserves it. In Los Angeles, we'd found that comedians do best in environments where audiences feel secure—such as dark rooms or in crowds planted with professional laughers, folks skilled in letting others know that everything is okay and therefore funny.

We found additional evidence for the "benign" half of the theory in comedy's potential downside, in how it signals that the stuff being joked about is harmless and doesn't have to be taken seriously. It's how people get away with derogatory humor by claiming, "It's just a joke," and it's likely why the funny sex-ed PSAs we created for the National Campaign to Prevent Teen and Unplanned Pregnancy might have been catchy but didn't get the job done.

Finally, our journey proved to Pete that both conditions of the benign violation theory have to be perceived simultaneously—that timing does matter. It's why most things in the world aren't funny, and it's why even so-called funny things are boring to some people and offensive to others. It's hard to find the balance between what's a violation and what's benign, especially when everybody has a different idea of what's okay and what's not, what's a horrible tragedy and what's a ho-hum mishap. That's why it helps to be diligent and observant like the stand-up comics we met in LA, not to mention creative and open-minded like the cartoonists we got to know in New York. All of those qualities are essential to landing your jokes in the comedic sweet spot.

"I can't say the theory is perfect," says Pete. There are funny things that don't easily fit the formula. But then again, he says, the benign violation theory certainly holds up better than its alternatives, theories like superiority, relief, or incongruity. "It's definitely better than what was out there before," he says. And even Victor Raskin, the theory's number-one critic, seems to have come around somewhat. "I hadn't realized that Peter was a psychologist," he writes in an e-mail to me once he's learned more about Pete's work. "His use of the term 'theory' is casual: it does not mean more than a certain feature that may be loosely associated with humor. Moreover, he measures the distance from a person or event and correlates it with humor appreciation. That's all there is to it." For someone like Raskin, that's downright effusive.

I've been impressed with the benign violation theory, too. But once again, I want to see the theory in action before final judgment. That's why we're here at the Just For Laughs festival, and that's why we asked Andy Nulman to provide a complete unknown and coveted spot at one of the festival's big, final-night events.

It's time, in other words, for the ultimate test.

"We have a little something different here," says Debra DiGiovanni to the Comedy Nest audience. "He's actually a professor at the University of Colorado, and he's studying what makes things funny. Please welcome up to the stage Peter McGraw!"

I could say that what happens next is a triumph, a coup, a stunning success. That every joke kills, that he turns that terrible audience around. That by the time his eight minutes are up, he's left in his dust his precursors, all those ringers from *Late Show with David Letterman* and *The Tonight Show with Jay Leno*. That the festival is soon buzzing about the unknown upstart who got on stage for the second time in his life and proved beyond a doubt that science has nailed comedy once and for all.

But I'd be lying.

Here's what happened:

"From studying comedy, I've learned that you have to get a laugh right away," begins Pete, flashing a confident smile. "Which is why I wore this sweater vest." The self-deprecating dig works, earning hearty guffaws from the audience.

"So does anyone know the famous quote by E. B. White about deconstructing humor?" he continues. "E. B. White wrote 'Analyzing humor is like dissecting a frog. Few people are interested and the frog dies of it.'"

Pausing for laughs, he carries on. "You know who says that? Comedians. Comedians say, 'If you figure out what makes things funny, that's like telling people the trick behind the magic. And then people won't like magic acts anymore.' But that's a silly argument. NO-BODY likes magic."

The punch line gets just a few meager chuckles. But we prepared for this. "Ah," Pete remarks thoughtfully, turning to a flip chart he's positioned on a metal tripod beside him. He flips over the first page, revealing an algorithm:

$$f(\text{LAUGH}) = a_0 + A/\pi r^2 *$$
$$\sum_{n=1}^{\infty} \left(a_n \cos \frac{n\pi x}{L} + b_n \sin \frac{n\pi x}{L} \right) *$$
$$e^x * 1 + \frac{x}{1!} + \frac{x^2}{2!} + \frac{x^3}{3!} + \cdots ,$$
$$-\infty < x < \frac{\infty}{\tan \alpha} + \sin \beta *$$
$$2 \cos \frac{1}{2}(\alpha + \beta) \cos \frac{1}{2}(\alpha - \beta)$$

He adds a square root symbol to the capital "A" on the first line. "We'll be good from this point on," he cracks, to the bemused laughter of the crowd. Then he continues.

"I do like hanging out with comedians. They are lot of fun. And they have a lot of advantages over professors. For instance, comedians can drink on the job. Scratch that. They HAVE to drink on the job. And they fall into one of three categories: they're either on their way to being alcoholics, they're alcoholics, or they're recovering alcoholics. So when someone comes up to me and says, "You know, Pete, I am thinking about getting into stand-up,' I have to ask them, 'How are you at alcoholism?'"

He pauses for laughter, but it's largely silent.

"But I haven't just been looking at comedians. I've actually been traveling the world, looking at humor in all of its forms. I recently was in Osaka, Japan. And if you don't know this, Osaka is the humor capital of Japan. The funniest people in Japan live in Osaka. You can walk up to someone on the street in Osaka and go BANG!"—Pete mimes pointing a gun at an audience member—"and they will spontaneously act like they've been shot."

He waits a beat. "What's fascinating about that is that no one has used this technique to rob the banks of Osaka." The laughs are back.

Pete wraps up with a discussion of our *Mad Men* experiment in New York. "I got an ad team from one of the big ad agencies drunk and asked them to create funny content." He turns to the flip chart. "I am going to show you the outcome of this study, in order from least-drunk to most-drunk Venn diagrams. This is after round one of drinks." He flips the page.

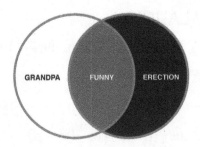

There's mild laughter. "After two or three drinks, they started to get a little more bold." Next page:

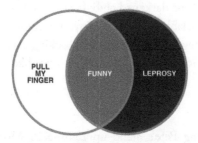

By now, a couple folks seem to be wheezing. So Pete pulls out all the stops. "And by the time that they were wasted . . ."

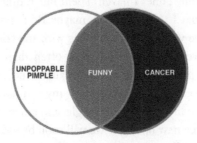

"Awwww." He's taken it too far. The laughter turns to groans. In this crowd, nothing about this diagram is benign.

"So, if jokes are like frogs, and this set is any type of example, there's a lot of sick frogs out there," Pete says in conclusion. "And I think cutting up a few frogs might actually benefit the world a little bit. So you can say, 'I've dissected this frog, and I know its problem.'" He holds aloft an imaginary amphibian, like Hamlet clasping the skull of poor jester Yorick. "It thinks that wearing a sweater vest is funny."

The crowd claps and laughs as Pete steps off the stage. "I didn't kill," he tells me. "But I didn't bomb, either." He's right: he got far more laughs than he scored at the Squire, and who knows, maybe more than if he'd developed his routine the traditional way.

"It's not surprising, knowing what we know," says Pete, standing in the back of the club with the other comics who've already gone on. A place like this is never going to be a perfect comedy lab, he says, gesturing around the darkened club. It's too wild, too messy, there are just too many variables outside of anyone's control. But that's okay, he says, celebrating with a whiskey and looking ever more like an old, road-tested comic. "After all," he says, "it's not like we were trying to cure cancer."

I'm still pondering Pete's stand-up routine in Montreal when my buddy Ron says something that surprises me. "You know," he tells me one night over beers a few weeks later, "I think you've gotten funnier."

"Really?" I'm taken aback. I've spent so much time scrutinizing other people's funny bones I haven't spent much time considering my own. But now that I think about it, maybe Ron's right. Maybe I am funnier. I'm more willing to crack jokes with my friends and family, even with relative strangers—and more often than not, these jokes work. I'm more playful, more quick to laugh, and, in truth, happier than I've ever been. I goof around with my son, Gabriel, try harder than ever to make my wife, Emily, giggle, and am excited to teach my clown tricks to the new baby girl we will soon be welcoming into our family. And while I've never been one for the spotlight, these days when I do speak in front of an audience, I'm more confident, even a bit cocky. It's as if I'm turning into a comedian.

Is it due to Pete's benign violation theory? Maybe in part. I have started to notice all the potential violations lying around that are waiting for me to make benign. And knowing what I now know about humor's balance of pleasure and pain, I've gotten more thoughtful and precise about what I joke about—and with whom.

But that can't be the full explanation for why I'm funnier. After all, as our time in Montreal demonstrated, we haven't managed to find a secret shortcut to becoming the world's greatest comedians. And that's okay. In fact, it's probably perfect. Yes, we've come a bit closer to cracking the code behind humor, a bit closer to comedy's underlying DNA. But we're far from finding the algorithm that will mass-produce great jokes like Big Macs. Humor is and will continue to be strange and complex and illusory and just a bit dangerous. It's always going to be part art and part science. That's what makes it so much fun. And if you want to become a world-class humorist, a good formula or two might set you in the right direction—but it won't get you all the way. To do that, you have to explore new ideas and challenge your assumptions. You have to venture out of your comfort zone.

That's exactly what we've been doing. We subjected our laughs to Hollywood's top humor headhunter, and acted out our Don Draper fantasies at one of Manhattan's ritziest watering holes. We tracked a mythical laughter disease across the African savanna and compared the size of our manhoods with Japanese game-show stars. We trudged through the frozen Swedish wilderness in search of an illegal fairy castle, embroiled ourselves in a Palestinian controversy of international proportions, and became way too touchy-feely with an Amazonian clown brigade. We now count among our friends stand-up comics and cartooning pariahs, joke connoisseurs and expat improv performers, rat ticklers and revolutionaries, and one sweaty Patch Adams. A couple of times we nearly got arrested. Traveling by airliner, rental car, bullet train, African dinghy, Israeli techno-cab, and clown-filled cargo plane, we each covered enough miles to circumnavigate the globe—repeatedly.

I'm not the same guy I was all those months ago, cowering in the corner at the Squire Lounge. For one, I have a lot more witty yarns in my comic repertoire. And now that I've hit five of the seven continents (Australia and Antarctica, we still hold you in our hearts), it's far easier for me to put my daily foibles and faux pas in perspective, to find a way to laugh them off. Let's not forget that I've tangled with Israeli soldiers and Scandinavian commandos, strapped on a clown nose in one of the poorest places on earth, and temporarily paralyzed my pinkie for the good of science. After all that, putting myself out there by telling a joke or two doesn't seem so daunting. All in all, I've found there's a lot more to life—not to mention a lot more to laugh at.

Credit has to go to the professor whose off-the-wall research started it all. Pete's no longer just another story subject for me. He's a colleague, a close friend, a partner in crime. He's pushed me out from behind my reporter's notebook and forced me out of my shell. The process hasn't always been easy, but it's been more than a little worthwhile. In return, he tells me, I've helped him think less like an academic and more like a journalist, an explorer, a vagabond. He's back in touch with his adventurous side, the part that got lost in the shuffle when he was busy engineering his life to be productive and comfortable. Now his hypotheses are a little messier; his variables aren't so constrained. He's learned it's okay for his experiments to not always go as planned.

Like the best *manzai* duos, we make a good team.

"I understand humor better now," Pete tells me; it makes sense to him in a much broader way. "Most people could stand to laugh more," he says. "Life gets serious. Our world is full of mortgages and careers and retirement funds and horrible headlines on the nightly news. And when you live in a world that's really serious," he says, "it's hard to be playful about things."

So how can we hope to change that? I ask. "One way to do so is to be really systematic about it," Pete replies—the way he usually goes about things. Watch fewer dramas and more sitcoms. Join a laughter yoga club. Increase your visits to your local comedy club.

But there's a better way to do it, he says: "Surround yourself with the people and things that make you laugh. Seek out interesting places and interesting people. Focus on the friends who make you laugh, not the ones who bring you down. Choose as a partner someone with whom you share a sense of humor, someone who helps you see the lighter side of life."

"And maybe it's clichéd," he continues, "but remind yourself that everything is going to be okay." That thing that seems so scary in the moment, so catastrophic and worrisome, is only scary because you're paying so much attention to it. It's okay to complain, but add a bit of wit to your grumbling. Figure out a way to make that violation benign.

Above all else, he concludes, "Remind yourself that life's meant to be enjoyed, to be delighted in, to be laughed at." In short, that our world is one big joke. Sure, the set-ups aren't always perfect, but keep an eye out. Sooner or later, you'll find a punch line waiting to happen.

ACKNOWLEDGMENTS

In the same way the best comedy is often a team effort, this book would never have been possible without a great many people helping us in many different ways.

Pete never would have made it to where he is today without the guidance of his academic mentors, Barb Mellers, Phil Tetlock, and Danny Kahneman. Now that he's made it, he's grateful to the University of Colorado at Boulder's Leeds School of Business, particularly Marketing Division Chair Donnie Lichtenstein and Dean David Ikenberry, for the plentiful resources and assistance they've provided him, support that was all the more generous considering part of the project occurred while he was on sabbatical.

I, on the other hand, have had the benefit of being coached, edited, and yelled at by some of the best people in journalism. But none of it compared to what I received from *Westword* editor Patty Calhoun, especially in the yelling department. From her I learned the secret of magnificent obsessives, the value of seeking out people whose passion draws readers into unparalleled worlds—people like Pete.

Pete's path and my own never would have crossed, much less taken us around the world, if not for a fortuitous string of helping hands along the way. I never would have heard of Pete if not for superhuman matchmaker Andrew Hyde. The resulting *Westword* story surely would have been the end of it, but Jonathan Levav kindly mentioned Pete's work to a literary agent in New York. And that agent just happened to be Sasha Raskin at the Agency Group, who took one look at what I'd written about Pete and came up with an idea as outlandish as it was brilliant. Chris Baker at *Wired* helped build momentum by taking a shot on a nutty story idea pitched by an unknown freelancer, Susan Davis and Andrew Hartman walked two neophytes through all the legalese, and Adam Cayton-Holland came up with the perfect longshot conclusion. Dominick Anfuso's enthusiasm helped seal the deal with Simon & Schuster. And we're grateful to Amy Gibb for helping us figure out how to get that deal done without going broke.

To pull off our global adventure, we are indebted to a small army of good Samaritans who connected us with just the right people and opened (if not barged through) just the right doors. In Los Angeles and elsewhere, no one worked harder to gain us entry to the world of comedy than Alonzo Bodden, though several others came close, most notably Dan Altmann, Geoff Plitt, Kevin Goetz, Gary Stiffelman, Ryan Kartels, A. J. Jacobs, Sarah Klegman, Judi Brown-Marmel, Brett Carducci, Jordy Ellner, Bart Coleman, J. P. Buck, Bruce Kaplan, and Neal Brennan. In New York, Bob Mankoff scored us access to all sorts of incredible places, including a few he probably shouldn't have. We never would have known where to start looking for *omuneepo* in Tanzania without the help of Latif Nasser, and even then we wouldn't have been able to get there without the wherewithal of William Rutta (it was our pleasure to be Rutta's "number-one most flexible and happy travelers"). Our excursion to Japan was far less daunting thanks to the tireless work of Goh Abe, Aki Yorihiro, Moka Umehara, Araki Takahiro, Jocelyn Martinez, Jessica Milner Davis, Daniel Feit, Terje Langeland, Nami Moto, Katsura Asakichi, Megumu Tanigawa, and several other members of the Japanese Humor and Laughter Society, not to mention the energetic and sometimes debaucherous assistance of Bill Reilly, Mike Staffa, and all their randy pirates. Jytte Klausen, in her work and over the phone, provided us the lay of the land in Denmark and Sweden. And when we got there, Kurt Westergaard and Lars Vilks had no good reason to let us into their homes, considering the sort of people who sometimes show up at their door. But they let us in anyway, and for that we are grateful. Naomi Zeveloff, Erin Breeze, Vanessa Rousselot, Yaniv Shani, Chaya Ostrower, and Rami Mehdawi prepared us for the places and issues we'd explore in the West Bank and Israel; hopefully someday we can all get together over a conciliatory Mediterranean breakfast. (If Israeli omelets and Palestinian yogurt can't bring about lasting peace, we don't know what can.) For professional and personal reasons, we are beholden to Steve and Pam Wilson for providing us access to the American Association for Therapeutic Humor, just as we are indebted to John Glick, Patch Adams, and everyone else we met in Peru for welcoming us into their clown family. And last but not least, much gratitude goes to Andy Nulman for granting us VIP treatment (twice) at the world's greatest comedy festival, before we had the guts to ask.

An equally sizable number of people helped on the academic part of our journey. Pete's Humor Research Team (aka HuRT) at the University of Colorado at Boulder never balked at his strange requests, so credit goes to team members Ryan Brauchler, Erin Percival Carter, Robert Collins, Caley Cuneo, Christina Kan (HuRL's Lab Manager), Robert Keenan, Bridget Leonard, Linds Panther, Roxanne Ross, Julie Schiro, Abigail Schneider, and Rachel Stermer. They were far from Pete's only collaborators. In the academic realm, Elise Chandon Ince, Phil Fernbach, Dan Goldstein, Gil Greengross, Jennifer Harman, Kathleen Vohs, Lawrence Williams, and Max Justicz contributed their time and expertise. Outside the ivory tower, Alex Sidtis, Alex Berg, and Joe Wengert at the Upright Citizens Brigade Theatre; Jaime Kopke, Sonnet Hanson, and Lindsey Housel at the Denver Art Museum; Steve Krauss and Ari Halper at Grey New York; Larry Swiader, Danny Rouhier, and Liz Sabatiuk at the National Campaign to Prevent Teen and Unplanned Pregnancy; and Jeff Richins, Ryan Smith, and Danny Anderson at Qualtrics Online Survey Software all provided access to their expertise, resources, work spaces, and humorists, no questions asked. Meanwhile, Andrea Grimes at San Francisco Public Library's Schmulowitz Collection of Wit and Humor and Reaux Flagg at U.C. Berkeley's Folklore Archive proved invaluable sleuths when detective work arose. Finally, our gratitude goes out to the entirety of the University of Colorado library staff, especially Janet Freeman and Betty Grebe, for handling with patience and grace our hundreds upon hundreds of book, journal, and interlibrary loan requests. Sorry about the late returns.

We can't forget the folks who helped spread the word about what we were up to, plus those who made sure what we were saying was a polished as possible. Tor Myhren at Grey New York was so taken with our idea that he gave us an offer we couldn't refuse. Lewis Wallace at Wired.com, Bryan Maygers at the *Huffington Post*, Lauren Friedman at *Psychology Today*, and John Swanburg at *Slate* offered us invaluable online soapboxes, and Josh Mishell crafted the logo and Venns we proudly sported there and a hundred other places around the world. John Wenzel and Grace Hood, among others, covered our exploits; Kristen Sink snapped our publicity photos; and Sean Guillory, Andy Wood, Ben Roy, Paul Ronca, and Alf LaMont helped get us on stage all over North America, before we had much to show for our efforts. We looked and sounded much better than we deserved thanks to a crack team of wordsmiths and videosmiths, namely Rick Griffith, Josh Johnson, Daniel Junge, Vanessa Martinez, Shane Mauss, and Evan Nix. We owe McKenzie Binder a weekend for the one she spent tidying our bibliography. Jane Le added a final sheen to our prose, courtesy of her passion for terminating dangling modifiers with extreme prejudice and her unrivaled knowledge of Yiddish. Ron Doyle, founder and president of the Humor Code Fan Club, understood what we were up to better than we did, and deserves his own media empire for the marketing work he did on our behalf. Brit Hvide, Marie Kent, Leah Johanson, Richard Rhorer, and everyone else at Simon & Schuster deserve accolades for their endless patience and support, despite all our odd questions and rookie mistakes. And of course, we are beyond grateful to our editor, Ben Loehnen, for his incredibly enthusiastic embrace of our project and his unrivaled skill at making every word, sentence, and paragraph shine.

Last but not least, there are a select few who were always there for us, providing feedback, encouragement, and support in numerous unquantifiable ways. For Pete, that includes his mother, Kathleen McGraw, Mark Ferne, Joni Klippert, Mike Koenig, Jeff Larsen, Julie Nirvelli, Michael Sargent, Janet Schwartz, Marcel Zeelenberg, Jaclyn Allen, Adam Alter, Adam Grant, Chip Heath, and especially Dan Ariely. Most of all, Pete wants to thank Caleb Warren and his sister, Shannon Sorino. His research would be rubbish if it weren't for Caleb's time, effort, and impressive intellect, and he never would have thought that he was funny enough to get on stage (twice) if Shannon hadn't always laughed at his jokes.

My shortlist of personal advocates includes George Smith, Vince Darcangelo, Jared Jacang Maher, Hester McNeil, Kelly Warner, and above all, my parents, Jim and Barb Warner. And I can never fully repay my family, Emily, Gabriel, and Charlotte, for the fatherless weeks, spotty Skype calls, unanswered e-mails, late nights in the home office, and moments of grouchiness. All I can say to them is through good times and bad, the funny and not-so-funny stuff, you've been a wonderful audience—and a wonderful team.

NOTES

Chapter 1: Colorado

1. Don L. F. Nilsen and Alleen Pace Nilsen, "Twenty-Five Years of Developing a Community of Humor Scholars," http://www.hnu.edu/ishs/ ISHS Documents/Nilsen25Article.pdf (accessed December 30, 2012).
2. Caleb Warren and A. Peter McGraw, "Humor Appreciation," *Encyclopedia of Humor Studies* (forthcoming).
3. Elliot Oring, *The Jokes of Sigmund Freud: A Study in Humor and Jewish Identity* (Philadelphia: University of Pennsylvania Press, 1984), 114.
4. John Morreall, "A new theory of laughter," *Philosophical Studies*, 42(2) (1982), 243–254.
5. Howard R. Pollio and Rodney W. Mers, "Predictability and the Appreciation of Comedy," *Bulletin of the Psychonomic Society* (1974): 229–232.
6. Caleb Warren and A. Peter McGraw, "Beyond Incongruity: Differentiating What Is Funny From What Is Not" (under review).
7. Thomas C. Veatch, "A Theory of Humor," *Humor: International Journal of Humor Research* (1998): 161–215.
8. A. Peter McGraw and Caleb Warren, "Benign Violations: Making Immoral Behavior Funny," *Psychological Science* (2010): 1141–1149.
9. Ibid.
10. Sarah-Jayne Blakemore, Daniel Wolpert, and Chris Frith, "Why Can't You Tickle Yourself?" *NeuroReport* (2000): R11–R16.
11. McGraw and Warren, "Benign Violations," 1141–1149.

Chapter 2: Los Angeles

1. Willibald Ruch, ed. *The Sense of Humor: Explorations of a Personality Characteristic* (Berlin and New York: Mouton de Gruyter, 1998), 7–9.

2. Alan Feilgold, "Measuring Humor Ability: Revision and Construct Validation of the Humor Perceptiveness Test," *Perceptual and Motor Skills* (1983): 159–166.

3. Herbert M. Lefcourt and Rod A. Martin, *Humor and Life Stress: Antidote to Adversity* (Berlin and Heidelberg: Springer-Verlag, 1986), 17.

4. Victor Raskin, *Semantic Mechanisms of Humor* (Dordrecht, Holland, and Boston: D. Reidel, 1985), 32.

5. Greg Dean, *Greg Dean's Step by Step to Stand-Up Comedy* (Portsmouth, NH: Heinemann, 2000), 125.

6. Salvatore Attardo and Lucy Pickering, "Timing in the Performance of Jokes," *Humor: International Journal of Human Research* (2011): 233–250.

7. Salvatore Attardo, Lucy Pickering, and Amanda Baker, "Prosodic and Multimodal Markers of Humor in Conversation," *Prosody and Humor: Special Issue of Pragmatics & Cognition* (2011): 194, 224–247.

8. Joe Boskin, ed., *Humor Prism in the 20th Century* (Detroit, MI: Wayne State University Press, 1997), 111.

9. Lawrence Epstein, *The Haunted Smile: The Story of Jewish Comedians in America* (New York: PublicAffairs, 2001), x.

10. Mel Watkins, *On the Real Side: A History of African American Comedy* (Chicago: Lawrence Hill, 1999), 26.

11. Jonathan Levav and R. Juliet Zhu, "Seeking Freedom though Variety," *Journal of Consumer Research* (2009): 600–610; J. Meyers-Levy and R. J. Zhu, "The Influence of Ceiling Height: The Effect of Priming on the Type of Processing That People Use," *Journal of Consumer Research* (2007): 174–186.

12. Joseph A. Bellizzi and Robert E. Hite, "Environmental Color, Consumer Feelings, and Purchase Likelihood," *Psychology & Marketing* (1992): 347–363.

13. C. B. Zhong, V. K. Bohns, and F. Gino, "Good Lamps Are the Best Police," *Psychological Science* (2010): 311–314.

14. Edward Diener, "Deindividuation: The Absence of Self-Awareness and Self-Regulation in Group Members," ed. P. B. Paulus, *Psychology of Group Influence* (Hillsdale, NJ: Erlbaum, 1980), 209–242.

15. Timothy J. Lawson and Brian Downing, "An Attributional Explanation for the Effect of Audience Laughter on Perceived Funniness," *Basic and Applied Social Psychology*, 243–249.

16. Richard Zoglin, *Comedy at the Edge: How Stand-up in the 1970s Changed America* (New York: Bloomsbury, 2008), 5.

17. "Richest Comedians," http://www.therichest.org/celebnetworth/category/celeb/comedian/ (accessed February 15, 2013.)

18. Jimmy Carr and Lucy Greeves, *Only Joking: What's So Funny About Making People Laugh?* (New York: Gotham Books, 2006), 103.

19. Gil Greengross, Rod. A. Martin, and Geoffrey Miller, "The Big Five Personality Traits of Professional Comedians Compared to Amateur Comedians, Comedy Writers, and College Students," *Personality and Individual Differences* (2009): 79–83.

20. Gil Greengross, Rod. A. Martin, and Geoffrey Miller, "Personality Traits, Intelligence, Humor Styles, and Humor Production Ability of Professional Stand-up Comedians Compared to College Students," *Psychology of Aesthetics, Creativity, and the Arts* (2011), 74–82.

21. A. Peter McGraw, Erin Percival Carter, and Jennifer J. Harman, "Disturbingly funny: Humor production increases perceptions of mental instability" (working paper).

Chapter 3: New York

1. Russell Adams, "How About Never—Is Never Good for You? Celebrities Struggle to Write Winning Captions," *Wall Street Journal* (2011), A1.

2. Judith Yaros Less, *Defining* New Yorker *Humor* (Jackson: University Press of Mississippi, 2000), 10.

3. Judith Yaros Less, *Defining* New Yorker *Humor*, 56.

4. Ibid., 11.

5. Arthur Koestler, *Act of Creation* (New York: The Macmillan Company, 1964), 35.

6. Caleb Warren and A. Peter McGraw, "Beyond Incongruity: Differentiating What is Funny From What is Not" (under review).

7. Arthur Koestler, *Act of Creation*, 45.

8. A. M. Isen, K. A. Daubman, and G. P. Nowicki, "Positive Affect Facilitates Creative Problem Solving," *Journal of Personality and Social Psychology* (1987): 1122–1131.

9. Barry Kudrowitz, "Haha and Aha!: Creativity, Idea Generation, Improvisational Humor, and Product Design" (PhD diss., Massachusetts Institute of Technology, 2010).

10. Chloe Kiddon and Yuriy Brun, "That's What She Said: Double Entendre Identification," Proceedings of the 49th Annual Meeting of the Association for Computational Linguistics (2011): 89–94.

11. Graeme Ritchie, "Can Computers Create Humor?," *AI Magazine* (2009): 71–81.

12. C. F. Hempelmann and A. C. Samson, "Computational Humor: Beyond the Pun?" in *The Primer of Humor Research*, ed. V. Raskin (Berlin: Mouton de Gruyter, 2008), 335–341.

13. Koestler, *Act of Creation*, 93.

14. Fred K. Beard, "*Humor in the Advertising Business: Theory, Practice, and Wit*"(Lanham, MD: Rowman & Littlefield, 2008), 2.

15. Charles S. Gulas, Kim K. McKeage, and Marc G. Weinberger, "Violence Against Males in Humorous Advertising," *Journal of Advertising* (2010): 109–20.

16. Ibid., 112.

17. Caleb Warren, and A. Peter McGraw, "When Humorous Marketing Backfires: Uncovering the Relationship between Humor, Negative Affect, and Brand Attitude" (under review).

18. Judith Yaross Lee, *Defining* New Yorker *Humor*, 159.

19. A. Peter McGraw, Phil Fernbach, and Julie Schiro, "Humor Lowers Propensity to Remedy a Problem" (working paper).

20. Judith Yaross Lee, *Defining* New Yorker *Humor*, 159.

21. Sasha Topolinski and Rolf Reber, "Gaining Insight Into the 'Aha' Experience," *Current Directions in Psychological Science* (2010): 402–405.

22. A. Peter McGraw, et al., "Too Close for Comfort, or Too Far to Care? Finding Humor in Distant Tragedies and Close Mishaps," *Psychological Science* (2012): 1215–1223.

23. Geoff Lowe and Sharon B. Taylor, "Effects of Alcohol on Responsive Laughter and Amusement," *Psychological Reports* (1997): 1149–1150.

Chapter 4: Tanzania

1. Robert Provine, *Laughter: A Scientific Investigation* (New York: Penguin, 2001), 27, 37, 40.

2. McGraw, et al., "Too Close for Comfort, or Too Far to Care?," 1215–1223.

3. Provine, *Laughter*, 45.

4. Ibid., 157, 163, 172, 173.

5. A. M. Rankin and P. J. Philip, "An Epidemic of Laughing in the Bukoba District of Tanganyika," *Central African Journal of Medicine* (1963).

6. Susan Sprecher and Pamela C. Regan, "Liking Some Things (In Some People) More Than Others: Partner Preferences in Romantic Relationships and Friendships," *Journal of Social and Personal Relationships* (2002): 463–481.

7. Robert H. Lauer, Jeanette C. Lauer, and Sarah T. Kerr, "The Long-Term Marriage: Perceptions of Stability and Satisfaction," *The International Journal of Aging and Human Development* (1990): 189–195.

8. Dacher Keltner, Randall C. Young, Erin A. Heerey, Carmen Oemig, and Natalie D. Monarch, "Teasing in Hierarchical and Intimate Relations," *Journal of Personality and Social Psychology* (1998): 1231–1247.

9. Rod A. Martin, *The Psychology of Humor: An Integrative Approach* (Burlington, MA: Elsevier, 2007), 187–188.

10. V. S. Ramachandran, "The Neurology and Evolution of Humor, Laughter, and Smiling: the False Alarm Theory," *PubMed* (1998): 351–354.

11. Matthew M. Hurley, Daniel Dennett, and Reginald B. Adams, *Inside Jokes: Using Humor to Reverse-Engineer the Mind* (Cambridge, MA: MIT Press, 2013), 4.

12. André Parent, "Duchenne De Boulogne: A Pioneer in Neurology and Medical Photography" (2005): 369–377; Guillaume Duchenne, *The Mechanism of Human Physiognomy* (1862).

13. Matthew Gervais and David Sloan Wilson, "The Evolution and Functions of Laughter and Humor: A Synthetic Approach," *The Quarterly Review of Biology* (2005): 395–430.

14. Marina Davila-Ross, M. Owren, and E. Zimmermann, "The Evolution of Laughter in Great Apes and Humans," *Communicative & Integrative Biology* (2010): 191–194.

15. Jaak Panksepp and Jeff Burgdorf, "'Laughing' Rats and the Evolutionary Antecedents of Human Joy?" *Physiology & Behavior* (2003): 533–547.

16. L. Alan Sroufe and Jane Piccard Wunsch, "The Development of Laughter in the First Year of Life," *Child Development* (1972): 1326–1344.

17. Rod A. Martin and Nicholas A. Kuiper, "Daily Occurrence of Laughter: Relationships with Age, Gender, and Type A Personality," *Humor: International Journal of Humor Research* (1999): 355–384.

18. Martin, *The Psychology of Humor*, 233, 239–240.

19. Jane E. Warren, et al., "Positive Emotions Preferentially Engage an Auditory Motor 'Mirror' System," *The Journal of Neuroscience* (2006): 13067–13075.

20. Karen O'Quin and Joel Aronoff, "Humor as a Technique of Social Influence," *Social Psychology Quarterly* (1981): 349–357.

21. John A. Jones, "The Masking Effects of Humor on Audience Perception of Message Organization," *Humor: International Journal of Humor Research* (2005): 405–417.

22. Christian F. Hempelmann, "The Laughter of the 1962 Tanganyika 'Laughter Epidemic,'" *Humor: International Journal of Humor Research* (2007) 49–71.

23. Leslie P. Boss, "Epidemic Hysteria: A Review of the Published Literature," *Epidemiologic Reviews* (1997): 233–243.

24. Robert E. Bartholomew and Benjamin Radford, *Hoaxes, Myths, and Manias: Why We Need Critical Thinking* (Amherst, NY: Prometheus, 2003), 94.

25. Susan Dominus, "What Happened to the Girls in Le Roy," *New York Times Magazine*, March 11, 2012.

Chapter 5: Japan

1. Mahadev Apte, *Humor and Laughter: An Anthropological Approach*, 33, 51.

2. A. R. Radcliffe-Brown, "On Joking Relationships," *Journal of the International African Institute* (1940): 195–210.

3. Jessica Milner Davis, *Understanding Humor in Japan* (Detroit: Wayne State University Press, 2006), 8.

4. Christie Davies, *Jokes and Targets* (Bloomington: Indiana University Press, 2011), 41, 82–93, 198–201.

5. Jan Bremmer, *A Cultural History of Humour from Antiquity to the Present Day*, ed. Herman Roodenburg, 16–17, 98.

6. Carr and Greeves, *Only Joking*, 193.

7. Christie Davies, *Jokes and Targets*, 255.

8. Eric Romero et al., "Regional Humor Differences in the United States: Implications for Management," *Humor: International Journal of Humor Research* (2007): 189–201.

9. Salvatore Attardo, "Translation and Humour: An Approach Based on the General Theory of Verbal Humour (GTVH)," *The Translator* (2002): 173–194.

10. Mahadev L. Apte, *Humor and Laughter: An Anthropological Approach* (Ithaca, NY: Cornell University Press, 1985), 17.

11. Laura Mickes, Drew E. Hoffman, Julian L. Parris, Robert Mankoff, and Nicholas Christenfeld, "Who's Funny: Gender Stereotypes, Humor Production, and Memory Bias" *Psychonomic Bulletin and Review* (2011): 108–112.

12. Martin D. Lampert and Susan M. Ervin-Tripp, "Exploring Paradigms: The Study of Gender and Sense of Humor Near the End of the 20th Century," in *The Sense of Humor: Explorations of a Personality Characteristic*, ed. Willibald Ruch (Berlin and New York: Mouton de Gruyter, 1998): 231–270.

13. Thomas R. Herzog, "Gender Differences in Humor Appreciation Revisited," *Humor: International Journal of Humor Research*, (1999): 411–423.

14. Christopher J. Wilbur and Lorne Campbell, "Humor in Romantic Contexts: Do Men Participate and Women Evaluate?" *Personality And Social Psychology Bulletin* (2011): 918–929.

15. Dan Ariely, "Who Enjoys Humor More: Conservatives or Liberals?" *Psychology Today*, http://www.psychologytoday.com/blog/predictably-irrational/200810/who-enjoys-humor-more-conservatives-or-liberals (October 23, 2008).

16. Arnold Krupat, "Native American Trickster Tales," in *Comedy: A Geographic and Historical Guide*, ed. Maurice Charney (Westport, CT: Praeger, 2005), 447–460.

Chapter 6: Scandinavia

1. Martin, *The Psychology of Humor*, 43–44.
2. John Morreall, "Comic Vices and Comic Virtues," *Humor: International Journal of Humor Research*, 23.
3. Martin, *The Psychology of Humor*, 47.
4. Clark McCauley, Kathryn Woods, Christopher Coolidge, and William Kulick, "More Aggressive Cartoons Are Funnier," *Journal of Personality and Social Psychology* (1983): 817–823.
5. Lambert Deckers and Diane E. Carr, "Cartoons Varying in Low-Level Pain Ratings, not Aggression Ratings, Correlate Positively with Funniness Ratings," *Motivation & Emotion* (1986): 207–216.
6. Willibald Ruch, "Fearing Humor? Gelotophobia: The Fear of Being Laughed at Introduction and Overview," *Humor: International Journal of Humor Research* (2009): 1–25.
7. Paul Lewis, et al., "The Muhammad Cartoons and Humor Research: A Collection of Essays," *Humor: International Journal of Humor Research* (2008): 1–46; Ted Gournelos and Viveca S. Greene, *A Decade of Dark Humor: How Comedy, Irony, and Satire Shaped Post-9/11 America* (Jackson: The University Press of Mississippi, 2011), 220.
8. Jytte Klausen, *The Cartoons that Shook the World* (New Haven, CT: Yale University Press, 2009), 14.
9. Ibid., 107.
10. Ibid., 137–138.
11. Art Spiegelman, "Drawing Blood: Outrageous Cartoons and the Art of Outrage," *Harper's Magazine* (June 2007).
12. Klausen, *The Cartoons that Shook the World*, 125.
13. A. Peter McGraw, Lawrence Williams, and Caleb Warren. "The Rise and Fall of Humor: Psychological Distance Modulates Humorous Responses to Tragedy" (2013) (under review).
14. Alan Dundes, "The Dead Baby Joke Cycle," *Western Folklore* (1979): 145–157.
15. Alan Dundes, "At Ease, Disease—AIDS Jokes as Sick Humor," *American Behavioral Scientist* (1987): 72–81.
16. Alan Dundes, "Many Hands Make Light Work or Caught in the Act of Screwing in Light Bulbs," *Western Folklore* (1981): 261–266.
17. Klausen, *The Cartoons that Shook the World*, 157.

18. Ibid., 152.
19. Catarina Kinnvall and Paul Nesbitt-Larking, *The Political Psychology of Globalization: Muslims in the West* (Oxford, UK: Oxford University Press, 2011): 140.
20. Dacher Keltner, et al., "Teasing in Hierarchical and Intimate Relations," *Journal of Personality and Social Psychology* (1998): 1231–1247.
21. Thomas E. Ford and Mark A. Ferguson, "Social Consequences of Disparagement Humor: A Prejudiced Norm Theory," *Personality and Social Psychology Review* (2004): 79–94.

Chapter 7: Palestine
1. Lloyd M. Bucher and Mark Rascovich, *Bucher: My Story* (New York: Doubleday, 1970), 348.
2. Mark Twain, *Following the Equator* (American Publishing Company, 1898), 119.
3. Christie Davies, *Jokes and Targets* (Bloomington: Indiana University Press, 2011), 227.
4. Ulrick Marzolph, "The Muslim Sense of Humor," in *Humour and Religion: Challenges and Ambiguities*, ed. Hans Geybels and Walter van Herck (London: Continuum, 2011), 173.
5. Ibid., 179.
6. Khalid Kishtainy, "Humor and Resistance in the Arab World and the Greater Middle East" in *Civilian Jihad: Nonviolent Struggle, Democratization, and Governance in the Middle East*, ed. Maria J. Stephen (New York: Palgrave Macmillan, 2010), 56–57.
7. Sigmund Freud, "Humour," *International Journal of Psycho-Analysis* (1928): 4.
8. Davies, *Jokes and Targets*, 264.
9. Ibid., 251.
10. A. Peter McGraw, Lawrence T. Williams, and Caleb Warren, "The Rise and Fall of Humor: Psychological Distance Modulates Humorous Responses to Tragedy (2013) (under review).

Chapter 8: The Amazon
1. Paul Schulten, "Physicians, Humour and Therapeutic Laughter in the Ancient World," *Social Identities* (2001): 71.
2. Norman Cousins, *Anatomy of an Illness as Perceived by the Patient* (New York: W. W. Norton, 2005), 40.
3. Madan Kataria, *Laugh for No Reason* (Mumbai, India: Madhuri International, 1999), 11.

4. M. D. Shevach Friedler, et al., "The Effect of Medical Clowning on Pregnancy Rates After In Vitro Fertilization and Embryo Transfer," *Fertility and Sterility* (2011): 2127–2130.

5. R. A. Martin, "Is Laughter the Best Medicine?: Humor, Laughter, and Physical Health," *Sage Journals* (2002): 217.

6. Sven Svebak, Rod A. Martin, and Jostein Holmen, "The Prevalence of Sense of Humor in a Large, Unselected County Population in Norway: Relations with Age, Sex, and Some Health Indicators," *Humor: International Journal of Humor Research* (2004): 121–134.

7. Carr and Greeves, *Only Joking*, 53.

8. "No More Clowning Around: It's Too Scary," *Nursing Standard* (2008): 11.

9. Cath Battrick, Edward Alan Glasper, Gill Prudhoe, and Katy Weaver, "Clown Humour: the Perceptions of Doctors, Nurses, Parents and Children," *Journal of Children's and Young People's Nursing* (2007): 174–179.

10. Dacher Keltner and George A. Bonanno, "A Study of Laughter and Dissociation: Distinct Correlates of Laughter and Smiling During Bereavement," *Journal of Personality and Social Psychology* (1997): 687–702.

11. Charles V. Ford and Raymond C. Spaulding, "The Pueblo Incident: A Comparison of Factors Related to Coping with Extreme Stress," *Archives of General Psychiatry* (1973): 340–343.

12. Michelle Gayle Newman and Arthur A. Stone, "Does Humor Moderate the Effects of Experimentally Induced Stress?" *Annals of Behavioral Medicine* (1996): 101–109.

13. A. Peter McGraw, Christina Kan, and Caleb Warren, "Humorous Complaining" (2013) (under review).

INDEX

Aarhus, Denmark: McGraw and Warner's
    visit to, 132–40
Abbas, Mahmoud, 160
Abraham (biblical person), 156, 171
Abu Ghraib prison (Iraq) photos, 124–25,
    141
The Act of Creation (Koestler), 49
Adams, Hunter "Patch," 181, 183, 186–87,
    191, 192, 196, 211
Addams, Charles, 56
advertising
    creating humor for, 43, 51–54
    about *Paradise Island* show, 136, 139
    See also alcohol: humor and
Africa
    See Tanzania
age: humor and, 35, 95
"Aha!" moment, 56, 199
Ahmadinejad, Mahmoud, 145
Al-Abi, 157
alcohol: humor and, 62–66, 208–9
Allen, Melanie, 48
Amazon, trip to
    benign violation theory and, 205
    clown brigade and, 175–76, 181–94, 205
    McGraw and Warner's, 175–76, 181–94,
        196, 205, 211
    McGraw and Warner's lessons learned
        from, 200, 205
Amelia (survivor of laughter epidemic),
    84, 86–88
*Anatomy of an Illness as Perceived by the
    Patient* (Cousins), 122, 177

animals
    laughter of, 79–81
    Mohammad cartoons and, 143–46
Annual Association for Applied and Ther-
    apeutic Humor Conference, 176–77,
    178, 179, 180
Ansari, Aziz, 39–40
anthropologists: comedians compared
    with, 30
anti-Israeli jokes, 164–65
Arab comedy ladder, 158
Araki, Takahiro, 106, 116, 118
Ariely, Dan, 112
Aristophanes, 165
Aristotle, 6, 11, 84
Attardo, Salvatore, 26–27
attention-grabbing jokes, 54
audience: role of, 23, 32–34, 86, 200, 205
Awad, Manal, 160–61, 162, 165
Aykroyd, Dan, 27

Bartholomew, Robert, 90
batsu game, 116, 117
Bekoff, Marc, 81
Belén project (Peru), 181, 183–89, 191
Bell, Nancy, 129
Belushi, John, 27
benign violation theory
    alcohol-humor study and, 63–66
    Amazon trip and, 205
    and balancing benign and violation, 200,
        205–6
    C.K.-McGraw discussion and, 18

benign violation theory (*cont.*)
  creativity and, 49, 52
  criticisms of, 11–12, 13
  development of, 9–13
  everyday life and, 212
  fly-down experiment and, 128
  and humor as coping, 189
  Japanese humor and, 205, 208
  and Just For Laughs Festival invitation, 203–5, 206–10
  laughter and, 72, 78
  and pain as source of humor, 154
  Palestine trip and, 205
  purpose of, 201
  Sarah Silverman Strategy and, 12
  Seinfeld Strategy and, 12, 15
  timing and, 205–6
  Warner's thoughts about, 210
  and what makes people funny, 18
  and what makes successful comedians, 38–39
Berg, Alex, 39
Bergson, Henri, 157
Between Heaven and Mirth (Martin), 156
bin Laden, Osama, 160
Binder, McKenzie, 35
birth-control campaign, 52, 53–54, 167, 205
black comedians, 35
"black swan" arguments, 167–69
bladeless fans experiment, 120
Bloomberg, Michael, 42
Bodden, Alonzo, 201
boke (Japanese comedy partner), 106, 205
Boosler, Elayne, 20
Born Standing Up: A Comic's Life (Martin), 30
bowling-ball cartoon (Kanin), 47, 55–58, 64–65
Brady, Jordan, 31
Brockovich, Erin, 90
Brooks, Mel, 163
Brown, Tina, 45
Bruce, Lenny, 25, 36, 63, 112, 120
Bucher, Lloyd, 153–54
Bukoba, Tanzania: McGraw and Warner's visit to, 73–75, 83–85
Burgdorf, Jeffrey, 80–81
burlesque show, African, 75

Carell, Steve, 27
The Caricature Crisis (Larsen), 138

caricature.dk (website), 148
Carolla, Adam, 108, 109
Carr, Jimmy, 36
Carter, Erin Percival, 38
cartoons
  aggressive, 124
  "Aha!" moment for, 56
  and aspiring cartoonists, 54–58
  captionless, 49
  context for, 56
  and definition of cartooning, 47
  disadvantages of, 142
  fact-checkers for, 56, 58
  as failures, 128–30, 132
  Gruner's views about, 123–24
  McGraw and Warner's lessons learned from, 206
  Mohammad, 124–30, 131–32, 133–37, 138–39, 140
  See also the *New Yorker* cartoons
The Cartoons that Shook the World (Klausen), 127
cat-as-sex-toy story, 9, 10
censorship, 130, 160
Center for Applied Nonviolent Action and Strategies (CANVAS), 169
Central Casting (Los Angeles), 33–34
Chaplin, Charlie, 112, 113
charging woman: in Denmark, 119
Cheezburger Network, 13
Chesterfield, Lord, 123
children, 84–85, 193–94
  See also laughter epidemics; Tanzania
church raffle–Hummer story, 4, 10
C.K., Louis, 17–18, 40, 72
"clash of two mutually incompatible codes," 49–50
cleverness: creativity and, 50
Clinton, Bill, 63
Close, Del, 28
clowns
  Amazon trip and, 175–76, 181–94, 205
  benign violation theory and, 205
  and Glick's Parkinson's disease, 191–92
  image of, 187
  McGraw's views about, 188–89
  nose of, 182–83, 187, 196, 198, 211
  as outsiders, 187
  training for, 186
The Colbert Report (TV program), 62, 111
Colbert, Stephen, 27
Collins, Robert Merrifield, 120

comedians
  audience relationship with, 23, 32–34,
    86, 200, 205
  earnings of, 35, 106
  as inherently unhappy, 37
  Jews as, 30
  as outsiders, 30, 72, 199, 201
  production process impact on, 59–62
  therapy programs for, 36
  and who is funny, 17–41, 199
  See also specific person
comedy
  "bibles" about creating, 48
  and comedy writing as orgasm, 48
  commonalities among types of, 29–30
  comparison of American and Japanese,
    117–18
  compartmentalization of, 102
  context of, 30–32, 103–4, 128
  creation of, 41–66
  diversity in, 93
  emotions as key in, 60
  and exceptionally difficult circum-
    stances, 169–72
  experience and experimentation as key
    to, 25, 40
  failures of, 128–30, 200
  formal instruction about, 25
  humor differentiated from, 117–18
  Koestler's views about creating, 48–50, 51
  performing environment for, 31–32
  truth and, 28, 30
  unexpectedness in, 7
  worldwide popularity of, 113–15
  See also humor; joke(s); laughter; *type of
    comedy*
"Comedy Bang Bang" (UCB stand-up
  show), 39–40
Comedy Central, 35, 105
comedy club
  what is a, 31–32
  See also specific club
Comedy at the Edge (Zoglin), 34
Comedy Nest (Montreal): McGraw's
  stand-up comedy routine at, 197–202,
  206–10
Comedy Store (Los Angeles), 19–21, 107
Comedy Store (Tokyo), 107
complaining, humorous, 190–91
computers: creativity and, 50–51
condom jokes, 53–54
conflict situations

improvisation and, 28
successful comedians and, 38
conservatives: sense of humor of, 112
context
  for cartoons, 56, 128
  of comedy, 30–32, 103–4, 128
  of humor, 200
Cook, Dane, 104
Copenhagen
  See Denmark
coping/relief, humor/jokes for, 7, 8, 12, 134,
  163–64, 167, 173, 189–91, 200, 206
Cosby, Bill, 7
Coser, Rose, 85–86
Cousins, Norman, 122, 177, 179, 196
creativity
  in advertising, 43, 51–54
  benign violation theory and, 49, 52
  "bibles" about, 48
  as "clash of two mutually incompatible
    codes," 49–50
  cleverness and, 50
  communal/team-based, 57, 199
  complexity of, 128
  computers and, 50–51
  humor as help to, 50
  Koestler's views about, 48–50, 51
  and mass-produced comedy, 41–62
  and McGraw and Warner's lessons
    learned from travels, 199
  New Yorker cartoons and, 41–46, 54–58
  risk and, 144, 147
  as solitary, 57
  in stand-up comedy, 57
  terrorism and, 60–61
cruel joke cycle, 135
culture
  influence on humor of, 93–118
  joking relationships and, 95
  sense of humor and, 95
  and worldwide popularity of comedy,
    113–14
Cycowycz, Gizelle, 162, 163, 164, 170

Daiku, Tomiaki, 104–5, 106
The Daily Show (TV program), 54, 60, 62
dark humor, 119–48, 200
dating profiles: humor and, 109
David, Larry, 35
Davies, Christie, 95–99, 167
Davila-Ross, Marina, 79–80
Davis, Susan, 121, 122

"Day of Rage," 126–27
Day, Spring, 107–8
dead-baby joke cycle, 135
dead-monkey joke, 8–9
Dean, Greg, 23–25, 26, 49
Debatable Humor: Laughing Matters on the 2008 Presidential Primary Campaign (Stewart), 111
DeLuca, Rudy, 19
Democrats: comedy and, 111–12
Denmark
    charging woman in, 119
    and "Day of Rage" activities, 126–27
    derogatory jokes in, 169
    McGraw and Warner's trip to, 119–21, 124–25, 130–42
    Mohammad cartoons and, 124–30, 131–32, 133–37, 138–39, 140, 141, 142, 145
    Muslims in, 125–26, 131–32, 138–40, 145, 148
    Warner/McGraw–police exchanges in, 130, 132, 133
    See also specific person
Denver Art Museum: as comedy club, 32
Denver, Colorado: Squire Lounge in, 1–2, 5–6, 13–15, 202, 209, 211
Denver Laughter Club, 178
derogatory jokes, 142, 169, 205
DEviaNT (Double Entendre via Noun Transfer) program, 50
Dice Clay, Andrew, 20
Dick, Andy, 35
dick jokes, 117, 118
DiGiovanni, Debra, 198–99, 206
"digit affair"
    See Hawaiian good luck sign
Diller, Phyllis, 7
dirty jokes, 7, 11, 29, 121–22, 163
disparaging jokes, 142
doctor-wife joke, 24
Dotombori district (Osaka, Japan), 102–3
Downtown (Japanese comedy act), 106–7
Drescher, Fran, 33
Du Bois, W.E.B., 30
Duchenne, Guillaume, 77–78
dumb-blonde jokes, 96–97
Dundes, Alan, 134–36
Dunham, Jeff, 104

earnings: of comedians, 35, 106
Ebert, Roger, 45

Edwards, John: Huckabee comment about, 112
Ellen DeGeneres Show (TV show), 32
Ellner, Jordy, 201
emotions: as key in comedy, 8, 60
"encrypted humor," 111
Encyclopedia of 20th-Century American Humor, 13
Encyclopedia of Humor Studies, 6
everyday life
    benign violation theory and, 212
    how humor is used in, 29
    laughter of, 72, 92
    in Palestine, 173
evolution: of laughter, 76–79

"F" parking lot cartoon, 45
fact-checkers: for cartoons, 56, 58
failures, comedy, 128–30, 200
Fallon, Jimmy, 27
Farajin, Imad, 160
Farashat, Bashar, 171, 172–73
Feingold, Alan, 22
Fernbach, Phil, 35, 45, 53
Ferrell, Will, 27
Ferri, Sam, 55
Fey, Tina, 27
Fiqh Council of North America, 127
fireworks show gone wrong, 204
The Flamingo Resort and Casino (Las Vegas), 35
fly-down experiment: benign violation theory and, 128
football: Dundes's views about, 134–35
Ford, Thomas, 142
Foxworthy, Jeff, 104
France
    and French folklore, 135
    and French love of Jerry Lewis, 97–98
    and randy-Frenchmen bon mots, 96
free speech: Mohammad cartoons and, 130, 144–45
Freedom Theatre (West Bank), 165–66, 167, 169, 171
Freud, Sigmund, 6–7, 134, 164
Frevert, Louise, 136
Friedman, Josh, 20–21, 23, 40
Fry, William, 48

Gacy, John Wayne, 187
Galifianakis, Zach, 41–42
game: humor as a, 123–24, 141

game shows, Japanese, 116–17
Gaza Strip, 149–50
  restrictions in, 157
"gelotophobia," 124
gender
  as bias in comedy, 108–10
  and humor in dating/mating, 109
  Japanese humor and, 107
  joke-writing competition and, 110
  and jokes about women, 108
  laughter and, 89–91, 92
  Martin's studies of humor and, 108–9
  political jokes and, 112
  sense of humor and, 95
  and what makes a successful comedian, 35
Gervais, Matthew, 76–79
Gesundheit Global Outreach, 181–82, 183–89, 191
  See also Amazon, trip to: clown brigade and
Gesundheit! Hospital (West Virginia), 181
"Giggleometer," 114
Glick, John, 181–82, 183, 187, 191–92
Goldstein, Dan, 37
The Goodies (sketch-comedy show), 129
Gordon, Rae Beth, 97
Gotham Comedy Club (New York City), 38
Gottfried, Gilbert, 61
Gough, Jacob, 166, 169, 171
Great American Lawyer Joke Cycle, 97
Greengross, Gil, 37, 38
Greeves, Lucy, 36
Grey New York (advertising company), 63–66, 208–9
grief: humor and, 194–96
Groupon (website), 58
Gruner, Charles, 123–24, 141

HAHAcronym Generator, 50
"Haiti" text experiment, 60–61
"Hakuna matata" ("no worries"), 70, 73, 92
Hall, Arsenio, 20
Hall, Edward, 104
Halpern, Charna, 28
Hammerschlag, Carl, 192–94
Handey, Jack, 112
Handler, Chelsea, 104
Hanson, Todd, 59–60, 61–62, 205
Harlan, Patrick, 110
Harman, Jennifer, 38

"Harold" technique, 28
Harris, Sidney, 55
Harvard Lampoon magazine, 47
Hawaiian good luck sign, 154, 155, 190
health: humor and, 175–96, 200
Heaven Spa (Osaka, Japan), 102
Hebron (West Bank): McGraw and Warner's trip to, 171–73
Hempelmann, Christian, 89
Hicks, Bill, 112
Hitchens, Christopher, 108
Hodzic, Nihad, 139, 140, 141, 148
Holocaust, 162, 163–64, 170, 173
homophobic jokes, 141
Hook, Theodore, 140–41
Hotz, Kenny, 203–5
Huckabee, Mike, 111–12
Huh, Ben, 13
human rights, 124, 204
humor
  Adams's views about, 186–87
  as balance of pleasure and pain, 210
  cause of, 52, 154
  comedy differentiated from, 117–18
  comparison of American and Japanese, 117–18
  complexity of, 210–11
  as coping/relief tool, 134, 163–64, 167, 173, 189–91, 200
  creation of, 41–66
  dark side of, 119–48, 200
  enjoying your own, 189, 193–94, 200
  evolutionary origins of, 109
  as a game, 123–24, 141
  health and, 175–96, 200
  Koestler's definition of, 49
  McGraw's thoughts about, 212
  purpose of, 6–7
  selling of, 51–54
  as subversion tool, 165, 173
  team-based, 201
  universal, 114–15, 118, 200
  See also comedy; joke(s); laughter; sense of humor; specific topic; type of humor
HUMOR (quarterly publication), 6, 8, 9, 13, 26, 89
Humor Research Lab (HuRL) (University of Colorado)
  benign violation theory development at, 10–13
  birth control campaign study by, 53–54, 167, 205

Humor Research Lab (HuRL) (*cont.*)
and dark side of humor, 120
founding of, 2
and "Haiti" text experiment, 60–61
and importance of information to fun-
niness, 128
McGraw-Warner's first meeting at, 2–3
McGraw's founding of, 2
New Yorker cartoon study by, 45
purpose of experiments at, 3, 15
Humor Research Team (HuRT), 2–3, 110
See also specific person
Humorous Behavior Q-sort Deck, 28–29
HUNT-2 study, 180
hunter joke, 114–15
The Hurricane Club (New York City):
alcohol-humor study at, 63–66
Hurricane Sandy, 170
Hutcheson, Francis, 123

I Am Comic (documentary), 31
Ibrahimi Mosque (Hebron), 172–73
Improv Olympic Theater (iO) (Chicago), 28
improvisation, 27–28, 29–30, 37–39, 40
Ince, Elise Chandon, 97
incongruity theory, 7, 8, 12, 206
infants: laughter of, 84–85
Inoue, Hiroshi, 99, 100
instincts: and what makes comedians, 18
intangibles: and what makes a person
funny, 22–23
International Humor Conference (Co-
penhagen, 2006), 124
International Society for Humor Studies
(ISHS), 6, 13, 44, 95–96, 123
intifadas humor, 158–59, 164, 165
"Into the End Zone, Trying to Get a
Touchdown" (Dundes), 135
Iquitos (Peru)
McGraw and Warner's trip to, 176,
183–85, 186, 188, 192–94
Punchana neighborhood in, 193–94
See also Belén project (Peru)
Irish jokes, 98
Irving, Washington, 98
Isen, Alice, 50
Israel: and anti-Israeli jokes, 164–65
Israeli-Palestinian friendship, 173

Jackson, Victoria, 111
Japan
benign violation theory and, 205

characteristics of humor in, 95, 99
compartmentalization of comedy in,
102
Davies comment about, 99
as homogenous, 103
McGraw and Warner's lessons learned
from, 200, 205
McGraw and Warner's trip to, 93–94,
205, 211
political jokes in, 110
samurai as central to humor in, 99, 100
U.S. influence on, 113
See also Osaka, Japan
Japan Society for Laughter and Humor
Studies, 99
Japanese Humor and Laughter Society,
93–94, 102
JAPE (Joke Analysis and Production Engine) (robo-jokesters), 50
Jenin (West Bank): McGraw and Warner's trip to, 165–67, 169
Jerichow, Anders, 130–32, 137
Jerusalem, McGraw and Warner's trip to,
162–64
Jewish humor, 164
Jews: as comedians, 30
"Jihad Jane" (aka Colleen Renee LaRose),
145, 146
joke-writing
of Dean, 24–25
gender and, 110
of Raskin, 24–25
joke(s)
boring, 129–32
characteristics of, 141
as coping/relief tool, 134, 163–64, 167,
173, 189–91, 200
culture and, 95
dark, 148, 159
delivery of, 201
difficult circumstances and, 169–72
as failures, 128–29
as a game, 123–24, 141
offensive, 129–32
Palestinian, 158–59
purpose of, 134
for self-preservation, 163–64
in Soviet Union, 154–55
stereotypes and, 141
translations of, 104
world's funniest, 114–15
See also type of joke

Jokes and Their Relation to the Unconscious (Freud), 6–7
"Jon Stewart Effect," 54
Just for Feet commercial, 53
Just For Laughs Comedy Festival (Montreal)
   and McGraw-Warner decision to participate in, 15
   McGraw and Warner's invitation to participate in, 203–4, 206
   McGraw's stand-up comedy routine for, 197–202, 206–10
   Singer as talent scout for, 21
Jyllands-Posten (Danish newspaper)
   incendiary imagery in, 134
   Mohammad cartoons in, 124–30, 131, 133
   survey about immigrants by, 138
   threats against, 131

Kahneman, Daniel, 4
Kamala, Jason, 69–71, 88
Kan, Christina, 190
Kanaana, Sharif, 158–59, 161, 164, 165, 171
Kanin, Zachary, 46–48, 49, 51, 54, 55–58, 64–65
Kansai University (Osaka, Japan), 100
Kaplan, Bruce Eric, 43
Kashasha, Tanzania
   laughter epidemic in, 68–69, 74, 83, 89
   Rugeiyamu visit with McGraw and Warner in, 88–91
Katagelasticists, 124
Kataria, Madan, 178–79
Kaufman, Andy, 20
Keltner, Dacher, 140
Kinison, Sam, 20
Kiroyera Tours, 70
Klausen, Jytte, 127
Klegman, Sarah, 21, 22
Klikushestvo shouting manias, 90
Klovn (TV comedy show), 136
knock-knock jokes, 6
Koestler, Arthur, 48–50, 51
Koran, 156–57
Koziski, Stephanie, 30

labor unions, for comedians, 20
Ladonia (micronation), 146–47
LaMont, Alf, 19, 20
LaRose, Colleen Renee "Jihad Jane," 145, 146
Larsen, Rune, 137–39

Las Vegas, Nevada: McGraw and Warner's trip to, 34–37
Laugh Factory (Los Angeles club), 36
LaughLab (website), 114
laughter
   of animals, 79–81
   benefits of, 178–79
   benign violation theory and, 72, 78
   in children/infants, 84–85
   as contagious, 68, 73, 86, 88–89, 200
   difficult circumstances and, 169–72
   as "disabling" mechanism, 76
   Duchenne and, 77–78
   in everyday life, 72, 92
   evolution of, 76–79
   gender and, 89–91, 92
   Gervais and Wilson's views about, 76–79
   and good versus bad audience, 33–34
   health and, 175–96
   madness and, 71
   as mass hysteria, 89–90
   McGraw and Warner as practicing, 33–34, 86, 205
   McGraw and Warner's lessons learned about, 205
   mimicked, 78
   as mysterious, 68
   as pathological, 74
   as protest, 89–90, 168–69
   Provine's explanation of, 71–73
   purpose of, 76–79, 92, 199–200
   at self, 199, 200, 201
   as signal that things are okay, 83
   social power of, 72–73, 85–86, 92
   solitary, 72
   stand-up comedy and, 72
   stress and, 90–91, 92
   tickling and, 79–80
   uncontrollable, 71, 74
Laughter: A Scientific Investigation (Provine), 71, 89
laughter epidemics, 67–71, 73, 74, 83–85, 87, 88–90, 91–92
Laughter in Hell: The Use of Humor During the Holocaust (Lipman), 163–64
Laughter Universities, 179
laughter yoga, 178–79, 212
laughtivism, 168–69
lawyer jokes, 97
Le Roy, New York: student outbursts in, 90
Lear, Norman, 48

Lee, Judith Yaros, 44
Legman, Gershon, 121–22, 124
Leno, Jay, 20
Leonard, Bridget, 97
Leore (Israeli cabdriver), 150, 152
Letterman, David, 20
Levity (comedy agency), 21
Lewis, Jerry, 97–98, 124
Lewis, Richard, 20
liberals: sense of humor of, 112
Lichtenstein, Donnie, 9
Life Studies of Comedy Writers (Fry and Allen), 48
lightbulb jokes, 136
lighting: role in comedy of, 31–32
Limbaugh, Rush, 111
linguistic theory of humor, 24
Lipman, Steve, 163–64
Lorena (Argentinian clown), 189
Los Angeles, California
  McGraw and Warner's lessons learned from, 199, 205, 206
  McGraw and Warner's trip to, 17–41, 211
  See also Central Casting; Comedy Store; Santa Monica Playhouse; Upright Citizens Brigade Theatre (UCB); *specific person*
Los Angeles Comedy Awards, 23
Louie (FX series), 17
Lubetkin, Steve, 20
Lutz, Chip, 177

Mad Men (TV show), 62, 107, 208
madness: laughter and, 71
Malin, Elisabeth, 112
Mamet, David, 56
Man Show (TV program), 142
Mankoff, Bob, 43–44, 45, 46, 47, 54–58, 64
manzai (two-man comedy style), 106, 107, 110, 113, 117, 205
Mark (Amazonian clown), 193
marriage: humor and, 75–76
Martin, James, 156
Martin, Rod, 108–9, 179, 180
Martin, Steve, 20, 25, 30
Marx, Groucho, 36
Masada, Jamie, 36
mass hysteria: laughter as, 89–90
mass-market jokes/comedy
  creation of, 41–62
  risks involved with, 58–59
  See also the *New Yorker* cartoons

mass motor hysteria, 90
Massachusetts Institute of Technology (MIT): idea generation study at, 50
Massou, Khalid, 160
Mauss, Shane, 201
Mazzilli, Chris, 38
McGhee, Paul, 85
McGraw, Kathleen (mother), 3, 194–96
McGraw, Peter
  educational background of, 3, 4
  first attempt at stand-up comedy by, 1–2, 5–6, 13–15
  impact of global expedition on, 212
  personal background of, 3–4
  personality of, 4
  second attempt at stand-up comedy by, 197–203, 206–10
  Warner first meets, 2–4
  Warner's relationship with, 211–12
  See also specific topic
McGraw, Shannon (sister), 3, 195
McNally, Martin J., 137
medicine
  laughter as best, 175–96
  See also health: humor and
Mehdawi, Rami, 161, 171
Mer-Khamis, Juliano, 165–66, 167, 169
Metzger, Darwyn, 27–28
Miller, Dennis, 111
Mitchell, Alex, 129
Mohammad cartoons, 124–30, 131–32, 133–37, 138–39, 140, 141, 142, 143–46, 147, 148, 149
Montreal, Canada
  See Just For Laughs Comedy Festival (Montreal)
moral violations
  McGraw's interest in, 4
  See also benign violation theory
Morishita, Shinya, 94, 100
Morreall, John, 123
Muslims
  in Denmark, 125–26, 131–32, 138–40, 141, 145, 148
  humor and, 157
  in Sweden, 145
  See also Mohammad cartoons; Palestine
Muslims in Dialog, 139, 141
Myers, Mike, 27

"N+V Theory," 8–9
Nagashima, Heiyo, 94, 102, 103

The Naked Gun study, 63
Namba Grand Kagetsu (Osaka, Japan), 107
Nasser, Latif, 90
National Campaign to Prevent Teen and Unplanned Pregnancy, 52, 53–54, 167, 205
New Star Creation (comedy school) (Tokyo), 104–6, 107, 110
New York City
    alcohol-humor study in, 62–66, 208–9
    McGraw and Warner's lessons learned from, 199, 205, 206
    McGraw and Warner's trip to, 41–66, 211
    See also Gotham Comedy Club; the *New Yorker* cartoons; *specific person*
the *New Yorker* cartoons
    cartoonist open-call day for, 54–58
    contest for, 41–42, 45, 54–58
    database of, 57
    gender responses to, 108
    HuRL study of, 45
    and Kanin's bowling-ball cartoon, 47, 55–58, 64–65
    laughter at, 71
    and selling of mass-market humor, 51
    uniqueness of, 44–45
The New Yorker Festival, 42
nicknames: McGraw's act about, 14
Nilsen, Don, 12–13
Nimis (Vilks sculpture), 146–47
"911 Café" (Ramallah), 158
No Laughing Matter (Legman), 122
North Korea: USS *Pueblo* incident and, 153–54, 170, 190
Norway: HUNT-2 study in, 180
nose, clown, 182–83, 187, 196, 198, 211
Nshamba, Tanzania: McGraw and Warner's visit to, 83–85
Nulman, Andy, 203–4, 206
Nutty Professor experiment, 97

Obama, Barack, 111, 160
O'Brien, Conan, 27
"Ogata Impossible" (*Power Purin* variety show), 116–17
Ogata, Takahiro, 116–17
Ojibwe Native Americans, 95
Old Testament: humor in, 123
Olympic gymnast joke, 103

omuneepo
    See laughter epidemics
Onion (film), 61–62
The Onion News Network (web broadcast), 61
The Onion (newspaper), 59–60, 61–62, 205
Only Joking: What's So Funny About Making People Laugh? (Carr and Greeves), 36
orgasm: comedy writing as having an, 48
Oring, Elliot, 7, 164
O'Rourke, P.J., 111
Orwell, George, 165
Osaka, Japan
    benign violation theory and, 208
    as comedy capital of Japan, 100, 107, 208
    McGraw and Warner's trip to, 99–104, 203, 208
    post–World War II, 100–101
    rakugo performance in, 94–95
    silence in, 101
    smallest bar in the world in, 103, 104
Osaki, Hiroshi, 112–13, 116
Otpor! (Serbian youth movement), 168–69

pain, 154, 173, 210
    See also dark humor
Pakkun Makkun (*manzai* act), 11
Palestine
    benign violation theory and, 205
    censorship in, 160
    geography and economy of, 150–51
    Israeli-Palestinian friendship in, 173
    Israeli settlers in, 171
    as laughter-free zone, 170–71
    McGraw and Warner's lessons learned from, 200, 205
    McGraw and Warner's trip to, 149–53, 155–62, 164, 205, 211
    Ramadan in, 150–52, 156, 159
    restrictions in, 157
    See also Gaza Strip; Hebron (West Bank): McGraw and Warner's trip to; Ramallah (West Bank): McGraw and Warner's trip to; West Bank
Panksepp, Jaak, 80
Paradise Island (show): advertising about, 136, 139
Paramount Theatre (Denver), 17–18
Parkinson's disease: Glick and, 191–92

Pascal, Blaise, 7
penis questions, 18, 19
The Peregrine Penis (Legman), 122
performing environment, 31–32
 See also context
personality: and what makes comedians, 18, 37–38
Peruvian Air Force, 175, 176
PET (Danish intelligence service), 132, 133
Pew Research Center: Mohammad cartoon survey by, 127–28
Philip, P. J., 68, 74, 83
Philogelos (joke book), 98
Pickering, Lucy, 26
Pinsker, Sanford, 44
Pirates of the Dotombori (Osaka, Japan), 99
Pirates of Tokyo Bay (Tokyo, Japan), 99
Plato, 6, 122–23
play fighting: incongruity theory and, 7
pleasure: humor as balance of pain and, 210
Plucker, Alvin, 154, 170
Poehler, Amy, 27
Polish jokes, 98, 135–36
politics/political jokes, 95, 110–12, 167
 See also Mohammad cartoons
Politiken (Danish newspaper), 130–31
Popovic, Srda, 168–69
positive-humor movement, 122
post-traumatic stress disorder, 170
Power Purin (Yoshimoto variety show), 116–17
pranks/practical jokes, 140–41
"prejudiced norm theory," 142
The Primer of Humor Research (Raskin), 13
protest: laughter as, 89–90, 168–69
Provine, Robert, 71–73, 89
Pryor, Richard, 20, 25, 36
The Psychology of Humor (Martin), 108, 179
punch lines
 Dean's views about, 25
 delivery of, 201
 everyday laughter and, 212
 incongruity theory and, 7
 Japanese humor and, 103
 and Koestler's views about creating humor, 49
 linguistic theory of humor and, 24

in Soviet Union, 157
and who is funny, 26–27
puns, 7, 11, 49, 51, 123

Qualtrics, 97, 115

Rabbo, Yasser Abed, 160
race
 jokes about, 141, 142
 political jokes and, 112
 and what makes a good/successful comedian, 35
rakugo (Japanese storytelling), 94–95, 116
Ramallah (West Bank): McGraw and Warner's trip to, 155–62, 164, 170–71
Ramiro (Amazonian clown), 188
randy-Frenchmen bon mots, 96
Rankin, A. M., 68, 74, 83
Raskin, Victor, 13, 24–25, 206
Rasmussen, Anders Fogh, 126, 138, 139
rat-tickling experiments, 80–81
Rationale of the Dirty Joke (Legman), 121–22
Refn, Lars, 125–27, 128–29, 133, 148
refugee camp, Palestinian, 165–67
Reilly, Bill, 99–100, 101, 102
relationships: sense of humor and, 75–76, 212
relief: humor/jokes as, 7, 8, 12, 134, 163–64, 167, 173, 189–91, 200, 206
religion: humor and, 156–57
Remnick, David, 65
Republicans: comedy and, 111–12
Richards (Keith) story, 12
riffs, 25
risk
 creativity and, 144, 147
 mass-market comedy and, 58–59
Robbins, Tony, 24
robo-jokesters, 50
robots: and creation of funny, 50–51
Rock, Chris, 30, 35
Rock, John, 194
Roll Me in Your Arms and Blow the Candle Out (Legman), 122
Rose, Flemming, 130
Ross, Harold, 44, 54
Rubondo Island National Park: McGraw and Warner's trip to, 79–80, 81–83
Ruch, Willibald, 124
Rugeiyamu, Kroeber, 88–89

Rutta, William (Tanzanian guide), 70, 73, 74–75, 79, 81–82, 83, 84, 86–88, 91, 92

Saatchi & Saatchi, 53
safari, African: McGraw and Warner on, 79–80, 81–83
safety valves
  See coping/relief
Sahl, Mort, 36
samurai: Japanese humor and, 99, 100
Santa Monica Playhouse, 23, 25
Sarah Silverman Strategy, 12
sarcasm, 11, 99
satire, 134, 160, 164, 167
Saturday Night Live (TV program), 52, 60, 65, 111, 116
Scandinavia
  McGraw and Warner's lessons learned from, 200
  See also Denmark; Mohammad cartoons; Sweden; *specific person*
"Scattered Pearls" (Al-Abi), 157
Schiro, Julie, 32, 53
Schneider, Abby, 37
schools: laughter epidemics in, 68–71, 83–85, 89–90, 91–92
science: comedians' use of, 40
Second City (Tokyo), 113
Seinfeld, Jerry, 35, 37
Seinfeld Strategy, 12, 15
Seinfeld (TV program), 17, 43–44
self
  censorship of, 130
  and enjoying your own humor, 189, 193–94, 200
  making fun of, 199, 200, 201
self-preservation jokes, 163–64
Sellers, Peter, 97, 98
selling: of mass-market humor, 51–54
Semantic Mechanisms of Humor (Raskin), 24
Semmerling, Jeff, 182–83, 187
sense of humor
  definition of good, 22
  factors influencing, 95
  HUNT-2 study and, 180
  measurement of, 22
  politics and, 112–13
  relationships and, 75–76
  self-rating of, 22
September 11, 2001, 60–61, 205

Serbia: and "black swan" argument, 168–69
set-ups
  everyday laughter and, 212
  linguistic theory of humor and, 24
  and who is funny, 26–27
settlers, Israeli: humor about, 171
sex, 75, 141, 142
  See also dirty jokes; gender
Shakur, Tupac, 79
Shilimpaka, Margaret, 91
Shore, Mitzi, 19
Shore, Sammy, 19
sick jokes, 134
Sikh put-downs, 98
silence: in Osaka, 101
Singer, Jeff, 21, 22–23
Skelton, Red, 179
sketch comedy
  See Watan ala Watar
slapstick: superiority theory and, 6
smallest bar in the world (Osaka, Japan), 103, 104
Smalls, Biggie, 83
Smith, Moira, 140–41
Soviet Union
  collapse of, 167
  jokes in, 154–55, 157, 167
Spa World (Osaka, Japan), 101–2
Spiegelman, Art, 127
Squire Lounge (Denver), 1–2, 5–6, 13–15, 202, 209, 211
St. Claire, Lisette, 33–34
stand-up comedy
  audience-comedian relationship in, 23
  creativity in, 57
  Dean's class about, 23–24, 25
  experience as key in, 25, 199
  improvisation compared with, 29–30, 37–38
  laughter and, 72
  and McGraw and Warner's lessons learned from travels, 199, 206
  McGraw's first official attempt at, 1–2, 5–6, 13–15
  McGraw's preparation for, 199–202
  McGraw's run-through for, 202
  McGraw's second official attempt at, 197–203, 206–10
  Osaki's views about American, 116
  personality and, 37–38
  politics and, 112

stand-up comedy (*cont.*)
  at Squire Lounge (Denver), 1–2, 5–6, 13–15
  Zoglin's views about, 34–35
  See also specific comedian
STANDUP (System to Augment Non-speakers' Dialogue Using Puns) (robo-jokester), 50
"Stars and Bucks Café" (Ramallah), 158
Steinberg, Saul, 56
Step by Step to Stand-Up Comedy (Dean), 25
stereotypes, 36, 141
Stewart, Jon, 111, 112, 165
Stewart, Patrick, 111
Storytelling
  experiment with, 38–39
  See also rakugo (Japanese storytelling)
stress: laughter and, 90, 92
stupidity jokes, 98–99, 137
subversion: humor as tool for, 165, 173
successful comedians: what makes, 34–35, 37–38
Superiority Theory, 6, 8, 12, 122–23, 141, 206
Supreme Court Building, U.S.: Mohammad image in, 127, 140
survival humor, 163–64
  See also coping/relief
Svebak, Sven, 180
Sweden
  derogatory jokes in, 169
  McGraw and Warner's trip to, 143–48, 211
Swift, Jonathan, 165
Syria: reactions to Mohammad cartoons in, 131–32

"Take my wife—please" quip, 26
Tanganyika
  See Tanzania
Tanzania
  laughter epidemic in, 67–71, 73, 74, 83–85, 87, 89–91
  McGraw and Warner's lessons learned from, 199–200
  McGraw and Warner's trip to, 67–92, 211
  sense of humor in, 95
teasing, 6, 140
terrorism
  creativity and, 60–61
  See also September 11, 2001

Terry (McGraw's friend), 202
theory of verbal humor, 13
therapeutic humor movement, 176–78, 180
therapy programs: for comedians, 36
"ThriftOnline" (fictional company): creating advertising headlines for, 43
Thurber, James, 56
tickle robots, 11
tickling, 7, 11, 79–80
timing
  and benign violation theory, 205–6
  difficulty of, 60
  and humor in tragedy, 60–61
  Japanese humor and, 99
  and "too soon" jokes, 61
  and who is funny, 26–27
Tokyo, Japan
  McGraw and Warner's visit to Yoshimoto in, 112–17
  New Star Creation comedy school in, 104–6
The Tonight Show (TV program), 17, 20
"too soon" jokes, 61
tragedy
  humor and, 60–61
  See also type of tragedy or *specific tragedy*
translations of jokes, 104
trickster motif, 113–14
truth: comedy and, 28, 30
Truth in Comedy: The Manual of Improvisation (Halpern), 28
tsukkomi (Japanese straight-man), 106
Twain, Mark, 60, 154
tweets: about Hurricane Sandy, 170
"two-ness," 30

Uganda: McGraw and Warner's trip to, 67
Understanding Humor In Japan (Milner-Davis et al.), 113
United Nations, 124
United States
  diversity of humor in, 103–4
  influence on Japan of, 113
  political jokes in, 111–12
  See also Los Angeles, California; New York City; *specific comedian*
universal humor, 114–15, 118, 200
University of California, Berkeley: Folklore Archive at, 135
University College London: tickle robot at, 11

University of Colorado
  See Humor Research Lab (HuRL)
University of Sheffield: clown study at,
  187
University of Southern California: aca-
  demic comedy concentration at, 19
Upright Citizens Brigade Theatre (UCB)
  (Los Angeles), 27–28, 37–38, 39, 115
USS *Pueblo* incident, 153–54, 170, 190

variety shows, 113
vaudeville, 113
Veatch, Thomas, 8–9
Venn diagrams, 63–66, 208–9
Vilks, Lars, 143–46, 147, 148
Vohs, Kathleen, 110

Wallace, George, 35–37
Warner, Gabriel (son), 4, 182, 188, 210
Warner, Joel
  family background of, 150–51
  impact of global expedition on, 210–12
  personality of, 4
  See also specific topic
Warren, Caleb, 9–10, 12, 32, 43, 52, 110,
  128, 170, 190
Watan ala Watar (TV comedy show), 150,
  159–61, 162, 164, 165
Wengert, Joe, 27, 29–30, 38
West Bank
  McGraw and Warner's trip to, 149, 150,
  152–53, 165–66
  restrictions in, 157
  See also Ramallah (West Bank): Mc-
  Graw and Warner's trip to
Westergaard, Kurt, 133–37, 139, 143, 148
Westword (Denver newspaper), 2, 5

White, E. B., 207
Why the French Love Jerry Lewis (Gordon),
  97
Wiig, Kristen, 27
Williams, Lawrence, 128, 170
Williams, Robin, 20
Wilmer Grace and His Dog (made-up
  movie): Warner in, 27–28
Wilson, David Sloan, 76–79
Wilson, Pam, 180
Wilson, Steve, 180
Wiseman, Richard, 114, 115
With, Aaron, 58
wolfman in a barbershop (cartoon), 41,
  43, 46–48
wood-mill accidents study, 190
World Humor and Irony Membership
  (WHIM), 6
World Laughter Tour, 15, 180, 210–12
  See also specific nation or city
world's funniest joke, 114–15
Wright, Steven, 34

Yelp.com: study of business ratings on,
  190–91
"yo mamma" jokes, 36
yoga, laughter, 178–79, 212
Yorihiro, Aki, 106, 116
Yoshimoto Kogyo (Japanese comedy
  company), 105–6, 107, 112–16
Youngman, Henny, 26, 27

Zamen (Ramallah cafés), 156, 157, 161
Zebra (Danish artist co-op), 125
zingers, 50–51, 110, 114, 201
Zoglin, Richard, 34
Zubeidi, Zakaria, 165, 169